Surviving Mass Victim Attacks

Surviving Mass Victim Attacks

What to Do When the Unthinkable Happens

Gary M. Jackson

ROWMAN & LITTLEFIELD
Lanham • Boulder • New York • London

All statements of fact, opinion, or analysis expressed are those of the author and do not reflect the official positions or views of the U.S. Government. Nothing in the contents should be construed as asserting or implying U.S. Government authentication of information or endorsement of the author's views. This material has been reviewed solely for classification.

Published by Rowman & Littlefield
A wholly owned subsidiary of The Rowman & Littlefield Publishing Group, Inc.
4501 Forbes Boulevard, Suite 200, Lanham, Maryland 20706
www.rowman.com

Unit A, Whitacre Mews, 26–34 Stannary Street, London SE11 4AB

British Library Cataloguing in Publication Information Available

Library of Congress Cataloging-in-Publication Data

Names: Jackson, Gary M., author.
Title: Surviving mass victim attacks : what to do when the unthinkable happens / Gary Jackson.
Description: Lanham : Rowman & Littlefield, [2018] | Includes bibliographical references and index.
Identifiers: LCCN 2018006801 (print) | LCCN 2018008025 (ebook) | ISBN 9781538110881 (Electronic) | ISBN 9781538110874 (cloth : alk. paper)
Subjects: LCSH: Violent crimes—Prevention. | Mass murder—Prevention. | Terrorism—Prevention. | Self-defense. | Self-preservation.
Classification: LCC HV7431 (ebook) | LCC HV7431 .J325 2018 (print) | DDC 613.6/9—dc23
LC record available at https://lccn.loc.gov/2018006801

The paper used in this publication meets the minimum requirements of American National Standard for Information Sciences—Permanence of Paper for Printed Library Materials, ANSI/NISO Z39.48-1992.

Printed in the United States of America

Contents

Introduction

Mass Victim Attacks are surprise attacks that kill multiple innocent people simultaneously. It is a growing worldwide problem. Mass victim attacks are committed by diverse types of attackers noted by different motivations. For the purpose of this book, I define a mass victim attack in the following manner:

A mass victim attack is defined as a planned individual or multiple perpetrator violent assault against a group of people, using a single, multiple, or improvised set of weapons with the end result being the deaths of three or more innocent victims.

In the United States we have: (1) international terrorism, (2) domestic terrorism, (3) self-radicalized terrorism, (4) attackers with mental health issues, and (5) those attackers motivated by hate/bias. Although there are motivation differences, all mass victim attackers have one thing in common: They all attack multiple innocent people by surprise, with no mercy, and with the objective of slaughtering as many as possible in the shortest amount of time.

Mass victim attackers are dedicated to their killing plans—so much so that they are prepared to be killed or to commit suicide. I chose the term mass victim attacks because of the focus on the victim. We tend to think of those attacked as either being killed or wounded. However, there are other ways of being a survivor victim. Those who develop Acute Stress Disorder (ASD) or longer-term Post-Traumatic Stress Disorder (PTSD) because of being caught in a mass attack suffer as well. This book has a chapter devoted to such effects.

This book addresses the topic of mass attacks differently than other works.

1

My focus is on victims and not a singular focus on the attackers. Analyzing all forms of mass victim attacks and attackers, I have focused on how people have survived such attacks. This first-time, universal focus on survival provides a guide for how to live through future mass victim attacks. Bombs, hijacked airliners used as weapons, semi-automatic guns and rifles, shotguns, knives, chemicals, biological agents, and even trucks driven into crowds have been used as weapons. Just as weapons have varied, the attackers themselves have been different.

The major feature of mass victim attacks is not weapons but the attackers' intent to kill innocent victims in such a way as to strike fear into the hearts of all. Although all mass victim attacks are terrorizing, not all attacks are committed by terrorists. We must know the differences and similarities across attacker types. We must be better aware and understand the threat that we face today if we are to increase our chances of survival if the unthinkable happens—that is, being caught in a mass victim attack.

As an example, the deadliest international terrorist attack in the United States was the September 11, 2001, Al Qaeda attack in New York City and Washington, D.C. Forcefully gaining control of four airliners, 19 international terrorists worked as coordinated teams. Two hijacked airliners were flown into the World Trade Center Twin Towers, and one into the Pentagon. The fourth was a failure due to passengers fighting back, but it flew into the ground killing all aboard. The devastating attack resulted in 2,996 deaths with a minimum of 6,000 injuries.

Adam Lanza is an example of mental health issues. On December 14, 2012, 20-year-old Lanza shot his mother to death while she was sleeping and then drove five miles to Sandy Hook Elementary School in Newtown, Connecticut. Working alone, he was armed with two semi-automatic pistols, a rifle, and a shotgun. Forcefully entering the school by blowing out the windows adjacent to the front door of the school, he ended his own life about five minutes later. However, in that chaotic five minutes he managed to swiftly kill 20 children while they were hiding in vain under desks or in restrooms. All children were between the ages of 6 and 7, and all were shot multiple times. He also slaughtered six adults who were trying to protect the innocent children.

There are also mass victim attacks driven by hate and prejudice. On August 12, 2012, Wade Page armed himself with a semi-automatic pistol to kill Sikhs. Recognized as a white supremacist, his hate raged to the point of targeting a Sikh temple in Oak Creek, Wisconsin. He decided to act, approached the temple, and viciously killed six people and wounded four others—all members of the Sikh faith that he despised.

Self-radicalized terrorism is a more recent concern within the United

States. Without being recruited, attackers choose to follow and model themselves after radical Islamic terrorism. Contact with an organized terrorist group could be present but is not necessary. All that is required is a self-proclaimed allegiance to the idolized group. Such attacks as the assault on the Pulse nightclub in Orlando, Florida, on June 12, 2016 (49 killed and 53 injured), and the attack on the Inland Regional Center in San Bernardino, California, on December 2, 2015 (14 killed and 23 injured), demonstrate the viciousness associated with these attacks.

Why did I write this book? I am a psychologist with analytical and operational experience. I have worked in the areas of individual, group, national, and international threat my entire career. I was a psychologist in the U.S. Secret Service, an intelligence officer in the CIA, and in contracted threat-analysis positions across many aspects of the military and most intelligence agencies.

I have headed up a behavior-analysis team that tracked terrorists and headed a threat team at the Pentagon throughout the 9/11 attack and following threat. I have escaped from an attempted kidnapping, and I have met and interviewed despicable killers. For 31 years, I have focused on the development of innovative technology to anticipate threat from all types of adversaries.[1] These methods are currently in use within the U.S. government. This background has left me with knowledge that I am committed to share, knowledge that can help you to survive if the unthinkable happens—that is, being caught in a mass victim attack. By reading and studying this book, you will likely be more aware and prepared than you are now.

There are several key points to emphasize about how this book is presented. First, I have used repetition on purpose. There have been numerous mass victim attacks that have characteristics fitting into different sections and are used for emphasis. Second, key points to survival are repeated across the book with different examples to enhance learning and memory of important content. Last, the book is divided into three parts as described below.

PART I: THE TOP THREE THINGS YOU CAN DO TO STAY ALIVE

Escaping harm or death in mass victim attacks depends on more than one factor. Part I highlights the three major factors that can increase your chances of survival. Combined, these three points can replace fear of the unknown and sense of no control with what can be done to increase your chances of survival. These three factors are: (1) understanding past attacks to know how to survive, (2) recognizing warning signs, and (3) knowing how to react when caught in an actual attack. This important information will increase your situational awareness and better prepare you for the future.

PART II: ESCAPE, HIDE, STAY IN PLACE, OR ATTACK THE ATTACKER?

This second part of the book focuses on what to do to stay alive. Contrary to popular view, we do have options. Mass victim attackers use the element of surprise. Whether using a bomb, semi-automatic weapon, knife, vehicle, or any other form of weapon, the attacker strikes quickly and without mercy. Gender, age appearance, race, and even illness or disability is not considered. Because anyone in a selected target area can be a victim, we must know how to react. This part of the book covers the specifics of how and how not to respond in detail.

PART III: HOW TO SET UP YOUR PERSONAL PROTECTION PLAN

Part III is the final part of the book, which was written to assist you in establishing a personal protection plan. Tips are provided on how to focus on being prepared for specific types of locations visited based on your personal characteristics. Survival also includes coping with the effects of ASD and longer-term PTSD, as a result of being a victim of a mass attack. The book addresses all facets of survival, including surviving with long-term physical and psychological effects.

I

**THE TOP THREE THINGS YOU
CAN DO TO STAY ALIVE**

1

Understanding Past Attacks to Know How to Survive

Mass victim attacks are surprise attacks to kill multiple innocent people simultaneously or at nearly the same time. These attacks are devastating, both for actual victims and their families. By means of recorded video and television coverage, we cringe repeatedly when we see events replayed. During these replays, we can imagine just how frightening it would be to be a victim. However, most people typically do not dwell on such horrible thoughts. First, we tend to avoid dwelling on painful events if we were not directly affected. Second, we know the chances of being a victim are extremely small. The result is that most simply are not prepared for such a low-probability event. But for those who were victims, probabilities didn't matter—being a victim was a certainty.

We prepare for many events that have a small chance of happening. We follow road rules while driving and faithfully use our seat belts to avoid that fatal car accident. There is a 1 in 8,469 chance of being killed in an automobile accident. But we prepare. We take precautions, and we know what to look for if a bad driver is spotted. We drive defensively to stay as safe as possible through a variety of road and weather conditions.

There is a one in 2 million chance of being killed in an airline accident. There is also a one in 2 million chance of being killed by a terrorist within the United States. Although the chances are the same, we are far better prepared for airline trips. There is careful maintenance, strong safety standards, safety equipment, and a passenger briefing before every flight. There is sometimes an armed sky marshal on board, and pilot actions are monitored and recorded. Weather conditions are monitored closely, and emergency landings occur to avoid danger. We are prepared to fly as safely as possible.

Most of us do not know how to react if caught in a mass victim attack. Is the probability so low that we don't need to worry? I don't think so. As mentioned, the chance of being killed in an airline accident is about the same as being killed by a terrorist. But we are prepared for airline travel, regardless of how low the chances are of being killed. Mass victim attacks are very real, and I believe we need to be better prepared—just in case. If we add to terrorism the chance of being a victim of a mass victim attack from a mentally ill person, a copycat, self-radicalized person, or just someone filled with hate and bias, the probability is much higher. The world has changed; it is more dangerous and threatening. We need to think differently to increase our chance of survival.

Why are we better prepared for airline flights and auto trips? Because the auto and airline industries have learned from past events. For example, studies of how deaths occurred in past auto accidents resulted in required seat belts and airbags. The increased rates of survival in such accidents have been focused on the use of both.

In 1905 George Santayana remarked, "Those who cannot remember the past are condemned to repeat it."[1]

I have taken the approach that we must study and learn from how people have survived mass victim attacks. This has led to strategies to be better able to survive attacks in the future. In the vast majority of cases, survival depended on what the victim did, not just on being saved by responding law enforcement or security. Yes, law enforcement has been effective, especially in preventing attacks from occurring. However, once an attack begins, it occurs rapidly before law enforcement personnel can respond, unless they are already present. As a general rule, you are primarily on your own. Rather than leave your safety to others, you need to be better prepared to ensure your own safety.

I have also taken a different approach to studying the past. Many works have focused on attack method or only on a single type of attack during past events. Instead, I have focused on victims and how they managed to survive across all forms of mass victim attacks. Analyzing survival in these attacks has led to commonalities that we can use defensively. Why are there commonalities?

A terrorist is very different from an attacker suffering from mental health issues—they have totally different motivations. Some attackers commit their act alone and others with accomplices. Some kill themselves, and some try to escape capture. However, the fact that many people are killed and injured at one time is a strong commonality. Mass victim attacks require a mass of people being together at the same time. This limits attacks to locations with many individuals present. When we add to this what motivates mass victim attackers, we can narrow the potential list of targets to an even smaller list.

If attack locations are studied, we can determine how survival occurred within these locations. We will cover this in detail, but just as an example, many locations that can house a considerable number of people have multiple exits, adjoining or additional rooms, restrooms, a kitchen if a restaurant, closets, and so on. These additional areas can be keys to survival if an attack begins.

To study the past, we first need to know what types of mass victim attacks have occurred. We also need to know something about the types of mass victim attackers. In my analysis, I have identified five classes of mass victim attackers, driven by totally different motivators. These are:

- International Terrorism
- Domestic Terrorism
- U.S. Self-Radicalized Terrorism
- Mental Health Issues
- Hate/Bias

There is much said about "lone wolf" attacks. This is not a "type" of attacker with a specific form of motivation but a method of attack. The term creates some confusion, and is used in different ways. Some describe any mass attack committed by a single person as a lone wolf attack. Others use the term synonymously with self-radicalized attacks committed by a single attacker. Any type of attacker could act alone. In addition, the line between acting alone or with others has become unclear. If a sole bomber is communicating with and getting instructions from an international terrorist organization, is that a lone wolf attack? Due to this confusion, I don't use the term in this book. Instead, separating mass victim attacks by what serves as motivation provides clearer commonsense distinctions aiding understanding as to *who*, *what*, *where*, *when*, and *how* such attacks occur.

One of the more common points of confusion about mass victim attacks results from the absolute horror of the events themselves. Killing many innocent victims with semi-automatic weapons, bombs, or any other form of weapon leaves shocking events and horrific images. This leads to labeling such events as terrorism because of the *terrorizing* outcome associated with all mass victim attacks.

Adding to the confusion is the fact that there simply is not a single, universally accepted definition of terrorism. Attacks have received much attention from media, military, intelligence, public safety, and academicians. Studies and analyses have focused on weapons, targets, motivations, tactics, and message. Different perspectives have simply led to different definitions.

Although there is not a single accepted definition of terrorism, and experts point to their favorite definitions, there is a common thread across most definitions, regardless of the perspective taken. This common thread is the underlying need to deliver a political, religious, ideological, or anti-country (e.g., anti-U.S.) message. Attacks fueled by hatred of a specific type of target and attacks associated with mental health issues most likely are not associated with an ideological or politically inspired message. Adam Lanza, who had mental health issues, killed 20 children and 6 adults at the Sandy Hook Elementary School shooting after killing his mother. Why? We still are not totally sure. There was no message.

When studying past attacks, we see that weapon choice, targeting, and location choice for mass victim attacks flow from motivation. Studying attacks by type of attacker helps to determine how attacks have occurred and how victims have survived. In the following section we study the past, discussing five types of attacks and attackers in more detail.

INTERNATIONAL TERRORISM

Definition: An international terrorism mass victim attack is committed by non-U.S. citizen(s) to violently kill multiple innocent and random people in a single or coordinated event with an objective of making a political, religious, ideological, or anti-U.S. statement. Perpetrators have the motivation, will, and resources to strike on a global basis (e.g., Al Qaeda's September 11, 2001, airliner attacks against the World Trade Center and the Pentagon).

International terrorism is likely recognized as the most significant threat to the United States and is noted by the backing of such organized groups as Al Qaeda and ISIS/ISIL. There is some confusion over the acronym used for the latter. Many terrorism experts and the media use the name ISIS (Islamic State of Iraq and Syria). Those in the Obama administration used the term ISIL for the same organization (Islamic State of Iraq and the Levant). The difference is the designation for a region. The word *Levant* covers a larger area. The Levant is an area from southern Turkey to Egypt, including Israel, Lebanon, Palestinian territories, and Syria. The overall goal of this effort, regardless of the name, is to establish an Islamic state, known as a caliphate.

Certainly there are differences between Al Qaeda and ISIS. In fact, Al Qaeda has even denounced ISIS. Their methods are different. Al Qaeda, formerly led by Osama bin Laden, is focused on the United States as a target, as we saw in the 9/11 attack and the bombing of the USS *Cole*. They have been exceedingly careful in selecting members of their organization. There is little doubt that the successful raid on Osama bin Laden's residence in Abbottabad, Pakistan, on May 2, 2011, resulting in his death had a significant and lasting effect on Al Qaeda. Additional U.S. military efforts have also resulted in the death of many former Al Qaeda leaders.

ISIS, not as selective, has been successful in recruiting those to assist their cause, including U.S. citizens. ISIS's reach is much broader. Both Al Qaeda and ISIS organizations are brutal and intent on killing massive numbers of innocent victims. Differences aside, both groups represent Islamic radical fundamentalism with beliefs that stray from mainstream, more peace-seeking Islamic beliefs. In addition, ISIS has acted more like a military organization and not just as an international terrorist organization.

The ISIS caliphate is a term used for the ISIS state—a primary objective of ISIS. The caliphate had been growing over several years, but in 2017, U.S.-backed forces/allies basically crushed the caliphate that had been centered in Iraq with Raqqa as the capital. However, as a decentralized terrorist organization, ISIS can be and has been effective at providing propaganda useful for self-radicalization. Given the Internet and the ease with which information can be obtained, U.S. citizens with a tendency to embrace radical Islamism may easily locate like-minded people, documents to read, and instructions on how to attack on the Internet/social media.

DOMESTIC TERRORISM

Definition: A domestic terrorism mass victim attack is committed by U.S. citizen(s) to violently kill many innocent people in one event with an objective of making a statement about "getting back" or revenge for a perceived injustice; it is not associated or identified with an international terrorist organization.

As an example, on April 19, 1995, Timothy McVeigh parked a truck filled with ANFO explosive in front of the Alfred P. Murrah federal building, left the scene, and then detonated the truck bomb, killing 168 and injuring approximately 700. ANFO is easily obtained ammonium nitrate fertilizer and diesel oil. The combination, when detonated with any small explosive device, can be devastating.

The damage caused by the truck bomb to the target was extensive. A significant part of the large structure was demolished, and damage was apparent to many buildings across a large 10- to 16-block area. The planners, Timothy McVeigh and Terry Nichols, who had met in the U.S. Army, had become increasingly outraged over federal government actions.

The first incident was known as the Ruby Ridge incident, which was a 10-day standoff between Randy Weaver and his family and a large federal officer force. Weaver's wife and son were killed in the incident, as was a federal officer. The second incident was known as the Waco siege. Beginning with an armed conflict between the Branch Davidian religious sect and government officers, six sect members and four federal officers were killed. The following 53-day siege ended in a law enforcement rush on the Branch Davidian compound. The result was that 76 additional sect members were killed in a massive fire, including David Koresh, the leader.

McVeigh detonated the truck bomb in front of the federal building on the second anniversary of the Branch Davidian incident. Driven by an enraged need for revenge, the bombing remains the largest instance of domestic terrorism in the United States.

U.S. SELF-RADICALIZED TERRORISM

Definition: U.S. self-radicalized terrorism is a mass victim attack to violently kill many innocent people in the same event, perpetrated by U.S. citizen(s) who embrace the ideology and often tactics of a radical Islamic international terrorist organization or group but is not officially a member of that organization. A primary objective is to seek recognition and acceptance as a "soldier" or member of that organization.

Self-radicalized terrorists emerging from within the United States who are sympathetic to Islamic radical fundamentalism is a growing problem. Self-radicalization can occur with or without actual communication with an international terrorist organization. Such self-radicalized terrorist attacks as the assault on Pulse nightclub in Orlando, Florida, on June 12, 2016 (49 killed and 53 injured), and the attack on the Inland Regional Center in San Bernardino, California, on December 2, 2015 (14 killed and 23 injured), demonstrate the concern over this still-emerging form of terrorism.

The world has changed. International terrorist organizations now include experts in the use of social media to spread their message. The typical vulnerable U.S. citizen interested in such organizations tends to desire a sense of belonging. This can lead to recruitment, whether male or female, or what I would call "assumed recruitment." The Internet has been indispensable for ISIS recruitment efforts, and they have made significant amounts of information available specifically for the purpose of enabling self-radicalization and with instructions on how to attack successfully.

In addition to assisting recruitment, the Internet has become a valuable tool for communication in which a "terrorist wannabe" can gain religious knowledge, tactics, and attack instructions. For example, the availability of the Al-Qaeda online magazine *Inspire* provided instructions for making a pressure cooker bomb. Brothers Dzhokhar and Tamerlan Tsarnaev followed these instructions to make the bombs used at the Boston Marathon finish on April 15, 2013.[2] The two bombs detonated 12 seconds apart, killing 3 and injuring almost 300 innocent people.

The Internet assists terrorists in a multitude of ways. To surveil a potential target for a mass victim attack, one can just view Internet images of potential targets to determine the layout of the location. The posted busiest times of some restaurants and other public places are available at a click. Even live webcams may be viewed up to the minute of an attack. Furthermore, there are many options for communicating covertly or in such a way that discovery would be difficult, at best.

I have worked in the area of counterterrorism for over 30 years. The changes have been dramatic. The Internet has become a tool used by the self-radicalized terrorist. Because they are U.S. citizens, or living comfortably within the United States, detection is difficult—they can be your next-door neighbor. However, to counter growing threat, law enforcement and intelligence experts have increased skills in Internet chat, social media, and how to track malicious content. They are becoming diligent in their monitoring efforts. Chapter 12 discusses the many successes of law enforcement in preventing mass victim attacks. Using monitoring methods, informants, and infiltrations, scores of attacks have been foiled.

MENTAL HEALTH ISSUES

Definition: A mass victim attacker with mental health issues is intent on violently killing many innocent people in the same event. He is typically a U.S. citizen operating alone, suffering from delusions and/or anger (e.g., December 14, 2012, Adam Lanza shooting at Sandy Hook Elementary School, Newtown, Connecticut, when 20 children 6 to 7 years old and seven adults, including his mother, were killed).

There is a public perception that the mentally ill are violent and dangerous. This is not generally the case. However, there are exceptions. If committed to treatment for danger to others, there is a professional determination that the individual could harm others. In my years as director of treatment programs for the incarcerated and violent mentally ill, I was attacked, choked, and physically assaulted numerous times. But these were programs designed to treat the violent mentally ill, and violent individuals with diagnosed mental health issues were overrepresented—that is why they were there.

In our everyday public settings, violence with mental illness as a cause or contributing factor is rare. When a person is suffering from mental health issues with a tendency toward violence, repeated outbursts usually bring the person to the attention of law enforcement and the courts. However, some do slip through the cracks.

On July 20, 2012, 24-year-old James Holmes propped open the back door to an Aurora, Colorado, Century 16 movie theater and left, planning his quick return. The Batman movie *The Dark Knight Rises* was playing. Holmes was a fan of Batman. He returned in tactical clothing, hair dyed bright red (Joker's hair was bright green), a donned gas mask, and well armed with shotgun, rifle, and handgun.

Holmes began his attack by tossing two tear gas containers. He then systematically produced a hail of gunfire without mercy, killing 12 people and wounding 70. Holmes was not a stranger to mental health services. He had been seen by three mental health professionals at the University of Colorado prior to the attack. A PhD student in neuroscience, Holmes was bright but troubled. He had started arming himself with weapons and ammunition after recently dropping out of school.

There were many warning signs prior to the incident. Holmes had come to the attention of the campus threat-detection professionals. There was concern. After the incident, the insanity defense was used. Although diagnosed as suffering from schizophrenia and entering an insanity defense, the defense was rejected. In the presence of mental health professionals prior to the attack, Holmes had mentioned thoughts of killing others. However, it does not appear that much was done other than informing campus police of the homicidal thoughts.

There is little doubt that mental illness played a significant role in this shooting. Unfortunately, many warning signs were not acted on quickly enough. It is interesting to note that Holmes had been diagnosed with schizophrenia. In my work as a psychologist for the U.S. Secret Service, this diagnosis surfaced often with those who have threatened the president of the United States or other protectees.

The incidence of violence involving those diagnosed with schizophrenia is significantly higher than the incidence of violence in the general public.[3] Just a decade ago, it was believed that this was not the case, and you can still find many professionals who say the incidence of violence perpetrated by people with this diagnosis is no higher than that of the general public. But new evidence indicates that we should be alert. For this reason, a person with a diagnosis of schizophrenia making threats or mentioning thoughts of killing others should be taken very seriously—immediately.

I have mentioned that terrorism is associated with a political, religious, ideological, or anti-country message. Holmes kept a notebook of his thoughts. In that notebook he wrote that terrorism is not the message. He stated, "The message is, there is no message."[4] This makes this type of attack, regardless of the slaughter, very different from terrorism where there is an intended message. Yes, the attack was horrific and terrorizing, but technically not terrorism.

HATE/BIAS

Definition: A U.S. hate/bias-inspired mass victim attack to violently kill many innocent people in a single event is typically perpetrated by a single U.S. citizen who holds significant prejudice or bias and inordinately strong anger against a specific religious, racial, ethnic, or despised group.

A hate-inspired mass attack is the end result of hate/bias stemming from prejudice toward a group of individuals that is despised by the perpetrator. Hate is so strong that the perpetrator will risk all to kill multiple individuals of the hated group. It is difficult to hide such hate, and there are typically early signs of the underlying bias and anger.

On August 12, 2012, Wade Page killed six Sikh people and wounded four others at a Wisconsin Sikh temple. Page was known as a white supremacist with a hatred for those of the Sikh faith. Arriving on the scene of the attack, police shot Page in the stomach. In response, Page killed himself with a gunshot to the head. Hate clearly fueled this event. It was so strong that he ended his own life after achieving his goal of killing others he truly despised.

Hate is a powerful driver of repulsive attacks against any member of a hated target. We all know the history of the Ku Klux Klan (KKK) in the United States. The hatred directed toward nonwhites is a sad chapter in U.S. history. However, hate is still alive and directed toward many groups of people. Page's deadly assault against those of the Sikh faith at a temple is a very sad and prime example of the motivation that drives this form of mass victim attack.

We have recently witnessed many attacks against police officers in the United States. Some of the attacks are generated from a firm belief that police have targeted African Americans for shootings. This is the foundational belief behind the Black Lives Matter movement. As an example, on July 8, 2016, Micah Xavier Johnson interrupted a protest against police violence in Dallas, Texas, by shooting and killing five police officers and wounding seven. Using a semi-automatic AR-15 rifle, Johnson turned his hate into an intense killing of numerous despised police officers. Although a veteran, his anger drove him to strike back against law enforcement. Johnson was killed when police, out of safety concerns, sent in a robot armed with explosives. When close to the perpetrator, the bomb was detonated, killing Johnson and ending the killing of his hated targets, police officers.

Although some might classify police killings as domestic terrorism, I consider this to be a combination of hate and domestic terrorism. Driven by hate, perpetrators want to kill any members of the despised group, but there is also an element of revenge and leaving a message. Domestic terrorism carries with it a specific message of revenge. As we saw with the Oklahoma domestic terrorism bombing, Timothy McVeigh sought revenge for the deaths arising from two specific incidents, the Ruby Ridge and Branch Davidians deaths.

In hate/bias-driven mass victim attacks, the target is simply random members of a despised group. We witnessed numerous examples of attacks directed at law enforcement during 2016 and 2017. Tactics may differ to some extent, but the hate that drives the killings is very clear as a prime motivator.

There are additional attacker types, but I consider them to be special cases of attacks or sub attacks that fit under the provided five types. First, there are copycat attackers. Mass victim attacks seem to motivate some to model these and follow with attacks of their own. There are those who are inspired by mass victim attacks and seek the opportunity for recognition. Attacks beget attacks. There is also much being made of "lone wolf" attacks. A lone wolf attack is one in which the attacker acts alone without any assistance from others. However, he may be influenced by others. Because copycats and lone wolf attackers can be subsumed across other categories, I will keep them under the motivational categories provided. In other words, a copycat attack could mirror any of the provided five types of attackers listed.

Notice that with the examples provided, methods vary. In this book, mass victim attacks can include any attack by any means in which three or more victims are killed at one time. For example, the worst attack in U.S. history was the 9/11 attack on September 11, 2001. Nineteen foreign terrorist attackers working together hijacked four airliners and used them as weapons to crash into the Twin Towers of the World Trade Center in New York City and the Pentagon. One airliner did not reach its target thanks to brave passengers who challenged the terrorists in flight. That plane perished in a field in Shanksville, Pennsylvania, with all being killed. Box cutters were used as the initial weapons to hijack the planes in flight prior to using the airliners themselves as weapons.

There have been many attacks with improvised weapons, even including homemade pressure-cooker bombs such as the two that exploded 12 seconds and one block apart at the finish of the Boston Marathon on April 15, 2013. Three people were killed and over 260 wounded. Self-radicalized brothers

Dzhokhar and Tamerlan Tsarnaev were the perpetrators. Four days later, Tamerlan died in the hospital after being wounded in a police shootout and after being run over by either younger brother Dzhokhar or a police SUV. Later that evening fugitive Dzhokhar was wounded and apprehended. He was later convicted and sentenced to death by lethal injection.

Mass victim attacks are about killing as many people as possible in the shortest amount of time with any form of weapon. We have witnessed attacks using handguns, assault rifles, homemade bombs, vehicle run-downs, box cutters, biological agents such as anthrax, and knives. Weapons are not the focus of mass victim attacks. Rather, the types of attackers are different because of underlying motivations of the attackers. Understanding motivation is important because it is what fuels all the steps leading to the attack itself. Any method or device that can be used to take multiple lives is fair game for those who are intent on committing a mass victim attack.

THE ATTACK PROCESS

We tend to view a mass victim attack as the horrific event itself, and the many deaths and injuries resulting from the vicious assault. Through media coverage, which is often almost immediate, we see the location, we may see first responders, and we may see images of the casualties. *We must keep in mind that the attack itself is the end step of a multistep process.* This is one example of how we must think differently. There is much preparation required for mass victim attacks of any kind. Such preliminary work and planning could have taken days to weeks to more than a year. In the case of the 9/11 attacks, serious Al Qaeda planning began at least two to three years before the attacks. One just does not pick up guns or a bomb and then attack. Attacks require planning. Such planning can provide warning signs, if we are alert and report what we see.

Figure 1.1 displays the process that leads to an attack. Why is this important? The best way to survive a planned attack is to prevent it from happening.

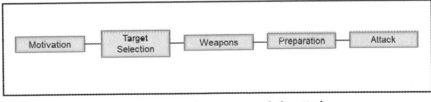

Figure 1.1   The process that occurs prior to a mass victim attack

When mass victim attacks are analyzed, more often than not there are the presence of attack-preparation warning signs. Unfortunately, we are often not tuned in to recognize these signs, or are reluctant to act on warning signs when observed.

Motivation

The first step in the process of attack preparation is for the attacker(s) to develop the motivation that would drive the entire process of preparation. This includes all steps up to and including the actual attack. There is *always* underlying and driving motivation. There could be an intense disgust for the United States, in general, or specific U.S.-based actions. Delusion and need for recognition could motivate the person with mental health issues. In an attack motivated by hate and prejudice, the motivation may be to kill as many of the hated group as possible with a single attack. Motivation of a mass victim attacker is much like filling the gas tank in your car. The available fuel must be sufficient to drive the perpetrator through the process to the final destination—the attack.

Target Selection

Target selection is critical for the attacker. Terrorism carries with it the need to make a statement. Therefore, target selection is likely to be fueled by considerations of the kind of statement that would be left after an attack. International terrorism is interested in symbolic targets, meaning that the target represents something much larger. For example, in the 9/11 attack, the World Trade Center Twin Towers were symbolic of U.S. economic dominance globally. The same day, the Pentagon was attacked, with the structure being symbolic of the U.S. military.

In some cases, it is not clear why a specific target was selected, particularly if mental health issues are present. It is still not clear as to why Adam Lanza picked Sandy Hook Elementary School for his attack. It may have been as simple as the school being just five miles away from where he and his mother lived. Hate-fueled attacks are clearer. An attacker targets a specific group of people that is truly hated. This is true of Dylann Roof's attack against African Americans during their worship service in Charleston, South Carolina on June 17, 2015. He stated during the shooting spree that he wanted to kill black people. So he attacked black worshippers during a religious service in church after sitting with them during the service.

Because it is important to the attacker to kill as many people as possible, we see attacks in locations where targeted people gather. What has changed over the past few decades within the United States is that no location is sacred. We have witnessed attacks in churches and temples, schools (including elementary, high schools, and colleges), nightclubs, workplace gatherings, restaurants, shopping malls, sporting events, and even military installations. This is very important because almost any location we visit where groups gather could be a target of some form of a mass victim attack. Therefore, we need to think differently when at any form of public gathering. The old saying "There is safety in numbers" is not true with mass victim attackers—numbers are part of target selection.

Should we stop going to public places? Absolutely not. But we need to know better how to survive if in a location that is attacked. As you will see in this book, details of how best to seek protection in locations visited will be highlighted.

Weapons

After developing motivation that will fuel the attack process and selection of a target, weapons choice becomes essential to the attacker. In some cases, target selection may occur after weapons choice, especially if the attacker already has weapons. Target selection and weapons choice go hand in hand. Although a weapon can be anything that can cause multiple deaths, we most often see two general types of weapons in mass victim attacks: bombs and semi-automatic guns. However, because of Al Qaeda and ISIS inspiration, we are witnessing more vehicle run-downs and stabbings with sharp objects.

The use of explosives takes many forms. An explosive device could be a homemade bomb, known as an improvised explosive device (IED). It could also mean using airliners with full fuel tanks to detonate when flying into the World Trade Center and the Pentagon. Don't underestimate the creativity of mass attackers. The element of surprise is on the attacker's side. Regardless of the form of explosive, the goal is the same: mass destruction and death.

To show the explosive power of homemade bombs, when I was in the U.S. Secret Service, we held a demonstration for White House staff. A car was placed in a field far away from the outside bleachers. The car trunk was loaded with common ammonium nitrate fertilizer soaked in diesel oil (ANFO). This form of easily obtained fertilizer when soaked in diesel oil is a very powerful explosive when ignited by a small explosive device. All that is left is to detonate it. In this demonstration, when detonated the car was blown at least 40 feet straight up into the air before landing in a flaming inferno. It would have been impossible to survive in or near the car. The truck bomb McVeigh used in the Oklahoma City bombing was very similar, except many times more powerful.

Semi-automatic guns, both handguns and assault rifles, are often weapons of choice. Their selection is obvious. They are small, can be concealed easily, and can shoot as fast as the trigger is pulled. Clips can be prefilled with extra ammunition to assist in rapid and continued firing. It is important to note that a semi-automatic weapon can shoot about two rounds of ammunition a second. With multiple weapons and not reloading, a single attacker could easily release well over 100 shots in the first minute of an attack.

Of course, a bomb explodes in a split second. It is frankly relatively easy to acquire materials to make IEDs and to purchase multiple semi-automatic weapons legally. Adam Lanza's mother, who he murdered before driving to Sandy Hook Elementary School to kill children, purchased the weapons used. She also accompanied him to the gun range to practice—and this in the presence of repeated warning signs. For example, if a family member increasingly isolates himself, becomes fascinated with mass victim attacks, keeps images of past mass killings, attempts to obtain semi-automatic weapons and/or ammunition, expresses strong hate, expresses hate on social media, or is appearing to gather any materials that could be used for an explosive device, concern should be heightened and activities reported. There are numerous warning signs that will be presented throughout this book. Loved ones may want to deny the presence of warning signs, hoping beyond hope that a son, daughter, father, or mother could not possibly commit any horrible act.

It is essential that if you see something, you say something. This is a common saying, but we will break it down into needed specifics. Getting a loved one or a friend help as a preventative measure is far better than coping with a suicide or forced law enforcement killing after he or she commits a horrific act. We will cover what to look for and how to report it in later chapters. Also, bombs and semi-automatic weapons require different strategies for survival. These strategies will also be covered as we move through the book.

Preparation

Once motivation is locked in, target selection has occurred, and weapons have been acquired, final preparation occurs. IEDs may be constructed and determinations made as to how to hide them. A tremendous amount of energy is stored in an explosive device. An IED can be as small as a pipe bomb or pressure cooker, or it could be a truck bomb with the cargo container loaded with ANFO. If guns are the choice, there may be multiple visits to a gun range to practice. There could also be surveillance of the target location selected. For example, it has been reported that Omar Mateen visited the

Pulse nightclub in Orlando, Florida, several times prior to his attack. On the last visit, he attacked.

We must also keep in mind that in today's world of technology, it is very possible to surveil a target from home using the Internet. There are pictures of locations inside and out, times of heaviest use, and even aerial photographs and maps. As mentioned previously, there are even detailed instructions on how to build a bomb, and materials are easily obtained.

The Attack

The attack itself is important to consider for survival. Given that no one had detected or reported warning signs that could have prevented the attack, the first indication we have that an attack has started is an explosion, the sound of rapid gunfire, a vehicle running over pedestrians, multiple stabbings, or any other calamity that hits multiple people in a group at the same time when it is clear that it is not an accident.

A bomb explodes with most energy released at the site of the explosion. The explosive energy reaches out equally in all directions but diminishes with distance. This is why we see many deaths at the location of the bomb and injuries through blast effects and flying shrapnel at distances away from the bomb.

One problem with rapid gunfire starting is that it is not unusual for eyewitnesses who survive mass shootings to report that they were not sure at first what the sound was. Some report a popping sound, or what sounded like fireworks. In addition, it can take a few seconds to gather thoughts to determine what is going on in a surprise armed assault. However, there could be a minimum of at least 100 shots fired within the first minute while the unaware are trying to determine what is happening. Each bullet could hit a victim. This book will help increase awareness. Awareness can shorten valuable reaction time, which is required to survive.

There are multiple strategies for survival with both bombs and semi-automatic gun attacks. Given that you are at the blast-effects distance and not near the location of the bomb, it is important to note that there could be another bomb near the first center of detonation. The Boston Marathon bombing had two pressure cooker bombs explode 12 seconds apart and near a block apart. Here the key is survival. Take cover when an explosion is heard to make sure that there is not a second blast that could be even nearer—with more shrapnel.

It is also possible that a bomb is used to make people move in a specific direction only to find an attacker with semi-automatic weapons shooting those who flee from the bombing. Also, and very important advice for all, know first aid and CPR! It is amazing how many simply do not know first aid. For example, if wounded and bleeding severely, how do you preserve life and prevent death? Take a first aid course and know how to treat wounds. This can pay off not just with mass victim attacks but in any form of accident. You, family, friends, or just someone near you could be severely injured and your actions could make the difference.

As a quick anecdote, I know first aid—as all should. Once on my sailboat I was alone and was knocked to the floor by a huge wave onto a knife I was holding. The knife left a serious cut in my hand. Help was not nearby. I was able to control the blood flow using first aid techniques while nervously threading a regular needle with black sewing thread. I was able to close the wound with eight stitches and stop the bleeding. The point here is that we can do amazing things in an emergency that can surprise even ourselves.

In a crisis, we do what we can do. There are numerous instances of how people have helped victims of attacks, even if wounded personally. Bottom line, know first aid. Just search on the Internet for American first aid courses, with your location, to find out where you can be trained. Be prepared. It can make the difference between life and death.

A mass victim attack is not a death sentence for all. Given distant blast effects and the availability of strategies to escape death in mass shootings, you can survive. That is the purpose of this book. Why a book? Because there is just too much detail to cover in a simple write-up or short video. To escape the deer-in-the-headlights reaction that occurs when an actual attack occurs requires thought and preparation. During those first seconds, awareness and practice thinking about how to react can save your life. This book provides that awareness and practice.

2

Recognize Warning Signs

Can terrorist attacks be prevented? According to the Heritage Foundation, as of July 22, 2013, 60 Islamist-inspired terrorist attacks had been prevented since the Al Qaeda attack on the World Trade Center and the Pentagon on September 11, 2001.[1] Primarily, elements of domestic and self-radicalized terrorism motivation accounted for the attempts. Alert law enforcement and intelligence staff deserve much credit for thwarting the attacks, but nonofficial observers assisted as well. Such success, as encouraging as it is, must continue to improve. The fact that numerous attacks have been prevented point to the absolute value of recognizing and acting on pre-incident activities and threatening behavior.

We tend to think of a mass victim attack starting when the first shots are fired, or a bomb explodes. Media start reporting as soon as they enter the scene, either during or right after the attack. We see and hear witnesses describe the horrific event, and we see the aftermath via videos and numerous replays on television. The horror of the attack remains with us as replays continue. Once a mass victim attack begins, it is typically completed in seconds to minutes, but can last for hours. However, preparation may have taken days to years.

Planning and preparation consist of a variety of behaviors on the part of the attacker. There are observable events, and the potential attackers may appear to be suspicious in many ways to an onlooker. In some cases, suspicious behavior is observed, reports are made, law enforcement intervenes, and attacks are prevented. However, in most other examples, suspicious behavior is observed, reports are *not* made, and the attack occurs. After the attack, we often see the interviews of onlookers, family, or neighbors, stating

23

that they knew something was wrong and were suspicious—but did not report.

The fact that numerous attacks have been prevented underscores optimism of prevention when reports are made of suspicious and threatening behavior. Although we have had successes in preventing actual attacks, we must be aware that plots and attacks are continuing. In April 2017, the then director of the Department Homeland Security (DHS), John Kelly, reported that there had been 37 ISIS-related plots since 2013.[2] Being more alert and knowing what to look for may, in fact, prevent an increasing number of mass victim attacks.

We have alarm sensors in our homes to detect smoke so that we can intervene to prevent catastrophic loss from fire. We also use burglar alarm sensors to detect a door or window as it begins to open to let us act to prevent theft. Because of early warning signs that could be associated with mass victim attacks, we must rely on human sensors to detect and report. With over 330 million people in the United States, we have human sensors in all locations that could be beneficial in spotting precursors to an attack and reporting what they see to the authorities. We must know what is suspicious and threatening, how to report, and we must actually report.

DHS has a term for detecting and reporting: *If you see something, say something*. They maintain a website of the same name that is useful.[3] The catchphrase is easy to remember, but it assumes that an observer knows what to observe and how to report. If I could rewrite it to be more specific, it would be:

If you see a person or persons engaging in behavior or some product of their behavior that is suspicious or dangerous and could result in harm to another person, call 911 if potential harm or danger is imminent or local law enforcement if suspicious without imminent harm or danger and report who is suspicious, why the observation is suspicious, what the specifics of the observation that concern you are, when the observation occurred, and where law enforcement attention should be directed.

The DHS website does describe suspicious behavior. For example, they list the following as warning flags. These are examples of activities that might precede an actual attack and fit "see something."

- *Unusual items or situations: A vehicle is parked in an odd location, a package/luggage is unattended, a window/door is open that is usually closed, or other out-of-the-ordinary situations occur.*
- *Eliciting information: A person questions individuals at a level beyond curiosity about a building's purpose, operations, security procedures and/or personnel, shift changes, etc.*

- *Observation/surveillance: Someone pays unusual attention to facilities or buildings beyond a casual or professional interest. This includes extended loitering without explanation (particularly in concealed locations); unusual, repeated, and/or prolonged observation of a building (e.g., with binoculars or video camera); taking notes or measurements; counting paces; sketching floor plans, etc.*[3]

This does not mean that we report behavior simply because it is unusual or different. A point should be made about anomalous behavior. An anomaly is: *something different, abnormal, peculiar, or not easily classified.*[4] If a person exhibits anomalous behavior, or something different, abnormal, peculiar, or not in the norm, it does not mean the person is a threat. There is anomalous behavior that is associated with threat and anomalous behavior that is harmless. As human beings, we often exhibit unusual behavior, or behavior that is not our normal behavior—this doesn't mean that it is harmful; it may just be different from what is normal for us. However, a person may also exhibit anomalous behavior that is an indicator of threatening behavior. We must use our judgment.

If we observe someone doing something strange or different, the context must be considered. I can't say how many times I have been in moderate to large cities and have witnessed very strange behavior. The person may be pushing a shopping cart full of objects, shouting aloud, cursing, and asking for money. Unfortunately, we observe those who may be suffering from obvious mental health issues, and could be homeless. The behavior may be anomalous, but not threatening from the perspective of mass victim attacks.

We may see another person at home working late into the night with the same acquaintances over several nights. They make early morning trips to the trash can to dump empty cans of spent chemicals, or place trash bags in their car trunk instead of in their home trash can. They may carry several pressure cookers into the house or place empty boxes visibly in the trash. These behaviors are anomalous as well, but of more concern.

If behavior is out of the norm and your concern is raised even though you don't know what the behavior means, you may be witnessing something that needs to be reported. Does the behavior fit the situation, or does it not make sense? Is your concern raised? Who do you call?

We tend to think of calling 911 when there is something unusual happening. This may be appropriate if it is an emergency. But remember we have two sets of numbers. If you are faced with an emergency, definitely call 911. If you observe suspicious behavior and there is not an immediate threat, call local law local enforcement. Most importantly, *definitely call* if you feel that there is threatening behavior occurring, whether immediate action is required

(911) or something strange needs to be investigated (law enforcement). The key here is to report.

Warning signs of mass victim attacks are always present, whether marked by weeks, days, minutes, or seconds prior to an attack, and can be divided into two categories: (1) attack preparation: those signs present well before an attack when it could be prevented, and (2) imminent attack: warning signs occurring just before or at the start of an attack. Obviously, the earlier warning signs are spotted and reported, the better. But, regardless, being informed as to what to expect is far better than being caught off guard.

As an additional complicating factor, *See Something, Say Something*, as sound as it may be, may just be too simplistic and certainly is not descriptive. What should we see? What should we say? These are important questions. What is suspicious to one person who observes someone photographing the insides of a metro tunnel is very different from a mother who is in denial and turns a blind eye to a son preoccupied with weapons, who espouses hate and threatens to harm others, and who may be withdrawing. Family members and friends may be in denial, not wanting to believe that a son, daughter, mother, father, friend, or acquaintance may be engaging in activities that are potentially dangerous to others.

Family members not reporting suspicious or dangerous behavior may be doing a disservice to themselves. Adam Lanza (the Sandy Hook Elementary School shooter in Newtown, Connecticut) first shot and killed his mother immediately before going to the school and killing 20 first- and second-grade children and six adults. Lanza's mother was not only aware of his strange behaviors, but she had taken him repeatedly to the shooting range. She had also purchased the weapons and ammunitions he used in the elementary school slaughter.[5]

One of the most noteworthy mass victim attacks with numerous missed warning signs, with many having been reported but not acted on, was the 19-year-old Nikolas Cruz attack within the Marjory Stoneman Douglas High School in Parkland, Florida, on February 14, 2018. On that day, Cruz, a former student who had been expelled, entered the school near the end of day and pulled the fire alarm. This would allow him to shoot students with his AR-15 assault rifle as they left their classrooms to exit the school. He killed 14 students and 3 adults and wounded 17 others. After six minutes of shooting, he left the school, blending in with students. He was later apprehended and is faced with 17 counts of premeditated murder.

For many years, Cruz was known to neighbors and the school as threatening. The police made scores of calls to his home because of his behavior. He had posted images of weapons and even dead animals on social media and claimed he wanted to be professional school shooter. Yet he was not stopped, and many lost their lives in what should have been a preventable tragedy. The police response during the attack was not adequate, with no armed officer entering the building to stop the attack. Multiple investigations resulted.[6]

Not a new phenomenon, on September 6, 1949, 28-year-old Howard Unruh was distraught and blamed neighbors for his perceived ongoing rejection as he walked through his neighborhood with a German Luger pistol in hand. In 12 minutes, called "the walk of death," he shot and killed 13 and wounded 3. He was apprehended, declared mentally unfit, and committed to what was then labeled as an insane asylum. He died in 2009 having been incarcerated for six decades. Unruh was declared a spree killer and was the first such killer in U.S. history. For several years, Unruh had numerous squabbles with others and disputes with neighbors. It was known that he had problems.[7]

On August 1, 1966, 25-year-old Charles Whitman killed both his mother and his spouse before he went to the University of Texas in Austin, Texas, climbed a tower, and with a rifle killed 16 and wounded 31 innocent people at random. One was a fetus. An expert marksman, all were shot near or in the heart except for the obviously pregnant woman, who he shot in the stomach.[8] It was clear that there were signs of his growing disturbance prior to the attack. Threatening behavior must be reported even if the concern is with a family member or friend.

TYPE OF ATTACKER

Although the type of attacker may not seem to matter that much to those caught in an actual attack, attackers select targets based, in part, on what motivates them to want to kill a group of innocent people. For example, terrorism, regardless of the type (international, domestic, or self-radicalized), involves symbolic targets as a statement that is political in nature or planned to influence policy. The Al Qaeda attack on September 11, 2001, focused on the World Trade Center and the Pentagon—symbolic U.S. economic and military targets. However, from a school perspective, attackers appear to target innocent students and staff more from a mental health issues perspective. Generally speaking, domestic terrorism tends to occur to correct some perceived injustice, while hate attacks are aimed at a very specific group of people truly hated by the attacker.

Why are such distinctions important? If you are in a school, movie theater, mall, or similar large venue, you are more likely to encounter an attacker with mental health issues. If you are in a government or military installation, then some form of terrorist attack must always be anticipated as a possibility. This is one of the reasons why such installations are well guarded. In this category, the attacker(s) could be external to the United States (e.g., the 911 attack) or an insider attack, such as Major Nidal Hasan, a psychiatrist at Fort Hood, Texas, who turned his gun against his fellow soldiers, killing 13 and injuring more than 30 on November 9, 2009. Hasan, who was in communication with Al Qaeda leadership, was an Islamic extremist who espoused anti-U.S. sentiment well before his attack, which surely can be categorized as warning signs that should have required close attention, reporting, and intervention.[9]

There are exceptions. To show how complicated attacks can be across types, U.S. Army specialist Ivan Lopez, five years later on April 2, 2014, again at Fort Hood, turned a gun against his fellow soldiers and killed 3 and wounded 14 before taking his own life. He had been treated for depression and anxiety and had no connection with terrorist organizations.[10] The attack was in the same general location as Hasan's but the motivation was different.

We should keep in mind that definitions of types do not provide clear distinctions. This is one primary reason why there is not a universally accepted definition of terrorism. We could have a domestic terrorist who also has mental health issues. We could have a self-radicalized terrorist who engages in what we might consider workplace violence (a form of hate). In other words, there can be crossover.

As figure 2.1 shows, there are similarities that occur across type. As the diagram depicts, there appears to be more crossover across types of terrorism because of a common motivation to provide a message by attacking a symbolic target. Some view terrorism as a form of mental illness, perhaps because of the vicious and noncaring way the attacks occur. However, terrorists, for the most part, do not suffer from mental health issues. Instead, terrorists perceive themselves to be soldiers fighting a war against the enemy. This is why the diagram depicts no crossover between mental health issues and forms of terrorism and only slight crossover between hate and domestic terrorism. However, historically there is some crossover between hate/bias and domestic terrorism, as in the case of Timothy McVeigh's truck bombing against a U.S. government building. The target was a building symbolic of the U.S. government, and McVeigh had learned to hate the U.S. government. The attack served to strike back at and gain revenge against hated government staff and a symbolic government structure simultaneously.

An attacker could also be motivated by both hate/bias and mental health issues, while other attackers may be motivated by only hate/bias or only mental health issues. But, importantly, types of attackers have more commonalities than differences because of similar characteristics within attacker type. These similarities are expressed in common warning signs.

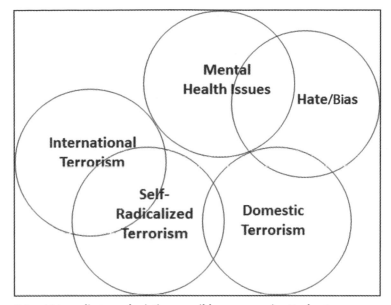

Figure 2.1   A Venn diagram depicting possible crossover in attacker types.

ATTACK PLANNING: WARNING SIGNS DURING ATTACK PREPARATION

Table 2.1 provides examples of what could be observed that would be suspicious and of concern. These are examples derived through many years of my experience and research. It should also be considered that new activities could surface that have never been observed in the past. Knowing typical activities that lead to concern can help in determining if something new is suspicious and should be reported.

Seeing something that could be early in the planning process of a mass victim attack, regardless of the type of attacker, provides an opportunity to prevent an attack. Knowing there can be observations early in the process is a very important realization. Most perpetrators of mass victim attacks display early signs. To attack a group of innocent victims to end their lives requires very intense emotions of hate, disgust, anger, fantasy, a strong desire for recognition, a need to belong to an adversary organization or to deliver a strong politically charged statement to influence policy. Such strong emotions are difficult to conceal. The expression could be private, in the case of posting clippings of past mass victim attacks / mass murders in one's room if suffering from mental health issues, or it could take the form of more open

Table 2.1   Pre-Incident Planning Warning Signs

Attacker Type	Examples
International Terrorism	Apparent surveillance of symbolic target; military-like preparation/practice; obtaining weapons, ammunition, knives, bags of fertilizer; making social media complaints about the U.S.; excessive target practice; open threats to kill U.S. citizens; vows of support for radical Islam; cheering successful mass victim attacks
Domestic Terrorism	U.S. person conducting apparent surveillance of symbolic target; obtaining weapons, ammunition, knives, bags of fertilizer out of context; social media complaints or making threats focused on the U.S. government, U.S. military, or political organization; statements of disgust about U.S. policies or politicians
Self-Radicalized Terrorism	U.S. person expressing strong anti-U.S. sentiment; threats made concerning the U.S.; repeated pro-terrorist or pro-Islamic radicalism, including these sentiments using social media; apparent repeated visits (apparent surveillance) of "despised" locations; attempts to communicate with or success in communicating with any international terrorist; any claim of being associated with a foreign terrorist organization
Mental Health Issues	History of violence-based mental health issues; preoccupation with firearms; collecting accounts of violent person's acts (newspaper/magazine clippings, movies, recorded programs); posting of dangerous person's acts on wall, computer, or social media; loner behavior; makes serious threats of harm or death; failure to take prescribed medications for depression or anxiety; attempts to seek help for homicidal thoughts; statements about the need to kill others
Hate	Often-stated disgust, bias, or hate for a specific ethnicity, religion, gender, race, or sexual orientation; threats of severe harm/death to hated groups; preoccupation with firearms or other forms of weapons (e.g., knives, bombs, vehicles); frequent displays of group-directed anger, including uncontrollable anger; statements threatening the life of others

social media rants. Nevertheless, there are typically early indicators. All forms of attacks require planning, acquiring weapons, and targeting—activities that have telltale signs.

It is especially important for friends and acquaintances to be aware of threatening behavior. A potential mass victim attacker may be converting a room to a bomb-making facility or the beginning of an arsenal. Someone suffering from mental health issues may have stopped his or her medication, shown a preoccupation with weapons, or made startling and threatening comments. It is far better for a loved one or a friend to not deny threat if it is present. It is far better to intervene to prevent a potential attack than to learn after the fact that many were killed, and the family member or acquaintance was killed or committed suicide to complete the attack.

I know of no examples of spontaneous mass victim attacks—they all require planning, and planning is not easy. It requires work, and there may even be a satisfaction gained from taking steps toward the end goal—the attack itself. Also, repeated planning efforts can lead to carelessness and less concern for concealment over time. Planners can get sloppy. This provides even more opportunity for others to see something and say something.

Attack preparation can give away clues that something is very wrong even if we don't know exactly what it could be. It is an understatement to say that those who witness suspicious behavior and do not report may have missed a very important opportunity to save lives in the future.

IMMINENT ATTACK: WARNING SIGNS JUST BEFORE AN ATTACK BEGINS

Warning signs can be present right up to the time a mass victim attack begins and, in some cases, during the actual attack. It may sound strange that warning signs can be present as the attack occurs because all in that location will know an attack is in progress. However, if an attacker enters the scene wearing a gas mask then it can be assumed that some form of a gas attack will follow.

As an example, James Holmes, wearing tactical clothing and a gas mask, entered the back-exit door at the Century movie theatre in Aurora, Colorado, on July 20, 2012. He released two tear gas grenades then started shooting. Holmes was well armed with rifle, shotgun, and Glock 9mm pistol. He mercilessly slaughtered 12 unknown, innocent victims and 58 were wounded. The Batman movie, "The Dark Night Rises" was playing at the time. Holmes was known to have been suffering from mental health issues.[11]

How an attack unfolds can provide invaluable information that can aid survival. A single shooter versus two or three shooters or a single weapon versus multiple weapons can make a very big difference. Strategies for survival must take such things into account. These issues are covered in detail later in the book.

There is a multitude of warning signs that a mass victim attack is imminent. I divide these into (1) warning signs of approach to the target location, and (2) the beginning of the attack. First, the focus will be on the final approach to the target.

The Final Approach

We must keep in mind that when mass victim attackers initiate the final approach to the target they are very much aware that this act could end with loss of their own lives. In some cases, they have planned to take their own lives. Living is not their primary concern as the final approach occurs. The focus is to kill as many innocent people as possible in the shortest amount of time before first responders arrive on the scene.

Attackers are aware that those targeted will have cell phones, and calls to 911 are immediate when the attack begins. This is true whether the attack is focused on shooting, detonating explosives, stabbing, running over victims, or the use of any number of weapons. It is not about the weapons—it is about killing with whatever weapons or set of weapons have been selected. At the first sign of attack, it is highly likely a 911 call will follow almost immediately. The attacker knows he must move quickly.

Because the final approach could be their last act, and their focus on spotting initial victims and the presence of any security is steadfast, approaching attackers have a different appearance than those around them. Facial expressions are more solemn. Others in the vicinity may be smiling, laughing, engaged in conversations, or engaged in many different activities. If a restaurant, visitors may be eating, servers serving, and tables being bussed. If a bar, conversation and drinking may be heavy with all engaged in a happy time. If a movie theatre, all are engrossed with the sights and sounds of the movie being played. In short, life is continuing as usual within the selected public target. The attacker knows to use this to advantage, and is well aware that it is all going to change shortly.

The attacker must have weapons, and they must be concealed. The attacker does not want weapons discovered before the act. Perhaps guns are concealed under a jacket or coat. This is an important consideration because most shooters bring several weapons and do not depend on only one. What if the one weapon jammed? There must also be extra ammunition to ensure that the attack goes as planned. Extra ammunition is required to make sure victims, who are often shot repeatedly, are killed. If first responders intervene, again extra ammunition would be required to halt their intervention.

If the weapon or one of the weapons is a knife, it is easily concealed. If it is warm outside and the attacker is approaching wearing a coat, the clothing may conceal the weapons but be out of context, particularly if no one else is wearing a jacket or coat. The jacket also may be necessary to conceal a suicide belt, or a chest-wrapped bomb. Different appearance, demeanor, clothing, behavior, expression, and carrying bags and backpacks that are out of place can all be warning signs. If more than one sign is present, concern should be even higher.

The psychology underlying the final approach to the target is very important. Attackers have worked out the issues concerning fear of death. If international terrorism or self-radicalized terrorism, the attack itself may be viewed as a positive way to serve God and to go a blessed way into the next life by being a good soldier for God. With others, the act may be viewed as a way to seek revenge for how they have been wronged in life and to end personal pain, particularly in the examples involving mental health issues. Attackers think differently—fear of death may be absent, and death actually a preferred end state.

If there remains concern for one's own life, the focus may be on escape without being caught, especially if the attack involves remote detonation of a bomb. For example, the Oklahoma City truck bomb of the Alfred P. Murrah federal building on April 19, 1995, was remotely detonated by Terry McVeigh, killing 168 people and wounding nearly 700 others, only after he had exited the scene to safety.

However, if the attack takes the form of a face-to-face armed assault, the shooter knows the attack may be the last act of his or her life. We can only imagine those last thoughts as the attacker closes in. Nevertheless, such thoughts must be there, and the reason why the attacker is going to appear to be preoccupied and not acting like others. There is a mission to accomplish, and failure at this point is not an option.

It is possible that attack activity occurs before entering the actual target location. There may be the presence of guards or off-duty law enforcement officers at the perimeter, serving as security. The objective is clear: Enter the selected location and kill as many people as possible. The attacker sees external security only as an obstacle to immediately overcome so that the objective can be completed.

Most mass victim attacks begin immediately when a location is entered, such as the Holmes attack at the Aurora, Colorado, movie theatre just mentioned. There has been much planning and preparation, and the attacker is primed to attack. Occasionally, there is an exception. On June 17, 2015, 21-year-old Dylann Roof entered the historic Emanuel African Methodist Episcopal Church in Charleston, South Carolina, and participated in a small Bible study with African Americans worshippers. After about an hour and before prayer, Roof stood, pulled out a Glock .45mm pistol, and shot and killed all but one person so that she could tell his story of getting back at *blacks.*[12]

Roof ranted as he shot, shouting about the need to hate and kill black people. He reloaded his gun five times as he systematically targeted his victims. He finally tried to kill himself by shooting himself in the head but was out of ammunition.[13] Roof killed nine innocent worshippers and is now in prison without the chance of parole. The white supremacist's hate crime was unusual in many ways, including the fact that he participated in the worship service for an hour prior to acting.

The First Seconds

Dylann Roof aside, most mass victim attacks begin without interaction with victims. Attackers use the element of surprise for many reasons. First, when an attack begins, regardless of the weapons used, it takes a few seconds for victims to process what is happening. The human startle response is complex both from physiological and psychological perspectives. Reflexively, we orient toward any disturbance to determine what is happening and then we process the sights and sounds that are invading our senses. The response, then, could be panic, running, hiding, or even attempting to fight. It is difficult to predict how anyone will act when confronted with a mass victim attack.

The more we know what to expect and how to increase the chance of survival, the more likely our responses will aid us. In short, we may be able to increase our odds by being able to react rapidly and follow a sound strategy such as how to escape.

As a more recent example of immediate attack, a hybrid self-radicalized terrorist and hate/bias attack occurred on June 12, 2016, in Orlando, Florida. Omar Mateen approached the gay nightclub Pulse. He was armed with a semi-automatic rifle and pistol. Encountering security near the entrance, an exchange of gunfire occurred, as the guard retreated. Mateen then entered the nightclub and began shooting indiscriminately. Mateen's objective was to kill all in the club. The attack persisted for over three hours until Mateen was killed by police officers who were able to get inside the club. The result of the attack was 49 dead and 53 injured.[14]

On December 2, 2015, a husband and wife entered a social gathering at the Inland Regional Center in San Bernardino, California. Twenty-eight-year-old Syed Rizwan Farook and 27-year-old Tashfeen Malik modified assault rifles[15, 16] to kill 14 people and wound 27. They were later shot and killed in a shootout after successfully escaping from the scene. They were discovered with thousands of rounds of ammunition and numerous pipe bombs in their possession. Self-radicalized, it still is not clear as to the reason for the attack. Those targeted were fellow employees.

When an attack begins, targets are startled, bewildered, and once immediate threat and danger are realized, they must determine what to do. This takes valuable time—time that could save lives if victims could act more quickly. Survivors of mass victim shooting attacks often report they heard popping sounds at the beginning of an attack and did not recognize the sounds as gunfire at first. There can be several reasons for not recognizing gunfire immediately. First, many people are simply not accustomed to hearing actual gunfire. Some report hearing fireworks, or a bag popping. Second, gunfire within a building can sound very different from gunshots outside or at a gun range and certainly different from what is heard in a movie, or on TV. A building has very different acoustics, and it can be difficult to determine the direction of the sounds, even after finally determining that gunshots are occurring.[17]

We must remember that in an active shooting, attackers will likely be using semi-automatic assault rifles and/or semi-automatic pistols. These weapons fire as fast as the trigger is pulled. Semi-automatic weapons also may have been modified to shoot on full automatic mode. In this way, the gun keeps shooting as long as the trigger is pulled—like a machine gun. In the October 1, 2017, attack on a live concert in Las Vegas, Stephen Paddock used a bump stock attachment to multiple semi-automatic rifles to shoot down at 22,000 concertgoers from his perch on a high-level floor of the Mandalay Bay resort. He killed at least 59 innocent people with over 500 sustaining injuries. The bump stock attachment turns a semi-automatic rifle into an automatic shooting device and allows the shooter to fire off many more rounds much faster than the speed of pulling a trigger with the finger.[18] The attachment resulted in the worst mass victim shooting attack in U.S. history.

If the attacker is a shooter, the assault begins with a hail of rapid gunfire meant to kill as many people as possible before they start springing into action, panicking, running, and hiding. We must also remember that it doesn't matter who you are—victims can include men, women, children, infants, the elderly, and the physically and mentally challenged.

Our first tendency when hearing such sounds is to look and see if we can find the cause of the sounds that startled us and may be continuing. This takes valuable seconds that could be spent on reacting in such a way that the chances of survival can be increased. If loud, gun-like popping sounds occur within an enclosure, my best advice is to: *assume the worst and don't hope for the best.* You want the first sign of extreme danger to be *recognized* sounds of gunshots, not the screams and panic that are sure to follow as life-threatening danger approaches.

If the attack begins with a bomb or the attack is a bombing, the closer victims are to the explosion, the more serious the blast effects. When a bomb explodes, it takes only a small fraction of one second to expend the energy stored in the bomb—less time than a blink of the eye. The sudden release of energy is immense.

In a bombing, there are those who are, unfortunately, caught within a primary blast effects center. This is the area that immediately extends out in a circle from the location of the bomb, the size of which depends on the explosive power of the bomb. This could be referred to as a kill zone for obvious reasons. A high-yield explosive such as dynamite, C4, Semtex, or an improvised explosive device constructed with ammonium nitrate fertilizer (ANFO), has a devastating shock wave that can instantly kill, maim, and destroy vision and hearing. Even low-yield explosives such as a pipe bomb or a pressure cooker bomb can have devastating effects.

The blast effects can vary widely. The domestic terror bombing of the Alfred P. Murrah building in Oklahoma City was constructed as a high-yield bomb using ANFO. The bomb was in a truck parked outside the building and detonated when Timothy McVeigh, the attacker, had safely left the scene. Much of the building was demolished, surrounding buildings damaged, 168 people killed, and over 650 injured.[19] The low-yield pressure cooker bombs planted by the Tsarnaev brothers at the finish of the Boston Marathon on April 15, 2013, killed three people and injured hundreds. Whether a high-yield or low-yield bomb and whether in a truck or a pressure cooker or pipe bomb, the effects can be horrifying.

When a bomb is detonated, there is no time to assess the sights and sounds as in an active shooter attack. It is immediate and leads to confusion. There will likely be those killed immediately, those injured and disfigured severely requiring immediate attention, and those hit with shrapnel and debris. There are also injuries that result from escaping as panic spreads. There may also be a second bomb. During the Boston Marathon bombing two pressure cooker bombs exploded approximately 16 seconds apart and were placed less than 100 yards apart.[20]

If the attacker uses a knife, the attack begins almost immediately with a stabbing and then the attacker goes after all nearby. We have also experienced vehicles being used as weapons to run over, kill, and injure pedestrians. In

May, 2017, the U.S. Transportation Security Administration (TSA) issued a security alert to trucking companies about potential stolen trucks used to follow ISIS recommendations to run over and kill pedestrians as a group.[21] For example, on July 16, 2016, a 31-year-old Tunisian driver drove his 20-ton rented truck into a crowd in Nice, France, and ran over as many victims as he could. He killed 84 and wounded 202, including 10 adolescents and children.[22] This is the largest vehicle type of attack at the time of writing this book. However, there have been others.

As highlighted by media, numerous vehicle attacks have occurred.[23] On December 19, 2016, in Berlin, during peak Christmas shopping, an ISIS sympathizer, Anis Amri, rammed a tractor-trailer into a group of pedestrians. He killed 12 and injured more than 40 people before being killed by police.

On March 22, 2017, an attacker rammed his rental car into pedestrians on Westminster Bridge in London. The bridge is near Parliament. After running over victims, he then entered Parliament grounds, confronted a policeman, and stabbed him to death before being killed by police. Five people were killed, including the police officer and a U.S. citizen.

On April 7, 2017, an extremist sympathizer stole a beer truck and ran over pedestrians before ramming into a department store in Stockholm, Sweden. Four people were killed and 15 were injured.

On June 3, 2017, three men targeted pedestrians on London Bridge in London and forcefully ran over them in a van. They then exited the van and went on a stabbing rampage at nearby bars. The result was eight victims killed and over 40 injured.

The United States has also experienced this form of attack. On November 28, 2016, an Ohio State University student, Abdul Razak Ali Artan, an apparent self-radicalized terrorist, ran his car into a group of students on campus. He then exited the car and started stabbing victims. He was later killed by police after exiting the scene. The attack resulted in 11 injuries.

On October 31, 2017, in Manhattan near the site of the 9/11 Al Qaeda terrorist attack targeting the World Trade Center, self-radicalized Sayfullo Saipov from Uzbekistan used a rental truck to run over innocent victims on a pedestrian/bike path.[24] He had shouted the all-too-familiar *Allahu Akbar* (God is greater) as he attacked. He killed eight people and injured 11 others, including three children. He finally exited his car after crashing into a school bus. He was wounded by a police officer as he wandered around the area brandishing a pellet gun and a paintball gun.

In some attacks the use of a vehicle to kill innocent people is immediately followed by stabbings. Although stabbings have occurred for some time, many do not result in mass fatalities. Again, there are exceptions. On April

26, 2016, in Sagamihara, a small town near Tokyo, Satoshi Uematsu, a former employee of a facility for the mentally ill, entered the facility and systematically stabbed and killed 19 people and injured dozens more. He attacked while the victims slept.[25] He had been placed in a mental health facility four months earlier for threats to kill the mentally disabled, but was released after two weeks.[26]

The Choice of Weapons

It is clear that mass victim attacks have many causes, and attackers have different motivations. In terrorist groups, bombers are revered and to be protected. Bomb-making if done correctly takes skill. Typically, if an attack is a bombing attack, then we are more likely to determine that international terrorism, self-radicalized terrorism, or domestic terrorism was the cause. If we observe a full-out assault with semi-automatic guns with no explosives, then often the motivation was a result of mental health issues or an attack driven by hate/bias. Motivation definitely affects weapons choice.

Much has evolved since the massive Al Qaeda attack directed against the World Trade Center North and South Towers and the Pentagon in 2001. The attack remains the most devastating in U.S. history, including the infamous Pearl Harbor attack that pulled us into World War II on December 7, 1941. The primary motive in international terrorism against the United States is to strike fear into our hearts and deliver an anti-U.S. message. The motivation is to create horrific death and injuries associated with U.S. symbolic targets, or at least that was the objective in 2001.

However, in 2014, ISIS spokesman Abu Mohammad al-Adnani said the following in the ISIS publication *Rumiyah*,

> *If you are not able to find an IED or a bullet, then single out the disbelieving American, Frenchman, or any of their allies. Smash his head with a rock, or slaughter him with a knife, or run him over with your car, or throw him down from a high place, or choke him, or poison him.*

Al Qaeda espoused a similar theme in their publication *Inspire*, aimed at devotees,

> *The idea is to use a pickup truck as a mowing machine, not to mow grass but mow down the enemies of Allah.*[27]

It doesn't take special expertise to determine that both ISIS and Al Qaeda have called for attacks against the West with whatever is available. Vehicles, knives, or any lethal means may be used. This is a simple message that lets anyone who is a sympathizer or self-radicalized enthusiast kill innocent victims and be considered a soldier. No special skills are required, and vehicles and knives, as they say, are easily acquired in any country.

There are commonalities among international terrorists, domestic terrorists, self-radicalized terrorists, those suffering from mental health issues, and those driven by hate toward a specific group of people. The following presents some of the major similarities:

- An attack is designed to show no mercy—all are fair game for killing whether man, woman, child, elderly, or the physically or mentally challenged.
- Attacks should be horrific, which adds to the power of the message, if terrorism, or the revenge, if fueled by hate or mental health issues.
- Weapon selection is simply a means to an end—an attacker uses whatever lethal means are familiar or available.
- Recognition is typically desired.
- Personal safety or staying alive is not a primary consideration—killing others is the objective.

Warning Signs

All mass victim attacks use the element of surprise to make optimal use of confusion, panic, and bewilderment, whether the attack is multiple stabbings, vehicle run-down, bombings, or armed assaults. The following warning signs should be remembered:

- Someone or several people approaching the location who do not fit the context (e.g., solemn faces, fixed stares, dressed inappropriately for conditions, threats, shouts of *Allahu Akbar*);
- Sudden loud sounds within a public/crowded location (e.g., explosion, loud firecracker, popping, or gun-like noise);
- Vehicle veering off path toward pedestrians or hitting multiple pedestrians;
- Panic, others running, screams, fear, crying, calls for help, and descriptive shouting of such words as *bomb, shooter, gun, or attack*;
- Immediate appearance of people down, apparent injuries, blood, or screams of pain.

This chapter focused on warning signs, or what to expect. In the next chapter, the focus will be on what to do if caught in an attack. The probability of survival is increased dramatically if warning signs are recognized early and knowing what to do is almost automatic. Time at the beginning of an attack is critical. To repeat, because it is so important, at the beginning of an attack, time is critical. Move, escape, and know what to do.

The act of reading this book can increase awareness. Knowing how to react when specific sounds are encountered can help to shorten reaction time and provide valuable seconds that can lead to survival. Awareness of threat, realization of an attack within the location you are in, and survival strategies for the situation are all key. In the following chapters, different scenarios are presented to provide practical awareness on how to respond.

3

Know How to React When Caught in an Actual Attack

The previous chapter focused on: (1) pre-attack planning and preparation, and (2) the beginning of the actual attack. In this chapter, we begin with the attack and how responses increase or decrease the chances of survival. This book is focused on the premise that visualization, understanding, knowing what to expect, and knowing how to react to different mass victim attacks better prepares us for an attack if it should occur to us. Facing the unknown with no preparation or knowledge is likely to enhance a startle response that can lead to panic and many lost seconds—and an increased probability of being a fatality.

I have covered types of attacks and attackers. The types were classified according to different motivators that drive attackers to their actions and target location selection. We can also focus on types of attack, because of similarities in tactics based on weapon choice. For example, bombings are similar, as are semi-automatic weapon shootings. We also see strong similarities in vehicle run-downs, as well as stabbings. The nature and restrictions of how specific types of attacks can happen dictate similarities. In the following sections, we will focus on shootings, bombings, vehicle run-downs, and stabbings.

In the following chapters, we will explore in detail how survival depends on a person's response at the beginning of a mass victim attack and during the attack. This differs from some current advice in several ways. First, typical responses are labeled Run, Hide, or Fight, at least for active shooter attacks. To quote Mike Wood, "The 'Run, Hide, Fight' campaign is a multi-agency effort, promoted most prominently through a widely-distributed training film produced by the City of Houston, with federal funding."[1] In Mr. Wood's analysis, the advice is flawed because it plays down a more active "fight" response.

I have a different view. The *Run, Hide, Fight* slogan has value but just as a start, even for active shooter cases. Although useful, my problem with it is that thorough defensive responses cannot be trained or adequately learned in a five-minute video,[2] which simply does not provide all the detail necessary for survival. It can demonstrate a single response to a specific form of attack, but mass victim attacks are as varied as their attackers. Second, this book is about all mass victim attacks and not just armed assaults. For example, we have stabbings, vehicle run-downs, and bombings in addition to shootings. But for mass victim attacks, the *Run, Hide, Fight* slogan is a good start for how to respond to all mass victim attacks, if extended properly.

Run, Hide, Fight designed for active shooter cases may be used as a foundation for all mass victim attacks—with needed modifications and additional detail. As will be seen in the following chapters, there are multiple options available based on the attack. I focus on four responses: (1) escape (2) hide (3) stay in place (4) attack the attacker. All are important, and can save lives if followed.

There are valid reasons for changing *run* to *escape*, *fight* to *attack the attacker*, and adding *stay in place* when considering mass victim attacks. *Hide* is *hide*, but much more detail will be presented as to how to hide properly. *Playing dead* is considered under the heading *Staying in Place* in this book—there are many dos and don'ts if staying in place. Staying in place can result in death or survival depending on the situation. Most importantly, you need to recognize that survival knowledge is not contained within a single article with a bulleted list or a short video. Mass victim attacks and how to survive is far more complex and requires a careful study.

Why change words? First *run* has the connotation of simply getting out of the area as fast as possible by running. Where do you run, how do you run, what do you do while running, do you run alone or with others, and why are you deciding to run? These are all very important questions. Survival is best achieved by planned escape, not just running. *Escape*, as I use it instead of *run*, has a stronger and more pointed meaning. Looking at a traditional definition, the word escape includes "to avoid a threatening evil" and "to get away."[3] In the case of mass victim bombing, running after an explosion could result in being in the vicinity of a second bomb. You could escape the first bombing only to enter the damaging range of a second bomb.

Second, in the case of a shooting assault, simply running could direct you into the range of a second shooter, or the only shooter if you don't know where he is. Noting the sounds of gunfire and the apparent direction can provide valuable clues as to whether there is a single shooter or multiple shooters. There are various ways you can escape in these two scenarios, and we will cover them in this book.

Why did I change the term *fight* of the common phrase *"Run, Hide, Fight"* to *attack*? If, as a last resort with few options left, then it may be appropriate to attack the attackers. When confronted with armed attackers, whether semi-automatic weapons, knives, or a vehicle run-down, you must know how to attack, not just fight. You will be at a distinct disadvantage. The attacker came prepared with multiple weapons and extra ammunition, or multiple knives, a vehicle to kill you, or a bomb.

The word *fight* is defined in many ways but most definitions include a battle of sorts or to "put forth a determined effort."[4] The objective of *attack* is not a struggle or an attempt to fight back, it is to kill the attacker. You must be ready and capable to know that to save lives, including yours, you will need to kill the attacker who is killing others. This is not a fistfight—this is not trading punches like in the movies. If you attack back, you must know what you can do, and be capable of doing it if you are to neutralize the threat. This does not mean that maiming, totally disabling, inflicting blindness, or any effort to neutralize the attacker cannot work, but these objectives are secondary. When faced with the need for very aggressive self-defense, you need to go for it and kill the attacker. There is no nice way to say this: You meet lethal force with deadly force.

Later in the book, we will cover the use of personal protection devices, PPDs, which are legal in all 50 states. They certainly can be part of *attack* and can debilitate an attacker. When attacked, all is fair game. You do what you must do to stop the threat and active killing of innocent victims. We simply are not accustomed to thinking about the need to stop an attacker at all costs. However, mass victim attackers are going to kill you if you are in their crosshairs. You cannot talk your way out of it or expect any form of mercy, whoever you are. Remember, even infants and young children are killed in mass victim attacks, as are the physically and mentally challenged and the elderly.

Of all mass victim attacks I have personally researched, I know of only two incidents when a person was purposely spared by an attacker. The first was mentioned previously. Dylann Roof in his attack in the Emanuel African Methodist Episcopal Church in Charleston, South Carolina, told one woman she would be spared so that she could tell the story of his attack. She was spared.

The second case was personal for me. On January 25, 1993, I was driving into the back gate of the CIA, where I worked. At the same time, Pakistani Mir Amal Kansi (or Kasi) exited his car and walked down the line of cars waiting at the red light to turn into the front gate main entrance. He systematically aimed into the cars with his rifle as he walked down the line toward the red light and killed two employees and wounded three. However, when encountering a car with a female driver, he passed the car to shoot the male driver in the car in front of her.[5] Although I headed up the behavior analysis of this event for years, we never discovered why he passed by the female. However, passing up any potential victims is indeed rare. Such shooters do not plan on, nor do they, spare anyone. After a very long search, Kansi was captured in Pakistan, extradited, and was executed by lethal injection on November 14, 2002, in the United States after having several appeals turned down. The secret of why he passed on the female died with him. I will never know why.

Even if attackers can spare people in shootings or stabbings, vehicle rundowns and bombings are indiscriminate. Whoever is in the path or in range will get hit, either fatally or with injuries. In short, you cannot depend on a mass victim attacker being merciful—you must act to save your life. In all seriousness, if faced with a mass victim attack and people are being killed, if you are not capable of facing this threat head on, then escape. In the following sections, I will provide details according to the type of attack encountered.

SHOOTINGS

When thinking of mass victim attacks, we likely think of shootings first. We have witnessed many mass victim attack shootings in the United States and around the world. Why? First, semi-automatic rifles and pistols, at least in the United States, are easily obtained. Second, it is easy to conceal a small semi-automatic weapon. Third, such weapons are extremely lethal and can be used to kill many victims in a very short period of time—seconds to minutes. Mass victim attackers do not have to worry about taking time to find a specific target. Everyone is a target.

Because semi-automatic weapons are small, multiple weapons can be carried—and concealed—by an attacker. There is even room in pockets for extra ammunition. When Dylann Roof entered the Emanuel African Methodist Episcopal Church in Charleston, South Carolina, he was dressed normally, and participated in the African American Bible study for about an hour. His goal was to start a race war. He was wearing a fanny pack, with a fully loaded Glock .45-caliber semi-automatic pistol hidden behind it. As previously detailed, he pulled out the gun, killed nine people and wounded three before fleeing the scene. Concealment was important for him to carry out his objective.

In some attacks, concealment isn't that necessary. For example, James Holmes, the perpetrator of the attack at the Aurora, Colorado, movie theater on July 20, 2012, had legally purchased the following in the week preceding the attack: a Smith & Wesson .223 semi-automatic rifle, two .40-caliber Glock pistols, and a Remington 870 shotgun. He also had purchased two teargas hand grenades used to start his attack.[6] The weapons were purchased from three different stores. He was dressed in full tactical clothing. Because he entered the fire exit door at the back of the theatre in reduced lighting while the movie was playing, he didn't need to worry about concealment.

The method of the attack will influence how difficult concealment is. If the attacker is dressed to match the attire of others during warm weather, with no coats or jackets, the objective is to blend in until the actual attack. In this case, weapons will be limited if a shooting is planned. There may be only a single weapon. However, if heavy clothing, or obvious tactical clothing to provide body protection, is worn—especially during hot weather—multiple semi-automatic weapons could be concealed.

However, the primary consideration for choosing semi-automatic rifles and pistols is the killing power. The number of shots that can be fired in a minute is limited only by how fast the attacker can pull the trigger and the amount of ammunition. Herein lies the reason for multiple weapons: It takes less time to switch to another previously loaded firearm than to reload during the attack. Also, at short distances typical of mass victim shooting attacks, accuracy is not that critical because of the ability to fire multiple shots within a very short time with anyone being a target.

Spraying bullets in the direction of many people confined within a selected space will meet the objective of killing innocent victims. Although semi-automatic weapons can be modified to shoot in a full-automatic mode, it really isn't necessary. Straight off-the-shelf semi-automatic weapons have more than enough firepower to kill many victims before first responders can arrive.

When it is apparent that an active shooting is going to occur (e.g., weapons observed, apparent tactical dress or gunshots begin), the best option is to *escape* followed by *hide*. At this point it is essential to understand that *fight* is a last-resort method. Likewise, *staying in place* is not a viable option (unless it is a special case, which will be explained). Given advancing rapid gunfire and given the attacker or attackers may be wearing protective clothing, immediate thoughts should go to any method of escape that is available.

Escape means to exit the premises for a location safe from threat. This can be accomplished through doors other than the one entered by the attacker(s) if they are still near the entrance. A kitchen door may provide a quick escape—almost all kitchens have a back door for delivery, trash removal, and employee alternate entrance or exit. A window broken with a chair can also provide a quick escape if on ground-floor level. Details will be covered later in the chapter focusing on escape.

If escape does not appear to be an option, then hiding should immediately be considered. Hiding is not preferable and is more dangerous than escape. Why? It all depends on how long first responders can intervene. The prevalence of smartphones usually results in immediate calls to 911. This results in rapid response, often within minutes. However, that does not mean that the attacker(s) will immediately be stopped, unless they take their own lives. In some cases, I am sorry to say, it has taken law enforcement officials a surprising number of hours to enter the scene of an attack.

As an example of how long a mass victim attack can drag on and why escape should be the number one concern, the attack by 29-year-old Omar Mateen at Pulse nightclub in Orlando lasted three hours. Thirty minutes after the beginning of the attack, Mateen himself called 911 and said, "I pledge allegiance to Abu Bakr al-Baghdadi of the Islamic State." He also acknowledged the Tsarnaev brothers, the Boston Marathon bombers. A self-radicalized terrorist, he entered by first having a shoot-out with a perimeter guard, but the guard retreated knowing that he was outgunned. After entering the facility, for several hours Mateen systematically hunted down those inside, and continued his senseless killing. Where was law enforcement? Remember, you are on your own for surviving. Know what to do!

Some trapped inside were fortunate enough to escape early. After two hours, more in hiding managed to escape through an air conditioning hole in the wall removed by law enforcement with the assistance of those hiding inside. There were indications that Mateen had a bomb and that his car may have had a bomb. For almost four hours he hunted down and shot patrons, made repeated cell phone calls to his wife, had repeated cell phone discussions with the police negotiator, and pledged allegiance to the Islamic State on a 911 call. The attack began at 2:02 a.m. and ended at 5:53 a.m., when police breached a wall, entered, and killed Mateen as he fired at them. At the conclusion, 49 were dead and at least 53 injured.[7] If an active shooter attack begins, the key is to escape, escape, escape in any way possible as a first resort. I have to ask again: Where was law enforcement and why did the Pulse attack continue for several hours?

BOMBINGS

A bombing is very different from an active shooter attack. In a shooting attack, there is a beginning to the attack, and it progresses in stages until it ends. Victims are shot one at a time until the conclusion. Many are shot repeatedly, just to make sure they are dead. In a bombing, there may be no warning until the detonation occurs. The explosion is literally faster than a blink of an eye. If caught within the killing range nearest to the bomb, the probability of survival is slim to none, depending on the power of the bomb. However, the explosive power of a detonated bomb diminishes quickly with distance.

What is a bomb? Bombs can be very different in makeup, size, explosive power, and how they are delivered. Most often, bombs used in mass victim attacks are improvised explosive devices, or IEDs. An IED is a homemade bomb, not existing military munitions. To be clear, very clear, constructing an IED is not difficult. Documents easily found on the Internet contain all the details required to find materials, construct, and detonate IEDs. In my opinion, less than a high school diploma is required to construct a bomb that can kill many people. On the smaller side, pipe bombs may be loaded with easily obtained gunpowder. More powerful bombs may use ANFO, a combination of ammonium nitrate-based fertilizer and diesel oil, to make military grade explosives.

Beginning at the exact location of the bomb and moving out in a circle, there are deaths, the severest of injuries, severe injuries, injuries, and fortunately, at a certain distance, no injuries. Bombs have enough explosive power that the blast alone can kill. However, mass victim attack bombs are likely to be packed with small shrapnel such as nails, BBs, and other sharp objects to increase damage nearby and at greater distances. These objects all become projectiles like individual bullets when a bomb explodes, much like many firearms going off at one time. Often there are injuries inflicted from the shrapnel alone.

Whether a bomb is placed or carried, there is an opportunity before detonation to report suspicious behavior. If you see any unattended package, whether it be a suitcase, backpack, shopping bag, box, or any other container that could conceal a bomb, tell others to move away immediately and contact law enforcement. Do not stay near a suspicious package with no apparent owner. When reporting to police, make sure to describe the package, the exact location, and all relevant circumstances.

There are some key points to consider if a bomb should go off in your vicinity. Not all bombs are equal. There could be structural damage, and walls or ceilings could fall. If the bombing is small, as devastating as it may be, running away blindly could place you near a second bomb. Stay in place if there are no apparent shooters! This is the only time it is appropriate. You may be able to give first aid to yourself, family, or others until first responders arrive, which is usually within minutes.

If you are not injured or are injured only slightly, and it is a smaller bombing, this is the one instance where it is wise to stay in place. Mass victim attackers do not place two bombs in the same location. If two or more bombs are used, they are placed at separate nearby locations to maximize damage. If you are OK after the bomb detonation, and you were close, you are not likely to experience another explosion in the exact same location. This is a controversial move. Others, such as the Department of Homeland Security, have suggested running immediately to be clear of dust, fumes, and other bomb effects.[8] Don't! It depends on the size of the bomb! If massive, escape. If smaller, stay and assist. As an example of a massive bombing that says *escape*, on February 26, 1993, a bomb exploded two floors below ground at the Vista Hotel within the same World Trade Center that would be brought down by terrorists just eight years later in the infamous 9/11 attack. The plan was to collapse the building into the other World Trade Center building amidst dispersal of chlorine gas. It was later discovered that the bomb was contained in a rented moving truck. Although the overall plot failed, and the chlorine burned, seven people were killed. Seven terrorists were arrested after careful investigation. Ramzi Yousef, the mastermind, was captured in Pakistan, extradited, and was sentenced to 240 years in prison.[9]

A smaller bombing calls for a different response. The Tsarnaev brothers placed two pressure cooker bombs concealed in backpacks within a block of each other. One detonated, followed by the other 13 seconds later. The bombs were placed near the finish line of the Boston Marathon on April 15, 2013.[10] They were loaded with metal objects such as nails to serve as shrapnel.[11] Observers and potential victims witnessed the grizzly site of three dead, many injured, severed limbs, and spattered pools of blood. If in the vicinity of a bombing on the smaller side, the tendency to run immediately could place you in the dangerous vicinity of a second bomb.

Be alert when at public events. A sporting or similar event that draws massive and distracting attention makes it more difficult to see someone leaving a package that could contain a destructive bomb. In the Boston Marathon pressure cooker bombings, it is likely that all eyes were on the runners at the finish line. It is simple: Massive distraction can make the placement of a bomb much easier.

VEHICLE RUN-DOWNS

The terrorist group Al Qaeda—responsible for the 9/11 attack in New York City and Washington, D.C.—was the first to call for killing innocent victims by running them over in a vehicle in 2010. The use of a truck or similar vehicle to run over people can result in many deaths and injuries. The driver does not have to have any special skills other than driving and a will to kill as many people as possible. The following is just a sample of actual attacks:

- 7/14/2016, Nice, France, a 20-ton rental truck driven by self-radicalized 31-year-old Mohamed Lahouaiej-Bouhlel killed a minimum of 84 people before the perpetrator was killed by authorities.
- 11/28/2016, Ohio State University, Columbus, Ohio, 18-year-old likely self-radicalized student Abdul Razak Ali Artan ran over a group of students in a car, which he then exited, stabbing people with a knife. Eleven people were injured before Artan was shot and killed.
- 12/19/2016, Berlin, Germany, 24 year-old ISIS-inspired Tunisian Anis Amri drove a tractor trailer into a crowd and killed 12 people. He was killed days later at the end of a manhunt.
- 3/22/2017, London, England, 52-year-old Khalid Masood drove an SUV over pedestrians for hundreds of yards on Westminster Bridge. In the process, he ultimately killed four people and injured more than 50. He then crashed into the gates of Parliament and killed an unarmed policeman by stabbing him to death before being shot and killed by an armed policeman.
- 4/17/2017, Stockholm Sweden, 39-year-old ISIS-inspired terrorist Rakhmat Akilov crashed into a store after running over several pedestrians, killing four. He was arrested just hours after the attack.
- 6/3/ 2017, London, England, three men in a van ran over pedestrians on London Bridge, then exited the van and ran to a nearby market. There, they launched a stabbing attack. Police killed the three attackers after the terrorists had killed seven people and injured 48.[12]
- 10/31/2017, Manhattan, New York, 29-year-old Uzbek immigrant Sayfullo Saipov killed eight pedestrians and injured 11 others driving his Home Depot–rented truck down a pedestrian path near the site of the 9/11 World Trade Center attack. Mercilessly running down anyone in his path, the self-radicalized terrorist was shot by a law enforcement officer and sent to the hospital.[13]

Vehicle run-downs are relatively new and effective. The typical tactic is for an attacking driver to suddenly veer off a roadway to hit pedestrians, turning a normal van or truck into a rapidly moving multi-ton weapon. If not among the first victims, there may be some warning. For example, in the Westminster Bridge attack, the driver drove for several hundred yards, hitting pedestrians along the way, including knocking one woman, who later died, over the bridge.

There are a small number of things that can be done prior to a vehicle run-down attack to minimize the probability of being a fatality. First, and foremost, always walk on the side of the road facing oncoming traffic. In the United States this means walking on the left side of the road—against right-lane driving. In those countries honoring the British standard of driving on the left, walk on the right side of the road. In this way, you can see what is coming toward you in the lane nearest you. A vehicle could still be coming from behind and cross lanes to hit pedestrians, but it is easier to just veer off the road without crossing lanes.

The question is what to do given one has only a few seconds warning of a rapidly approaching vehicle heading directly toward you. Certainly, the first thought should be not to just stand in place. The startle response must be overcome, and the key is to get out of the projected path as fast as humanly possible. Second, don't run in the same direction as the attacking vehicle. The probability is high that you will be overtaken. This leaves the option of running to the left or the right of vehicle's path.

Be constantly aware when walking alongside any road anywhere. This doesn't mean you are looking for terrorist-related attacks. It is just a solid safety practice. For example, according to the Traffic Safety Facts website, in 2014 65,000 pedestrians were injured and 4,884 killed in the United States.[14] Vehicles can be an unintended danger or an intended weapon. However, if hit, the intent is not the immediate concern. Be alert, pay attention to traffic, and don't get distracted when walking along any roadway or street. Given the speed that a vehicle may be moving, best practice is to always be prepared to get out of the way. As always, prevention and awareness are far superior to being caught unprepared. We have eyes to see, ears to hear, and a lifetime of experience to let us know if something is wrong that could be impending danger; trust all three, and don't use your cell phone while walking.

STABBINGS

The movies and TV have led many to believe that stabbing results in a quick death. This is not always true. Although death could come quickly, death from stabbing could take hours, depending on what part of the body is stabbed, whether single or multiple stab wounds, and what the condition of the body is, among other factors. The bottom line is that a stabbing is not an automatic death sentence. It does mean that medical care must be sought or administered as soon as possible. First aid can do much to save lives in a stabbing. Knowing how to reduce blood flow through direct pressure, or how to fashion a tourniquet, can be lifesaving. Again, I highly recommend that every reader take a first aid course. A search on the Internet for first aid courses on your area will provide multiple contacts and websites.

If you are faced with an attacker who is either producing a knife or wielding it in any manner ESCAPE! Thoughts of fighting the attacker should be secondary to escaping. Keep in mind that real stabbings are different from what is depicted in the movies or on TV. Entertainment is there to show drama, which may be played out for more than a minute. Real stabbings are quick, with the objective of cutting the victim as quickly and as many times as possible.

Mass victim attack stabbings are not an afterthought. The attacker has planned to use a sharp and deadly weapon that could be a knife, machete, hatchet, or ax. Why? First, they are easy to acquire and strike fear into all. The attacker is familiar with the weapon, and has likely practiced. Second, it doesn't require much practice to use a knife. Lunge, slash, stab, and cut—as long as there is forceful contact, there will be damage.

I would like to provide a warning to those who are intent on searching the Internet to find out what to do to protect against a stabbing attack. There is some very bad online advice on this topic. The worst advice I have seen, not referenced here, is to get as close as possible to the attacker so that a stabbing motion can't be effective. The advisor has watched too many movies. Another site recommends fighting as a first step, while another recommends that you just shoot and kill the stabber. Many of these sites have official-sounding names. Just be cautious. If recommended action consists of anything other than run/escape, I would discount the advice. The major disadvantage of stabbing is the short reach of the attack. If you can't be reached, you are not likely to be stabbed.

Just to be clear, the best advice is to *escape* if you can. If the attacker is a mass victim attacker, he is prepared to die. His objective is to kill, not scare or threaten. If escape is not possible, make sure there is something between you and the attacker. You could use a chair, maneuver around a table, wrap a jacket or anything around an arm for protection. Use your extremities and try to protect face, abdomen, chest, and back. It is better to get cut on the arms and legs than stabbed multiple times in the stomach or back. If there is no out, fight for your life because that is exactly what you will be doing.

This bears repeating: If you see a sharp weapon, *escape*. Do not wait to see what situation unfolds. As a last major point, it is clear that some vehicle run-downs conclude with the driver and others in the attacking vehicle exiting after running over victims and start a stabbing attack. Use caution if you see multiple victims being run over—if clear of the vehicle, you may be faced with a knife-wielding extremist who wants to kill all that are near.

There are major things to remember across all types of attacks. First and foremost, if an attack unfolds, do not try to take pictures or record video. We all have smartphones, and most are quick to take photos or videos. You can be killed in those seconds. You can observe this happening in some videos replayed after an attack. How is there a video anyway? Who took it and why? Capturing images is not a defensive action, it is highly risky. Instead, use that valuable device to call 911 as soon as possible. If in Europe, the number is 112. If traveling, determine the emergency number and store it in your phone for that location. Most of all, if you are forced to hide, turn off the phone's ringer! You do not want the phone to give away your location.

Although the most common forms of mass victim attacks have been covered in this chapter, keep in mind that there can be significant variations and hybrids, although rare. For example, as mentioned, some vehicle run-overs have been immediately followed by stabbings. These hybrids are actually two attacks with different tactics. First, there is a vehicle run-over. That attack ends and then a stabbing attack begins. The objective in both attacks is to kill indiscriminately. Don't ever believe that you can talk your way out of being a victim by reasoning, begging, or praying. Praying is fine, but do so as you follow sound advice for surviving.

September 11, 2001, saw the most significant coordinated international terrorist attack ever to occur within the United States. At the time of writing this chapter, that was 16 years ago. Yet those older than mid-20s remember it well. Americans were in shock as two airliners crashed into the World Trade Center towers and the Pentagon, with one failing to reach its target due to passenger intervention and crashing into a field in Shanksville, Pennsylvania. The attack was orchestrated by Al Qaeda and was a combination of hijacking and a form of mass destruction bombing. First, terrorists working together across the four hijacked airliners used box cutters to threaten crews and gain control of the airplanes. They had been training for years, including how to pilot. Osama bin Laden, the then leader of Al Qaeda, took responsibility two days after the attack.

The surprise attacks began at 8:45 a.m. in New York City when American Airlines Flight 11, full of fuel, crashed into the North Tower of the World Trade Center. The crash resulted immediately in a powerful and fiery explosion. At 9:05 a.m., just 20 minutes later, United Airlines Flight 175 crashed in the same manner into the South Tower of the World Trade Center. At 9:37 a.m. American Airlines Flight 77 crashed in a ball of fire into the Pentagon in Washington, D.C., and at 10:03 a.m. United Airlines Flight 93 crashed into a field near Shanksville, Pennsylvania. Within 1 hour and 18 minutes, four hijacked airliners were exploded in purposeful crashes. At 9:59 a.m. the South Tower collapsed, and 29 minutes later, at 10:28 a.m., the North Tower collapsed.[15] Both towers were 110 floors high and at one time were the tallest buildings in the world.

Almost 3,000 innocent people died in these attacks, including passengers, those working in the World Trade Center towers, the Pentagon, and the airliner crashing into the ground in a field in Pennsylvania. The attack highlighted the desire, determination, and creative deadly intent of international terrorism. Nineteen terrorists carried out the surprise attack that ended the lives of these innocent people and left indelible, horrific images in the minds of many hundreds of millions worldwide.

The 9/11 attack in the United States underscores the resourcefulness of those intent on inflicting mass victim attacks against targets. We must remember that even a domestic terrorist, with some limited assistance, was able to bring down the Alfred P. Murrah Federal Building in Oklahoma City with a vehicle bomb parked in front of the building, killing 168 people and injuring over 700. We must be aware of our surroundings. Any suspicious activity must be reported. Vehicles have been used in vehicle run-overs and in bombings. Attackers do not use their own vehicles. *Therefore, suspicious activity when renting a vehicle should be reported, as well as immediate reporting of any stolen vehicles.* There are many examples of suspicious behavior when renting a vehicle. A sample includes repeated rental of trucks especially of increasing size within a short amount of time (e.g., weeks), discomfort in completing information for a rental contract, "nervousness" while renting, and using large sums of cash to pay for the rental instead of credit card. I refer the reader to the truck rental section under suspicious behavior in the Los Angeles Police Department website: www.lapdonline.org/iwatchla/pdf_view/44070.

It is important to mention trends in mass victim attacks that could adversely affect us. Although this book is focused on what to expect and how to react, there are forms of possible attacks that don't quite fit the usual patterns and are rare in occurrence.

The first category of such attacks fits the umbrella term CBRN, or chemical, biological, radiological, and nuclear. Some add E at the end of the acronym (e.g., CBRNE) for high-yield explosives. Perhaps it is human nature, but we tend to provide fixes for problems after crises. For example, after a number of accidents at a four-way stop, a stoplight may finally be installed. This is true to some extent with CBRN. There have been CBRN attacks in the past, but not in large numbers. However, we have paid attention after the fact, and now concern is increasing.

On March 29, 1995, five Asahara religious doomsday cult members in Tokyo each carried a plastic bag of liquified Sarin gas into five separate subway lines. Aum Shinrikyo, the blind cleric leader of the cult, admired

Adolf Hitler and the colorless and odorless Sarin gas, manufactured in Germany. At the appointed time, the cult members punctured the bags and released the liquid in the cars, creating deadly Sarin gas fumes. The method of the attack and location of the terrorists allowed the liquid contamination and fumes to spread throughout the different subway lines.

Seven people were killed in the attack, and 500 others were injured.[16] As an example of a mass victim attack, the Sarin gas attack in the Tokyo subway system demonstrates what damage can be done, even if the deadly chemical may not have been delivered in the most efficient manner. History is riddled with the use of chemical attacks associated with warfare, and many thousands have been killed including attacks on schoolchildren.

There is concern that a radiological "dirty bomb" could occur. Unlike a nuclear bomb, which is actually a nuclear-based explosion with tremendous devastating power (e.g., Hiroshima and Nagasaki bombs in Japan in World War II), a dirty bomb uses a conventional explosion containing radioactive material. The conventional explosion disperses the radiological material across a wide area, contaminating everything touched by the material. To make matters worse, there were at least 30 incidents where radioactive materials used commercially went missing in the decade ending in 2014.[17] In April 2017 a truck containing radioactive materials in Mexico was stolen. Nine states were placed on high alert. There were seven such incidents in Mexico in the year before this theft.[18] The obvious fear is that stolen material will fall into the hands of terrorists. These are just samples of missing materials. Added to the concern for missing radioactive material is the ease with which a dirty bomb can be constructed and detonated.

II

ESCAPE, HIDE, STAY IN PLACE, OR ATTACK THE ATTACKER?

4

Surviving by Escaping

$\mathbf{P}$ersonal security is a very valuable concept as it relates to surviving mass victim attacks. I offer the following definition.

Personal security for mass victim attacks is the self-reliance on knowledge, aware-ness, known limitations and strengths, and types of responses you personally can perform to increase the probability of remaining alive when attacked.

When mass victim attacks occur, first responders are often on the scene within minutes. However, the presence of law enforcement, SWAT, or any other responders does not automatically mean immediate intervention. The Pulse nightclub attack in Orlando lasted for several hours. Omar Mateen extended the time by taking hostages and "negotiating" with law enforce-ment. Security, law enforcement, SWAT, and any other official forces to enter the scene are extremely important, and I respect their predicament and admire their actions tremendously.

Surprise attacks are bewildering, they are all different, and the circum-stances are never the same. Be aware that when forces arrive, it does not automatically signal the end of a mass victim attack. First responders can be killed, as well as immediate targets.

Personal security means that you take responsibility for your own life-or-death decisions at a moment's notice. There must be a realization that you simply cannot wait for official forces to arrive to end a mass victim attack. There may be a tendency to run to a restroom or other adjacent room to hide. Surely law enforcement will arrive in a few minutes. Back exits, windows, and other options for escape may have been avoided or not noticed. Immedi-ate safety may be the concern. However, escape is in order, immediately if possible. There are other options if escape is not possible, and the following chapters will cover these options.

On September 11, 2001, we witnessed the worst terrorist attack in U.S. history in New York City, Washington, D.C., and in a field in Pennsylvania. There were over 6,000 injuries and 2,977 deaths. One could write many books about this one attack.

I had a small threat-detection team in the Pentagon at the time, and fortunately was not there at the time the airliner hit the Pentagon. However, one of my employees was walking out the front exit to bring me documents at the office when the airliner hit. We worked in the Pentagon the next day. Of special note, brave first responders heroically did all they could to save lives. Of the 2,977 deaths, 343 firefighters, 23 police officers, and 37 Port Authority responders were included in the fatality count. These responders gave their lives to help others. We must remember that first responders are human too, and they face even more risk than others as they purposely run toward the danger.

When you are caught in a mass victim attack, you are your own expert. You do not have to be a law enforcement official, or a security expert. You are not likely to be carrying a concealed weapon, although there are those who do; this is a different story covered in chapter 6. In short, you are the best resource available at the time. Hopefully, you are knowledgeable, aware of your surroundings, situationally aware, and able to make the best decisions for survival available to you at the time.

Knowing that you are responsible for your own survival can reduce the bewilderment, startle response, and the time it takes to figure out what to do if not prepared. Seconds count. How carefully you scanned that restaurant, bar, grill, theatre, or an enclosure when you entered may pay off as the shooting, bombing, stabbing, run-down, or other method of mass killing begins to occur. For example, if a restaurant seated you next to a back exit, near the kitchen, or even near a window, then escape options are immediately available should an attack occur.

Personal security begins when you enter any public space. You may have even made seating decisions before coming to the location. But, at least, you should scan and make such decisions on entering. It takes just a few seconds—seconds that can offset the early seconds of bewilderment if or when an attack occurs.

Keeping escape as the first option is especially important for those who are not in excellent physical condition. Many patrons are not young, athletic, and able to sprint. In fact, next time you visit a restaurant, look around and notice all in the restaurant. Patrons could be very young and helpless infants and children, the elderly, physically and maybe even mentally challenged.

This makes preplanning even more important. When entering public venues such as restaurants, bars, and malls take special care to note the location of the exits. This is important not just for mass victim attacks but also for fires and other surprise calamities.

If physically challenged always insist on being placed near an exit. Think escape, not hiding or fighting back. It is true that the probability of being caught in a mass victim attack is very low, but if you are the one caught in such an attack, statistics are meaningless. Approach every location as if there could be a mass victim attack. It only takes a few seconds, and the preparation could save your life. Do attackers care if you are with a child or infant, elderly, or physically or mentally challenged? No one needs to know that you are being careful and ensuring escape.

For the most part, we have been focusing on mass victim attackers who are active shooters. How about other types of attacks: vehicle run-downs, stabbings, or bombings? Being prepared for mass victim attacks means being aware of any type of tactic that could be used against those in a crowded location. Please note this very important fact: Mass victim attackers are not interested in small gatherings of people. They are pushing for that one big act to kill as many as possible. They are prepared to die, if it comes to that end. They are not going to waste their time and risk their lives to go after one or two people. Their desire is to draw attention to the attack itself, if not to themselves. The bigger the attack, the better.

Escape is almost always the preferred response, and should be everyone's first thought, regardless of the type of attack. It should be obvious that if you are facing danger and a quick escape can remove you from that danger, then escape is the defensive method of choice. Survivors of mass victim attacks have used escape, hiding, staying in place, and fighting by attacking the attacker. However, there have been many fatalities when true escape did not occur. Victims have been killed hiding, staying in place, and attempting to fight back. A true escape means that you are free from danger. Specifically:

Escape is the act of exiting a location of imminent threat and danger by moving to a location that is safe from harm.

Certainly, hiding, staying in place, and attack can result in survival, but under special conditions. The conditions under which other strategies should be used are complex enough to require their own chapters, which immediately follow this chapter. However, there is wide agreement that if you can exit a location of imminent death or severe injury by moving to a safe location, it is the better strategy. *Other strategies are used only if escape is not an option.*

There have been numerous mass victim attacks and all such attacks have fatalities and survivors. Past attack survivals help to frame future strategies.

For example, in mass victim attacks, what were the target actions that led to both death and severe injury versus successful escape? In some cases, survival could be considered good fortune or luck. In other cases, successful escape was the result of calm and quick thought-out action. Regardless, escape methods that have worked, whether by accident or not, can produce strategies that can be learned and put into action by design when necessary.

ESCAPING FROM ACTIVE SHOOTER ATTACKS

If an active shooting attack begins near the entrance of a restaurant or bar and you happen to be near a back exit or window at the time, you exit quickly. You have moved from imminent threat and danger to a location that is safe. You then can call 911 to report the emergency, giving the exact location with all details to aid first responders, as you continue to move away to ensure continued safety. Yes, the exit avenue was open to you by chance, and you took quick advantage of the exit route. Principles of survival that we may use in a planned manner surface when analyzing such escapes. The following are examples derived from survival stories.

Recognize the sounds of gunfire and escape immediately.

Be aware of the sounds and actions of others at the beginning of an active shooting attack. Loud "popping sounds" associated with people running and screaming means escape immediately. Remember that sounds of guns firing in a confined space can sound very different from what we hear in movies. There is no need to stay in place to see what is happening. You could lose your life waiting. Hopefully you noticed the location of exits when entering the public place you are visiting.

When in a crowded location that could attract an attack, seek a table or location near an exit.

The probability is extremely high that you will never be caught in a mass victim attack. However, the tragedies that have occurred, the severe injuries, and the horrific loss of life should not be thought of as statistics. Forget that the probability of being caught in a mass victim attack is very low. It is exactly like putting your seat belt on when getting in your car. Always be prepared. Therefore, I highly recommend that when visiting any public event or location, immediately notice exits and be near them. Choose seating wisely: The food will be the same, you can have the same enjoyment with others, and you can escape immediately, if necessary.

If a location near the back exit is not available, choose a location near a kitchen door that can lead to a back exit.

Many locations do not have back exits that can be seen as you enter the building. But, if an eating establishment, know that almost all kitchens have back doors. Sitting near a kitchen door can provide a two-step escape. First, the kitchen door blocks the attacker's view of you while you head quickly to that back door. Second, that back exit offers an escape from the killing field.

If a back exit or close proximity to a kitchen door is not apparent or may even be missing, what other avenues are present that would allow an escape?

When entering a public location and noticing where exits are located, it is natural to look for doors as the form of exit. However, many ground-floor locations also have windows. Such windows can open in some cases, or may be broken with a chair—especially in an emergency. It is amazing how small an opening we can squeeze through, especially if a shooter may be approaching in a few seconds or minutes.

Are there stairs that lead up or down a floor with access to an exit? Can you sit next to the stairs if no back exits or windows are available?

True escape, as opposed to hiding, staying in place, or attacking does not have to be a matter of luck. Planning where you sit in a crowded location can very much be a part of a quick assessment of any location entered. I find that when I enter a new location it takes me about 10 seconds to scan the premises to determine potential places within the location that could allow a quick exit. This includes sitting in such a direction that I can see the front first and the back second. Is this paranoid? No. It is a quick safety assessment exactly like looking to see where the exits are in an airliner when I board. Safety comes first.

Know that you are a paying customer when you frequent restaurants, bars, and other similar crowded public venues. You have choices. I often request a different table or sitting area if a waiter wants to place me at a certain table I do not like. What if reservations are required? I have also requested a certain location within a restaurant if I need to make reservations. Many restaurant websites have multiple photos of the inside and some even show a floor plan. These can be used as a guide to selecting a seating location at reservation time. I find that theatres or concert venues requiring that tickets be purchased in advance provide great online images of seating arrangements for tickets. I can pick my seats wisely.

In short, we have choices, and we should exercise planning and control when visiting public places. Just as some experience a fortunate turn of events and escape successfully, the fatalities weren't so lucky. The question is whether increased knowledge and awareness can increase the probability of survival, or do we just hope to be at the right place at the right time when an attack occurs? This is much like asking if practice driving and driving tests increase safety. Obviously, it is better to be prepared and knowledgeable than not. There is no substitute for planning, remaining calm to the best of our ability when in crisis mode, and creating an escape, if necessary.

Special mention should be made about remaining as calm as possible, given the situation. A mass victim attack often includes panic, screaming, running, and mass dashes for obvious and nearby exits. Injuries, even severe injuries, can occur at this time as a result of pushing, shoving, and trampling. This is another reason why planning your location when you enter is noteworthy. There is the obvious immediate danger posed by flying bullets; however, there is also the possibility of accidental injuries caused by well-meaning patrons running without a plan in a state of panic.

There have been creative examples of escape. On June 12, 2016, self-radicalized Omar Mateen, a 29-year-old security guard, entered Pulse night-club in Orlando, Florida, and began shooting with the objective of killing a massive number of patrons. The attack included hostage and barricade tactics, and lasted for several hours. At the conclusion of the horrific attack, Mateen had killed 49 people and wounded 58 others. Highlighted by the terrible loss of lives, there were survivors in what was one of the worst shootings in our country's history.

At the beginning of the attack, when shots were fired at the entrance of the nightclub, a former marine, Imran Yousuf, kept calm and purposely sought out an exit near the back. He found two doors—one that led back to the club and one that led out to safety. However, the door exiting the club was locked. He repeatedly yelled for others to open the door, but to no avail—all people were scrambling for their lives. So he climbed the wall, went over the top, and unlatched the door from the other side. The now-open door allowed many who were trapped to escape to the outside. The best estimate was that 60 to 70 potential victims escaped through this door with their lives.[1] This was one of the best examples that I have found of keeping calm to reach safety that would also help others.

At the same time, there were nine people who had fled to a dressing room. A 20-year-old woman in the room called 911 and stated there was a wall-installed air conditioning unit that she thought could serve as an escape—there was no other way to escape from the room. In the meantime, Mateen was busy killing others, laughing, and talking on the phone to police and his wife. SWAT first discouraged removing the heavy air-conditioning unit, thinking the noise might attract the attention of Mateen to those hiding. However, after about two hours, the nine in hiding heard a knocking on the outside of the wall. It was the police. It was time to push out the air conditioning unit and escape. The unit was pushed out with the help of the outside police officers. The unit was removed, leaving a hole in the wall large enough for an escape path. All nine persons trapped in the dressing room exited through the hole, escaped, and survived.[2]

As with most mass victim attacks, there are examples of both fatalities and successful escape. In the Sandy Hook Elementary School shooting on December 14, 2012, Adam Lanza shot his way through the locked front door entrance and immediately started targeting children and staff. He was met by the principal, Dawn Hochsprung, and the school psychologist, Mary Sherlach, as they ran toward Lanza to stop him and protect the school children. True heroes, they were both shot and killed by Lanza. Attacking the attacker, or fighting back, in this case was not successful.

Another worker turned on the intercom near the front office, so the entire school could hear the shootings and chaos as a warning to escape, hide, or follow whatever strategy could be used. The custodian bravely risked his life running through the halls to give warnings to all classrooms that there was an active shooter, and other staff did all they could to protect the lives in their classes.[3] Some were killed by hiding and some survived by hiding. One little girl lived by playing dead—she was the only survivor of a restroom of slaughtered children. Victoria Soto, a 27-year-old teacher, died while literally taking bullets, serving as a human shield for the children in her care.

The quick thinking of staff to provide specific warnings as to what was happening was surely responsible for many successful escapes. The death toll (twenty 5- and 6-year-old children and six adults) would have likely been much higher without the quick warnings and successful attempts at hiding children. There are strategies for surviving, but this example deserves special attention. Six adults ignored personal safety and heroically chose to protect children at the cost of their own lives. Such a decision is as personal a decision as humanly possible. Lanza, plagued with mental health issues, succeeded in an unthinkable massacre of the innocent. But, it is clear the death toll would have been much higher without the many acts of bravery.

On December 2, 2015, self-radicalized married couple Syed Farook and Tashfeen Malik entered a Christmas party in San Bernardino, California. There were approximately 80 fellow employees celebrating. Masked, Farook and Malik opened fire with multiple weapons. By all accounts, they fired indiscriminately and tried to kill as many people as possible in the shortest amount of time. Survivors reported hearing popping sounds or fireworks at first. Some took cover under overturned tables and other obstacles.

Most importantly, *there were three exit doors accessible to the large room where the shootings occurred—which were not used by any of the occupants in the room.* These doors should have been the first choice, but survivors reported thinking the event was a drill, and they hid as they had been taught.[4]

At the conclusion of the swift attack, 14 were killed and 24 were injured. Farook and Malik escaped, but four hours later were killed in a shoot-out with the police while in their SUV. We are left wondering what would have happened if the first option, escape through exit doors, was exercised. Speaking of no mercy, multiple reports stated that the employees attacked had some time earlier given Farook a baby shower.

I cannot overemphasize the principle of escape. By definition, escape is the only strategy that includes leaving the location of danger for another location that is free of danger. We think, of course, anyone would use escape if exits were available! But we have the San Bernardino massacre when three exit doors from the room were available but not used at all.

Why were obvious exits not used? There may be several reasons. First, employees had received past training about how to hide in such an emergency. Hitting the ground and immediate hiding were included in the training. That is what they did. Second, as survivors reported, they heard a popping sound or "fireworks." So it took some seconds to realize the true danger and that the popping sounds were, in fact, deadly gunfire. This is not unusual in mass victim shooting attacks. Third, it was difficult to believe it was real, and they kept waiting for those who fell to the floor to get back up from what they thought was an exercise to support their training. Because of training, they tried to hide, falling to the floor in the one room. In the meantime, innocent victims were being shot, killed, and injured.

There is often disbelief that must be overcome at the beginning of an attack. Disbelief acts to lengthen the startle response that all will encounter. Is this real? Is it an exercise? Is it a joke? During the beginning of the James Holmes mass victim attack at the Century 16 movie theatre in Aurora, Colorado, on July 12, 2012, survivors reported that, at first, they thought the shooter's entrance was part of the movie, or not real. When an active shooter attack begins, as in the Aurora, San Bernardino, Orlando nightclub, or any other mass victim attack, the first few seconds were key to survival.

The lesson learned: Treat popping sounds, what may sound like fireworks, or what could "maybe" be gunfire as the real thing. This is especially important if you cannot see the entrance and the attacker. You are relying on sounds only. Fireworks are not likely to be going off in a confined setting, and if a balloon, one balloon could pop but it is not likely that multiple balloons will keep popping. Be aware that gunfire in a confined public space will sound very different from what you would expect. Your first thought for yourself, if alone, or yourself and family or friends should be ESCAPE.

Question training. Who are the trainers? What are their backgrounds? Have the training methods actually resulted in saved lives in real situations? Trainers and training methods must be vetted to ensure practicality and effectiveness. If you have questions, have several local law enforcement officers (not a friend or just one officer) review training material to ensure authenticity. Most importantly, don't rely on simple lists on a website. As I mention repeatedly, survival during mass victim attacks is not a function of knowing items on a list. It is more complex than that.

The beginning of an attack is important in many ways. When an attack begins and you decide to warn others, be specific! Don't just say, "Run!" If you simply say "run," those who hear the warning will look around to see why they should be running. Maybe it is a joke. Maybe you are crazy! It doesn't matter how often you say it or how loudly you shout it, the typical response is to look around to determine the danger and *why* one should run. It is human nature. However, if you yell, "active shooter," "shooter," "someone has a gun and is shooting people," "a bomb has exploded," etc., then valuable information has been communicated that can be acted upon immediately.

Be aware of information contained in this book so that you can make your own personal decisions. Be careful following the loudest voice—it is your life, and you should make your own decisions. A booming or screaming voice that says, "run out the front door" or "hit the floor" may not be the best advice simply because it is authoritative or loud.

As a whole, we are basically followers. In a mass victim attack, our lives are at stake, and we deserve to make our own informed decisions. It is quite possible to follow someone who has made a faulty, if not fatal, decision. Know what to expect, and focus on escaping from the location. At the beginning of a mass victim attack, there may be those with the best intentions who try to lead and give suggestions. Be aware, and make your own decisions.

ESCAPE FROM BOMBING ATTACKS

All mass victim attacks are horrific tragedies. However, bombings present the least possibility of escape. When a significant bombing occurs, those caught in the kill zone simply do not have a chance to escape. The result can be immediate death, severe injuries including missing body parts, deafness, blindness, damaged lungs from breathing noxious fumes, blast pressure effects, and psychological trauma that can last a lifetime. Any survivor of a mass victim attack must cope with psychological effects which, in severest form, can result in Acute Stress Disorder (ASD) or Post-Traumatic Stress Disorder (PTSD). These disorders will be addressed in chapter 10.

We tend to think there is nothing that can be done in a bombing. It is so immediate that there may be no escape, and if alive after the blast, we focus on injuries immediately. However, this book also covers what can be observed before an attack. There is much that can be done prior to a blast. If suspicious behavior is observed, report it. If bomb-making material is present at a neighbor's house, report it. If a relative appears to be ordering explosives or even detonating small explosive devices, this could be practice for an attack, not harmless fun. Yes, if a bomb is detonated, our focus will be on injuries. But being alert to surroundings can have a profound effect. For example, if at a public gathering of any kind and a suspicious package is spotted, report it!

Remember, also, that even if there is little that can be done once a bomb is detonated except worry about injuries, there can be a second bomb. We can be ready for that one. More about this in chapter 5. If you are alive and maybe uninjured after the blast, don't run wildly. You may encounter a second bomb or a shooter. On December 22, 2017, 26-year-old Everitt Aaron Jameson was arrested for planning a mass victim attack on popular Pier 39 in San Francisco. An informant had provided a tip to authorities after seeing a social media post. Jameson, a former U.S. Marine, had become self-radicalized. His reported tactic was to use an explosive to funnel those running into one area so that he could shoot and kill them with semi-automatic weapons.[5]

To risk being repetitive, know first aid. It is a very important investment of your time and can pay off not only for mass victim attacks, but for many and varied situations. The following are helpful hints once a bomb is detonated.

- If near the blast, even if injured, remain as calm as possible. Thinking and decision making works best when not panicking.
- Use first aid for self and nearby others—first responders are likely to respond quickly, but those minutes after a bomb detonation before first responders arrive can literally save lives.
- Know how to make a tourniquet and apply direct pressure to reduce significant and serious blood loss.
- Help direct first responders to the most severely injured: Confusion, bewilderment, and panic follow such attacks, and first responders will have to sort out what has happened while conducting their triage.
- Make sure authorities have your contact information as a witness; this can be very helpful to investigators who must piece together what happened, what type of bomb, and who may be responsible.

ESCAPE FROM STABBING ATTACKS

You are at a bar or restaurant and an emotional person ranting and shouting pulls out a long knife that was concealed. It could also be a hatchet, machete, or even multiple knives, collectively known as sharp-edged weapons. It is clear he is focused on stabbing anyone. Stabbing as a mass victim attack method carries with it the intent to kill. The knife or other similar object should be viewed as a matter of life or death. There is no way to talk the attacker down, nor is there any way to reason. He is there to kill. I say *he* because stabbers have been male. What do you do? How can you protect yourself from a raging person with sharp weapons with the intent to kill?

When I was a psychologist in the U.S. Secret Service, I attended a training session for agents. The live scenario focused on an agent acting as the U.S. president and shaking hands while walking amongst a crowd held back by a rope. He was protected by two agents, one being the chief trainer. This was a real scenario. It was not just acting. Training sessions incorporated real knives and it was up to the trainer to actually stop a lunge with a knife.

A planned assailant jumped out of the crowd unexpectedly to stab the protectee. The chief trainer accompanying the protectee immediately assessed the threat, and within two or three seconds, disarmed the assailant, and both agents had the assailant on the ground. The chief trainer dislocated his thumb in the process—this was apparent because it was pointed in a backward direction. He said, "Excuse me," turned around, snapped the thumb back in place with his other hand, and to his great credit, continued with training, seemingly unfazed. We are not superhuman like this highly regarded and legendary trainer, but there are many things we can do to defend ourselves from a stabber. The incident left an indelible impression on me. Awareness, knowing what to do, and acting immediately made the difference.

In the example, the trainer was in total control. How can you be in control? You don't have to be superman, and you don't have to have special years of training with years of experience. The enraged and ranting individual is lunging at innocent victims, and now is focusing on you.

There are several points to keep in mind if unfortunately caught in a stabbing attack. A stabbing attack can occur very quickly and does not consist of a single stabbing motion. Typically, fueled by the objective of killing and not to just threaten, many stabbing motions can be made in seconds and can consist of slashing, jabbing, lunging, and swinging from different directions. A mass victim attacker intent on stabbing can cover a several-yard distance between him and you in one or two seconds. There are no threatening moves—just a forward assault to stab, slash, and kill.

It is important to understand why the first thought you should have is escape if caught in a situation with a knife-wielding attacker. Tremendous damage can be done in just a few seconds. Forget what you have seen in the movies. It is rarely a single jab. An attacker knows where to stab and how to stab to kill. The details can be very gory. If a wound hits vital spots, bleeding can be intense, and immediate attention is required. The best way to defend against such attacks is to escape. Of course, escape must be possible. If not possible, there are still methods to be used that can save your life.

What can you do if faced with an irate, incensed, crazy-appearing attacker with a sharp weapon. Trust me: Escape! Run. A sharp object can deliver wounds within seconds that rival gunshot wounds. I believe I must present this as a quote. It is powerful, and it lets you know why you need to escape, if possible.

On August 22, 1995, Officer Steven Alva punched five bullet holes into a suspect's chest, including one that went through his heart, but the deadly fight continued as the suspect attacked with a large knife.

After a five-block foot pursuit, the 6-foot 4-inch, 260-pound suspect led Alva and his partner, Officer Jay Chambers, inside a house. The suspect ran into the kitchen area as Alva and Chambers entered the house. "As soon as we were inside we saw the suspect with a large knife held in the 'ice pick' grip, just like in the movie *Psycho*," recalled Alva.

Immediately the suspect lunged to cover the 11 feet between himself and Chambers, who didn't have a chance to draw his gun.

Alva fired three shots, all of them hitting the suspect's chest.

But the suspect didn't seem to notice that he had been shot as he began to slash Chambers and a struggle for the knife ensued. The suspect knocked Chambers down and landed on top of him, slashing the officer's face and making a deep cut from his left eye, across his nose, and down to his chin. All of this happened very quickly.

The slashing continued as Chambers and the suspect struggled for the knife. Knowing that his partner was taking potentially lethal wounds, Alva quickly got into position and fired two more shots into the suspect.

Now Alva was so close that he was able to wrest the knife out of the suspect's hands. Then he pushed him off Chambers and handcuffed him.

In the aftermath, 180 stitches were needed to sew Chambers' face back together and they discovered that his Kevlar vest had protected his chest from a deep slash attempt.[6]

A stabber with intent to threaten versus a stabber with the intent to kill are two entirely different situations. Be prepared for both, and be prepared to escape. The details provided in this chapter are relevant for stabbing attacks, as well as for shooting attacks. The precautions taken when entering a public location provide suggestions for moving from the imminent threat to a location that is safe. The first advice is not to underestimate a stabber. The immediate thought is likely that a shooter directing gunfire around a confined space is much more dangerous than a stabber. Remember that a stabber can move, run, lunge, and be very mobile in the midst of an attack to kill multiple people.

In this chapter, we are assuming that escape is possible. The same exit scanning should occur, noting the location of all exits, windows, kitchen location, and adjacent rooms that may have exits. When a stabbing begins, we may witness similar panic, running, and general pandemonium. Escape from the location and call 911 immediately so that law enforcement can enter the scene as soon as possible. The probability is very high that individuals will be stabbed and will be suffering from potentially grave injuries.

If escape is not possible, and hiding is not possible, you may need to attack the attacker to save your life. The stabber will have to be at arm's length to stab, which is very different than a shooting situation. This is a frightening situation, but also presents possibilities for survival. The lack of escape possibilities makes hiding and attacking-the-attacker options possibilities that may be necessary. Because it becomes complex if escape is not possible, the following two chapters covering surviving by hiding and surviving by attacking will provide details of how other options may be used.

ESCAPE FROM VEHICLE RUN-DOWNS

Escaping from vehicle run-downs is different from escaping within confined public gatherings. First, vehicles are outside, and victims are typically in an open environment. Vehicles are fast and accelerate at the time of attack, so running in the same direction as the moving vehicle is a sure way to be run over and killed, at worst, or severely injured, at best. Both Al Qaeda and ISIS have called for the use of vehicles to run over pedestrians and kill them.[7] They also have recommended stabbings. Why? Knives and vehicles are easy to obtain and do not require special skills—and they can be deadly for multiple victims at one time.

The key to survival of a vehicle run-down is escape! It is the only option. There is no time to hide because the vehicle suddenly accelerates with no warning. You cannot stay in place, or you could be hit for sure if you are in the path. You can't play dead—there is no reason to be dead, and the driver knows it. You can't attack, or fight back. Even if armed, you are not going to stop an accelerating vehicle coming straight for you. Again, forget the movies. If you were armed and shot the tires, these vehicles have momentum and they are accelerating, and they will hit you. This is all common sense, but we simply are not accustomed to thinking about such an attack. Regardless, when it is apparent that it is a vehicle run-down attack, you must already be escaping.

So, what can you do? You practice safe walking always. The following are key points for safety, many of which we learned early in life.

When on foot, walk on the side of the road that is facing oncoming traffic

Walking on the side of the road with traffic approaching you from the back is very dangerous. You need to constantly assess any approaching danger posed by oncoming vehicles. This goes for spotting the intoxicated driver, an accident coming at you, or even a terrorist who is driving a vehicle to kill pedestrians. No one knows it is a terrorist—it is a vehicle coming at you at high speed.

Be alert always when walking near traffic

In 2015, 5,376 pedestrians were killed and over 70,000 were injured in traffic within the United States. These were not terrorist attacks, but were traffic accidents with 90% involving a single vehicle. Surprisingly, 38% of pedestrian fatalities involved drinking—not the driver but by the killed pedestrians.[8] It is essential when walking near traffic or congregating near traffic that you remain totally aware of the traffic and surroundings. When walking, drinking can impair judgment and affect balance, as well as impair the ability to respond quickly.

Being in the proximity of traffic is not a time for cell phones or other distractions. Walking safely in the vicinity of traffic is a survival strategy to counter many types of traffic threats. It just so happens that the same principles can help you survive if an attacker in a vehicle heads in your direction. You have to see the threat—you may only have one to a few seconds—you have to be clear headed, and you must move.

When you are walking, try to walk near buildings and not on the edge of the street. This can allow a quick duck into an alley or a building if a vehicle is heading rapidly toward you. If near a building, go to the back immediately. If caught in the open, escape quickly to the left or right of the path—never in the same direction as the oncoming vehicle. You can't outrun a rapidly accelerating vehicle. To state another concern, be careful using a parked vehicle for protection unless absolutely necessary if there are no other obstacles to get behind.

On August 12, 2017, a heated white nationalist protest turned violent in Charlottesville, Virginia. Twenty-year-old white supremacist and Nazi sympathizer Alex Fields ran his Dodge Challenger at high speed into the back of two cars at a crowded intersection. The momentum of his car resulted in the other two cars surging forward, killing a 32-year-old female and injuring 19 other people.[9] Fields was arrested in the domestic terrorism attack.

5

Surviving by Hiding and Staying in Place

There is only one reason to hide when caught in a mass victim attack. The reason is that escape is not currently possible. But, first, we must answer how we know it is a mass victim attack? The answer is that we don't know for sure. If a shooter starts shooting at random, a vehicle begins running down multiple victims, or if a stabber starts slashing at random, we can assume that it is a mass victim attack, and there is not a specific target. You could be next. There are also situations where staying in place is necessary—but under very specific conditions that will be covered in this chapter.

If gunshots start, people are being run over, or if someone with a sharp-edge weapon starts slashing and stabbing, it is time to move—immediately. There is no reason to remain and see what is happening. There is absolutely no reason to remain and capture video or attempt to capture images on your smartphone; these could be your last images or video. Your first thought must be to escape through any exit, any window (even if you break it), back door, side door, or any avenue that is clear. If no escape is clear, then hiding must occur first. Always remember, escape is the number one method to secure your safety during any attack, but hiding can keep you safe until escape is possible. If escape is clearly not possible, then exceptional care must be taken as to where to: (1) hide and stay in place, or (2) hide and take the first opportunity to escape.

WHEN TO HIDE

Unfortunately, escape is not always possible if there is not a clear path to another location that is safe. The attack starts, you are caught in the immediate vicinity of the attack, and there is no obvious exit: It is time to hide.

71

To hide in a mass victim attack means that escape is not currently possible, and you protect yourself by immediately moving to a location that prevents an attacker from seeing or hearing you while you wait for the first opportunity to escape.

To complete the move successfully, it is obviously important for the attacker to not see you move to the hidden location. This is particularly true for shootings and stabbings. When we think of hiding, we typically think of being in a location where the attacker cannot see us. However, to successfully hide means that you also can't be heard. Remember to turn your cell phone ringer off if forced to hide. You do not want to be seen, AND you do not want to be heard.

Hiding is not always a definitive move that can protect you for the duration of the attack. Hiding can occur in stages as you move to a position of escape. If at the beginning of an attack a successful escape is not possible, you want to immediately get out of view of the attacker. This could mean hiding behind a door, on the other side of a wall, entering an adjacent room, or placing yourself behind any obstacle that can prevent direct view from the attacker. However, if the new location can lead to quick discovery, you need to immediately start scanning for another more secure location to move to at the right time.

Attackers do not remain stationary—they move while they attack. The constant movement increases the number of people that can be killed. However, even a quick move behind a door can provide valuable seconds to regroup and plan the next move to a more secure location or escape route. Extending discovery from seconds to minutes can save lives. Much can happen in the initial stage of an attack. In the past, first responders have often arrived on an attack scene within a few minutes. There may be law enforcement nearby when an attack begins. There may even be a patron or visitor present with a concealed carry permit who is armed and can shoot back. The key is to seek hiding immediately and move when possible.

Immediate hiding can provide the opportunity to move when the attacker moves. Attackers know that those inside will hide. After attacking those in his immediate view, he will tend to move about to find those who are in hiding. Restrooms appear to be high on the list for an attacker to check—most restrooms do not have an exit. These rooms are chosen quickly by fleeing targets, and it is not unusual to find out after the attack that restrooms contained multiple fatalities. For example, in the second worst mass victim shooting attack in the United States—the June 12, 2016, Pulse nightclub shooting in Orlando, Florida—of the 49 fatalities, 13 were found dead in the restrooms.[1]

In the December 14, 2012, Sandy Hook Elementary School mass victim attack, of the 20 children killed, 15 were killed with almost all crowded into one restroom where the teacher and a behavior therapist were trying in vain to hide and protect the children. They did their absolute best under the circumstances, with no possibility of escape. The two adults were also killed. One 6-year-old girl was the sole survivor.[2, 3] To her credit, she played dead by lying with the bodies and did not move. At 6 years old, this was an amazing accomplishment. After Lanza, the sole shooter, thought he had killed all in that location, he moved on to kill others, then killed himself with a single shot to the head.

At the conclusion, Lanza had killed a total of 6 adults and 20 children at the school, and had killed his mother right before going to Sandy Hook Elementary School to complete his slaughter. In other restrooms, students were successfully hidden and then made their escape. For example, although many were killed in one restroom, two young children were found alive in a restroom by law enforcement after the attack.

There are many unknowns in mass victim attacks, including the effectiveness of hiding. To be honest, sometimes it works, and sometimes it doesn't. When an attack begins, there are a few things we know for certain. If a shooting, the attacker will move around the location looking for victims after the easy targets are hit. Restrooms are often perceived as a hiding place by those who flee attacks. Many have the same idea, and this is why we find multiple fatalities in restrooms. Success in hiding in restrooms has depended on a number of variables.

- The restrooms nearest to the attacker are at greater risk of entry and discovery.
- A locked door does not provide a strong measure of detection because bullets can go through a door and can actually disable a lock.
- There are likely many individuals in a restroom because it appears to be a focus for hiding.
- The only way to make a restroom safe under the conditions of an attack is to blockade the door in such a way that the shooter cannot enter (see chapter 7).

If you must choose a restroom because escape is not possible, and there are no other hiding places, on the way to that hiding location grab whatever you can that could be turned into a weapon. If a restaurant, knives, forks, dinner plates, cups, glasses, serving trays, or any object should be grabbed on the way. A broken bottle, glass, or knife can be a self-defense weapon if necessary. Also, see "Barricade" below. If there is no lock, or even if there is, barricade the door. This is very important. Making entry difficult can convince an attacker to move on to other locations easier to approach and enter.

Yes, attackers know to look in restroom stalls and don't just look underneath the doors. They know that those fleeing an attack will stand on a toilet so that feet cannot be seen. Yes, you want to do this if there is no other choice, but it is better to also have any type of improvised weapon with you.

Because many people are likely to be in that hiding place, or any similar hiding place such as a coat room, kitchen with no exit, office, supply room, etc., realize that there is strength in numbers. Share what could be used as weapons. This situation is covered in chapter 7, "Surviving by Attacking," because it deserves detail. Still, as always, if the situation presents itself because of movement of the attacker, escape! Always be thinking of escape if the possibility should present itself, or if one can be improvised. Remember the example, cited earlier, at the Pulse nightclub in the Orlando, Florida, attack where an air conditioning unit was removed to allow a hole in the wall to the outside to provide a successful escape route. Be creative—your life may depend on it.

The concept of personal security presented in the previous chapter is very relevant for hiding. Although law enforcement can arrive within minutes, this does not always mean the attack is stopped. The Pulse nightclub shooting lasted over three hours because the attacker, Omar Mateen, took hostages and turned the attack into a hostage and barricade incident.

On April 20, 1999, 18-year-old Eric Harris and 17-year-old Dylan Klebold approached the Columbine High School in Columbine, Colorado, at 11:19 a.m. The two teens started shooting outside of the school in front of the cafeteria. Inside, students hid under cafeteria tables. At 11:23, as the first 911 call was made by a cafeteria worker, two students outside the school were killed and six were wounded. Police arrived within five minutes. Harris and Klebold entered the school after Harris exchanged gunfire with a deputy. Seven officers had arrived at that point.

As police positioned themselves around the perimeter of the school, the attacking teens headed toward the library. They shot and killed students, then moved to a public area of the school. Police helped students to escape, but remained outside. By noon, around 45 minutes after the first 911 call was made, at least 75 police officers were surrounding the building. At approximately 12:06 the first SWAT team members entered the building. At that time, Harris and Klebold both committed suicide by shooting themselves in the head; it was 12:08. No law enforcement officers had entered the school other than the SWAT team just two minutes before the suicides.[4]

The result was that 13 were killed—12 students and one teacher. This event led to controversy and lawsuits, with many claiming that law enforcement should have entered the school much earlier. In the meantime, approximately 75 police officers had surrounded the school with no entries as the pair continued to target and kill students.

Law enforcement training for such events has improved. However, we do see long delays for entering locations where active events are happening, such as in the three-hour Pulse nightclub attack. Given the prevalence and probability of attacks from international terrorists, domestic terrorists, self-radicalized persons, those filled with hate and prejudice, and attacks stemming from mental health issues, we must know that every attack is different. Every attack presents its own challenges. The challenges may delay law enforcement responses, even if they arrive on the scene quickly.

You must be astute and knowledgeable about how to spot danger and when and how to hide if escape is not possible. If escape and hiding are both not possible and you have been discovered, there are strategies to survive that involve attacking the attacker. Often, as a last and desperate means to survive, this topic is so important that chapter 6 provides the detail necessary. Being knowledgeable about escape, hiding, and attack methods can lead to survival. Although law enforcement can save your life, you need to be personally responsible for you own safety—just in case help is delayed.

STAYING IN PLACE

Staying in place during a mass victim attack does not sound like an effective strategy for staying alive. Most attempts to survive such attacks do not include this category. I have had some issues with the typical "Run, Hide, Fight" suggestions available on the Internet. The following are some reasons why much more detail is needed:

Such brief descriptions are just that—too brief.

Assessing survival across multitudes of past attacks led me to the conclusion that survival cannot be summed up with a simple video, bullet points on how to survive, or articles. In fact, such brevity could be misleading and could decrease chances for survival. Unfortunately, we have experienced many mass victim attacks, and the differences are greater than the similarities. Why? Because we have diverse types of attackers, using different weapons, focusing on different targets, and possessing different motivations.

Differences equate to an astronomical number of ways in which such attacks could occur. International terrorists, self-radicalized terrorists, domestic terrorists, those motivated by hate, and those suffering from mental health issues represent an amazing number of approaches and targeting, especially when considering hybrid, crossover attacks.

Staying in Place

As presented in this book, "run" is replaced with "escape," a more meaningful way of moving from danger to a safe location, as opposed to running blind. This is a distinctive difference, with a different mindset, and clearly different methods. "Fight" is replaced with "attack," a more considerate and targeted way of surviving. When caught face-to-face with an attacker, it is not a fight. It is a desperate last chance to attack to maim and kill the attacker. It is his life or yours. He has likely already proven that his objective is to kill. It is not a struggle—it is life or death. There is no nice way to say this. Your objective is to damage vulnerable spots on his body to kill him. It is kill or be killed.

"Staying in place" is often not mentioned, except in the context of never to do it. This is a serious error. In some cases, it must be the method of choice and requires special attention.

First, what is staying in place?

Staying in place is not moving during an attack. If there is no clear avenue of escape, hiding, or attacking the attacker, one must stay put—at least temporarily.

In unusual cases, escape, hiding, and even attack may not be possible, so what do you do? Before I can discuss what to do to stay in place, I must mention when NOT to stay in place. When a shooting, stabbing, or vehicle run-down attack begins, *DO NOT stay where you are.* Escape is the only thought you should have. Look for any direction that can put any obstacles between you and the attacker to block his view of you. Then, if the temporary location is not secure, immediately start looking for a more secure location.

The attacker is not going to stay in place, especially if a shooter, stabber, or one who is driving a vehicle to run others down. Because the attacker moves, if he moves away from you, it is time to escape if a clear path is available. This could be an actual escape, or it could be moving to a more secure location for safer hiding until true escape can occur. The main point is not to remain in place. If the attacker can see you, you are going to be a target.

Playing Dead

Playing dead is a special category that belongs in both *what not to do* and *what to do*. It depends totally on the situation. Playing dead is not escaping or hiding. There are those who have survived by playing dead, but we can't know how many times it was tried and failed. Playing dead basically means falling to the floor and acting like you are dead so that the attacker will pass you over; that is the purpose. It is an act of desperation and may be necessary if all other options are not possible.

The optimal time to escape or hide is at the beginning of an attack. Panic is highest at that point and is likely to be manifested as massive screaming, shouting, and running in the midst of the first gunshots or stabbings, people falling injured or dying, and screams of pain. At the initial stage of the attack, the attacker's focus is on killing anyone close. As an attack progresses, help-lessness can settle in, and deaths can start mounting. It will then be easier for the attacker to move around, see and hear others, and extend his or her killing range. During the beginning of the attack, you would be one of many moving and running. Minutes later, any movement is easier to spot. Lesson to be learned: The best time to escape is at the beginning of an attack when there is more likely to be chaos and pandemonium. Just a minute later, the attacker may well be into the hunt-and-kill mode based on any movement spotted.

Be aware! Many mass victim attacks have resulted in a shooter walking back and forth and shooting victims multiple times to make sure they are dead. If playing dead to avoid being shot, the shooter may come back and shoot you anyway. There are several accounts of survivors playing dead and feeling the shots rip through their bodies as the shooter returned multiple times to shoot those who had already been shot. Most importantly, if a shooter is killing victims on one side of a room and you are playing dead on the other side of the room, he knows you have not been hit. He will get to you shortly.

Staying in place and playing dead is not hiding. In many cases it is simply delaying the obvious. If escape is not possible, then hide—do not just play dead unless all other options are simply not possible. How to hide depends heavily on the characteristics of the location. If the attack occurs within a bar, restaurant, or similar setting, and escape does not immediately appear to be possible, the confined location may not present many hiding possibilities. You may be limited to hiding behind doors, in adjacent rooms, restrooms, under counters, bars, tables, or overturned tables, and even obscured by dra-peries as a temporary move.

If the attack is outside and in the open, hiding can be very difficult. For example, if caught in the path of an accelerating vehicle with a driver intent on killing anyone seen, you must first think about escaping by running to get out of the path—move left or right of the oncoming vehicle but not forward in the same path. Hopefully, you follow sound walking principles and walk alongside buildings and obstacles. If a vehicle is coming, and you are walking near buildings, you can hide by ducking in an alley or building. Even if not hidden, it is possible that a building, store entrance, or alley can save your life. As mentioned in chapter 4, vehicle run-downs are more of an escape scenario for survival. However, depending on the location, it may be possible to hide if there is enough warning.

When to Stay in Place

This is an important section. There are occasions when you do want to stay in place, and the situations are not common. Basically, you should stay in place when: (1) a bomb is detonated near you and you have escaped injury or are injured, or (2) escape is not possible and you must hide temporarily until you can escape, if possible.

A bomb is detonated near you

Large-scale bombings such as the Oklahoma City Timothy McVeigh vehicle bombing of the Alfred P. Murrah Federal Building on April 19, 1995, was a massive blast that essentially destroyed the building and damaged many other structures in the surrounding blocks. The victims numbered 168 dead and over 650 injured. McVeigh and his accomplice, Terry Nichols, were caught and prosecuted. McVeigh was executed on June 11, 2001. Nichols was sentenced to 160 consecutive life terms.[5] Such large-scale bombings occur as single bombings, partly because of the devastating effects.

Smaller-scale bombings can occur in multiples, on occasion two bombings. For example, the Tamerlan and Dzhokhar Tsarnaev brothers, on April 15, 2013, detonated two pressure cooker bombs between 50 and 100 yards apart within 8 to 12 seconds. Three were killed, with many receiving serious injuries. The older brother, Tamerlan, was killed in a shoot-out with police three days later and Dzhokhar was captured the next day.[6] The younger brother, Dzhokhar, was prosecuted and received the death penalty.

If a small-scale bomb and you have received injuries, major or minor, stay in place. It is better to tend to your own injuries, especially preventing blood loss, until first responders arrive. Rushing and running can accelerate blood loss and prevent adequate self-treatment.

There is not likely to be a second blast in the exact same vicinity. If you made it through the first blast, running could place you near a second bomb. Running from the blast could also place you in the killing range of a shooter who used the small bomb to funnel victims toward him. First responders are quick in such situations, and help is likely on the way.

Escape is not possible, and you must hide temporarily

If escape was not possible and you located a relatively safe hiding place, it is best to stay in place until there is a safer time to: (1) escape (this should always be the number one concern), or (2) move to a more secure hiding place. One of the primary indicators of knowing when to move is if the attacker is moving away from you. Again, attackers tend to move to find more victims. Either he is still in the process of moving to find more victims who could not escape or hide, or he is uncovering those who are hiding in a location away from you. Most importantly, when the attack begins, it is NOT the time to stay in place. Move to escape or, if not possible, move to get out of view of the attacker with the objective of escape at the first opportunity.

If in a shopping mall, know that almost every store has a back door. These doors are used for deliveries of merchandise. As we walk around a mall, we see almost as many back doors as we see storefronts. If a mass victim attack were to begin, escape to the nearest store and find the back door. During panic, most people are likely to rush to a regular entrance/exit. However, there can be many problems. Distance could be a problem; the person could be elderly or could be a child. If physically or mentally challenged, a dash across a mall to an established entrance/exit may not be possible.

Nearby stores provide many temporary hiding places, as well as escape routes. This is true of almost any store. When shopping at your local mall, take notice of the stores. If you drive around the back of the mall, you will likely see the many back doors used for deliveries. Many mall stores have a security gate that blocks the entrance during off-hours. If a store is nearby when an attack starts, escape there and state clearly that a stabbing or shooting attack is occurring and the security gate should be closed. Gates have been closed in attacks, with success. Then, move totally out of sight—again, out a back exit if available.

If no back exit (which is unusual) then hide amidst clothing, etc. The attacker is not likely to waste time trying to get through a security gate, which is very difficult. It is much easier for him to move on to search for other victims who are not in a secure setting, even if he knows there are people behind the security gate.

Those Requiring Assistance

The physically challenged, mentally challenged, elderly, and children present special concerns from a mass victim attack perspective. There is likely a designated individual to assist the person in a wheelchair move about. Even if on crutches, there is usually someone to accompany the person just to help with doors, getting meals, and for many other reasons. The elderly may have issues of their own, and range from the relatively healthy and independent to those who are physically challenged and require assistance. Children are basically helpless to respond to an attack.

Care must be taken not to panic children if in the process of moving them to safety. Cries and screams can become seemingly uncontrollable, and could easily give away a hiding place. Parents will know what I am talking about. Use your imagination. Move swiftly, do not alarm children, and get to the safest place you can find. Console, calm, distract, and focus on anything other than what may be threatening.

There are additional challenges to consider. Escape may be less of an option and hiding may take on much more importance. If alone, you may be able to sprint to an exit, but when in the position of taking care of others, hiding in the nearest location may be the only remaining option. Again, and it bears repeating, staying in place is not an option until well hidden or barricaded.

You must be astute, knowledgeable, and aware when accompanying anyone relying on you for safety. Knowing what to look for and knowing how to respond takes on special meaning. The time of an attack is not the time to start determining how to protect those under your care. It is important to think "prevention" as opposed to just "reaction." The information in this book takes on even more meaning for you if you are the designated responsible person. When you enter a location and you have others in your care, start looking for safe locations immediately as a routine practice.

We all have observed a gracious leader going through a mall or being at a public place such as a restaurant with a physically or intellectually challenged individual, or maybe a small group. This puts one person in charge because of the limited mobility and capabilities of the individuals he or she is accompanying. Know exits and sit near an exit or secure area to hide before going to the location. If an attack should occur, it is going to take more time to secure safety for those in your care.

Situational Awareness

Situational awareness is being tuned in to your immediate environment and knowing what is happening around you. This topic is taught in law enforcement, military, security, rescue, firefighting, emergency services, and any other service that must respond across a variety of settings. Key to survival in a mass victim attack is knowing the characteristics of the environment you are in, quickly assessing how you could escape or where to hide to give you more time to escape. Wherever you are and regardless of the situation, be aware of what is happening around you.

Given the relative ease with which mass victim attacks may be carried out and the potential threat that is present, we must be better prepared. When I was a child and even a young adult, we did not have to worry that much about mass victim attacks. It is different now. Whether at public events or gatherings, having dinner at a restaurant, at a movie or theatre, sporting event, or just walking, we can be a target. This is not an alarmist statement. It is simply a statement of fact and an acknowledgement that we need to be more situationally aware when in public—not only aware of what is going on around us, but knowing what to do if suddenly faced with life-threatening danger.

Being situationally aware is much like driving defensively. As we drive, we tend to view our rearview mirrors often to be aware of conditions behind us. We are attuned to oncoming traffic, we know what is happening in adjacent lanes, and we continually adjust our driving to meet existing conditions such as speed limits, traffic, weather, rain, snow, ice, storms, road construction, etc. It is an extensive list. When we first learn to drive, this is much more of a conscious effort. However, over time, with practice, safe driving and being alert becomes second nature. We can also learn and practice situational awareness in public places that could attract a mass victim attack.

As covered in the previous chapter, when entering a confined space and noting the location of exits and areas of escape, also take note of any locations to hide if escape is not immediately possible. Is there a bar or counter? Are there other rooms? Are there internal doors? Could tables be used to hide you from view, even temporarily? A quick scan of the location can provide valuable information to promote escape and hiding. After following this practice a number of times, it becomes almost automatic.

There are a number of key factors to consider if you are forced to hide because escape is not immediately possible. Perhaps the attacker is just too close.

- Seek any location nearby that can block the attacker's view and, once there, scan the environment for a more secure hiding spot.
- Move to a more secure hiding spot when possible while constantly seeking a way to escape.
- Make a hiding place more secure by using a barricade.

Barricade

If you enter a room to hide and it has a door, create a barricade to make entry more difficult. *A barricade temporarily blocks physical access to you by a threatening person or persons who could cause injury or death to you or others.* Many interior doors do not have locks, and even if a door has a lock, reinforce the door to make it more secure. Many objects can serve as a door stop—even a wallet or multiple wallets jammed under the bottom of the door can help to prevent the door from opening. Heavy objects can be moved to block the door from opening. More than likely, if the environment was crowded, you will have company in that room. Make sure that no one stands directly behind the door. Doors do not stop bullets. Grab anything that can be used as a weapon. See chapter 6 for more on this subject.

On September 17, 2016, on a Saturday, Dahir Adan, an ISIS-inspired loyalist, approached the Crossroads Center mall in St. Cloud, Minnesota, wearing a security guard uniform. He had been a security guard, but was unemployed at the time. He was brandishing two long knives. He had just committed a hit-and-run of a bicyclist and had run a red light. As he approached the entrance of the mall on foot, he stabbed a man and his pregnant girlfriend. He entered the corridor of the mall and stabbed five more people. Intermittently, he asked his targets if they were Muslim, then he stabbed them if they answered no.

Moving through the mall, he stabbed a father and son. As a clerk went to the entrance of a store to see what was happening, he was stabbed twice. Adan moved on to another store and stabbed another victim as an employee pulled down the security gate. He tried to enter but couldn't, so he moved on. He walked past Target, because employees had just locked the door. He approached Bath & Body Works and stabbed his 12th victim. There he encountered Jason Falconer, and asked if he was Muslim. Falconer answered no, and Adan turned away, but Falconer saw the knives.

Falconer, an off-duty policeman, was armed. Falconer identified himself as a police officer several times, showed his badge, and ordered Adan to stop. Adan continued moving away from Officer Falconer who continued showing his badge to others. Falconer ran in pursuit with gun pulled. He apparently was concerned that he was in plainclothes and had a gun pulled and aimed at a man wearing a security guard uniform. Adan finally went to the ground. However, he came up and went after the off-duty officer twice. Falconer fired, and Adan was shot six times and killed.[7]

I mention this attack specifically because it has all the elements of how to respond. Escape, Hiding, Staying in Place, and Attack were all in evidence as counterattack measures. The mall offered many avenues of escape, as well as places to hide. First, hearing the screams and sounds of an attack allowed some to immediately escape by leaving the target area. Second, some went to nearby stores, and security gates were closed, providing both hiding and barricades for protection. Once behind a barricade and especially if an exit wasn't present, then staying in place ensured safety. It is not worth the attacker's time to try to get through a barricade if easier targets are available.

Lastly, there happened to be an armed off-duty police officer who responded. He showed his identification repeatedly because he was in plainclothes and the attacker was in a security guard uniform. This unusual situation indicates the types of confusion that can be present during a mass victim attack. No two attacks are the same. To the officer's credit, he knew he had to make it clear to bystanders that he was the officer, even if dressed in plainclothes.

6

Surviving by Attacking the Attacker: A Last Resort?

Attacking the attacker is definitely not a preferred option. However, if there simply is no escape, no place to hide, you are in a confined space and can't run, and it is clear you are going to be a target in seconds, then attacking may be the only option. Mass victim attackers approach a target well armed and may be wearing personal protection tactical gear. Attackers have worn gas masks, bulletproof vests, and had extra weapons and ammunition. The attacker is likely to be young and fit.

The attacker is in that spot to kill . . . anyone—and is prepared to die either at his own hand or at the hands of others. When in a public place, we do not have protective gear, many are not young or are very young, we tend not to have weapons of any sort, and many are not fit. To say the attacker has a significant advantage is an understatement.

PREPARATION: INCREASING YOUR ODDS

I would venture to say that when most think of attacking, or fighting an attacker, the thought begins with the attacker suddenly there and you are face-to-face! There is a much better way. Think about it now, and how you can be better prepared if the seemingly unthinkable scenario occurs.

The scenario is frightening. You are in a public place, perhaps a restaurant. A shooter has entered the restaurant and has been mercilessly shooting everyone he sees. He is moving as he shoots. You have looked around and there is no way to escape. You have looked for hiding places, but it is just a room with no adjacent rooms and only one entrance. The attacker enters, and sees you. You wish you had a concealed carry permit and a gun; some people do—you don't.

There are only two likely scenarios: You can be proactive and be prepared for an attack, or you can use makeshift weapons when attacked. To be proactive means to be prepared before going to any public place. Does this mean carrying a gun? It can, but there are other defensive objects that can be carried at all times to improve your chances of survival.

If there has been no preparation and an attack occurs, there are many objects in most settings that can be turned into a weapon. There is a key here. If caught with no chance of escape or hiding, immediately look for anything that can be used as a weapon. Remember, an attacker already has a significant advantage. He is armed and wants to kill. Using your fists/hands is not likely to lead to survival, but if there are no other options, go for the eyes, ears, and throat.

BE PROACTIVE

To be proactive means you follow practices that will improve the probability of survival if you are attacked. There is a common view that the probability of being attacked is so small that we should not worry about it. I take great issue with this view. We just aren't accustomed to thinking about arming ourselves when going to public places. Be proactive and give it thought. Once you have an object that can be used as a weapon, you don't have to dwell on the weapon or defensive device. You know it is there should it ever be needed.

There are three categories of small, portable devices that can be used proactively to protect yourself. In other words, there are three categories of objects that can be carried at all times to be prepared should you ever be caught in a mass victim attack. Two of these categories consist of objects that can be lethal. The third category includes nonlethal objects to defend yourself as a way to immediately escape if used as a last resort. I refer to these categories as:

- Lethal Weapon: Gun
- Lethal Weapon: Knife
- Nonlethal Personal Protection Device (PPD)

There is a fourth category that is not proactive; it is more reactive and labeled as "Weapons of Opportunity." This latter category focuses on what objects happen to be present at the time of an attack that could be used as a weapon to assist an escape.

Lethal Weapon: Guns

The United States is a nation of guns, which has led to much controversy. This book does not focus on the controversy, but mentions guns as protection against mass victim attackers. Many may be surprised to learn that 12.3% of adults in the United States sometimes carry handguns, 5.4% carry handguns most or all the time, and 2.4% carry all the time. Most states require a concealed carry permit: however, there are 14 states that do not require a permit of any kind.[1] But, certainly, even with the prevalence of concealed handguns, unless you have one, you can't count on someone being present who would use a handgun to stop an attacker.

If there is an attack and you do have a concealed handgun, know that when you reveal the handgun, you had better shoot quickly. If an attacker sees you with a weapon, you will be the immediate target. You are posing a threat that could stop him. Do not yell "halt" or "put down your weapon" as you see in the movies. Shoot to kill. The attacker may be wearing some form of body armor—he likely came prepared. Shoot for the head or face. It may sound gruesome, but save your life and the lives of others. Whether he is a shooter or stabber, he is going to continue until he flees, is stopped, or kills himself. If he is an international terrorist or self-radicalized terrorist, he may even have a suicide belt holding explosives that he can detonate at any time.

All states in the United States allow some form of concealed weapon carry. The website http://handgunlaw.us is particularly useful. The site has an interactive map of all states. You can click on the state or states of interest and are directed to detailed information on the laws covering concealed carry laws for the state selected.[2] The site also includes U.S. territories.

Another site provides useful information on reciprocity, e.g., which states may honor your state-provided concealed carry permit).[3] Keep in mind that the list can change, so please keep a check on any state that has your interest. There are two tabs on the site. The first is labeled "States That Honor My Permit(s)." This means that if you have permit(s), you can check to see what other states honor your permit so that you can carry in those states using your existing permit(s). The second tab, labeled "Permits Honored by State," allows you to focus on any particular state to determine what permits are honored.

Notice two terms in the list that follows below: "*Shall* Issue" and "*May* Issue." *Shall* means that the state will issue a concealed carry permit if you meet requirements. *May issue* means that the state reserves judgment not to issue a permit if there is concern, even if all requirements are met. For example, there could be the obvious presence of mental health or mental disability issues great enough to cause concern about competence to handle a weapon safely, or concern over the potential presence of danger to self or others.

SHALL ISSUE TO RESIDENTS ONLY

Alaska, Colorado, Georgia, Guam, Indiana, Iowa, Kansas, Kentucky, Louisiana, Michigan, Mississippi, Missouri, Montana, Nebraska, New Mexico, North Carolina, Ohio, South Dakota, Vermont, West Virginia, Wisconsin, Wyoming

SHALL ISSUE TO RESIDENTS AND NON-RESIDENTS

Alabama, Arizona, Arkansas, Florida, Idaho, Illinois, Maine, Minnesota, Nevada, New Hampshire, North Dakota, Oklahoma, Oregon, Pennsylvania, Puerto Rico, Rhode Island, South Carolina, Tennessee, Texas, Utah, Virginia, Washington

MAY ISSUE TO RESIDENTS ONLY

California, Delaware, New York City, Virgin Islands

MAY ISSUE TO RESIDENTS AND NON-RESIDENTS

Connecticut, District of Columbia, Hawaii, Maryland, Massachusetts, New Jersey, New York

RIGHT DENIED

American Samoa

Some restrictions may apply. Check each state for its own restrictions. There are ways to take training, even online. Once certified, the carry permit can be good in over 25 states. Alaska, Arizona, Idaho, Kansas, Maine, Mississippi, Missouri, New Hampshire, North Dakota, Vermont, West Virginia, and Wyoming allow carrying a concealed gun without a permit.[4]

As a psychologist who has studied threat from many sources for an entire career, I feel the need for some disclaimers. It is a personal decision as to whether to carry a concealed gun with or without a concealed carry permit (depending where you live). This is a very complicated issue, and it cannot be solved with a few statements or attempted guidance. All depends on the makeup of the individual who would do the carrying. In making such a decision, I would offer the following for consideration.

The Potential for Making a Mistake

Situations, particularly in the midst of panic, are not always what they appear to be. I mentioned earlier the September 17, 2016, Dahir Adan stabbing attack at the Crossroads Center mall in St. Cloud, Minnesota. The self-radicalized attacker was wearing a security uniform as he stabbed innocent victims with two long knives. Jason Falconer, an off-duty law enforcement officer in plainclothes, was in the mall at the time and was armed. Falconer saw the long knives and pursued Adan with his firearm raised and visible. To the uninitiated, or to someone just walking onto the scene, it would appear that a man with a gun was chasing a security guard.

If you pulled out a concealed carry gun at the moment you saw Falconer in regular clothes pursuing Adan in a security guard uniform, what would you do? Falconer was aware that the scene could appear reversed, and he continued to identify himself as an officer and kept showing his badge. He eventually shot and killed Adan after Adan had lunged at him twice. However, this could have been an opportunity for a horrible, but well-meaning, error of judgment in which an officer could have been shot by an armed bystander because it appeared he was assailing a security guard.

Attackers often wear dark tactical clothing. They are typically young and fit. In many ways, they could look like law enforcement officers. They can also wear body armor. Furthermore, concealed carry permits are not skill based. It should be obvious that all who carry firearms are not equal in terms of judgment, skill, and how they handle crisis situations. There is a very big difference in target shooting for practice and facing an armed attacker who wants to kill you. If you pull out a concealed handgun, you had better know how to use it, and make sure you know the difference between the bad guys and the good guys!

The Potential for Being Outgunned

Extreme care must be taken in the event that a lethal weapon is used. An attacker comes with multiple weapons that are typically semi-automatic if guns, may have on body armor, carries extra ammunition, has likely done surveillance on the target area, and knows exits, nooks, and crannies. In short, he is there to kill as many people as he can and is determined to succeed. You will likely be outgunned. Furthermore, there could be more than one attacker. If cornered, there is no escape and no hiding and you are going to be killed; it is time to protect yourself. Remember the potential for body armor. This forces you into a lethal head shot, or shots, quickly. Just make sure it is the right person.

Training for Concealed Carry is Not Handgun Training

I would like to make one last point as it relates to the use of concealed carry handguns to provide protection against mass victim attacks. This is a two-part process. There is first certification in those states that require it.

Remember, some states do not require a permit. Then there is proper training on the safe use of handguns. This includes how to best handle the gun, and how to protect it at home. The training can include how to shoot properly and accurately. Don't skip this stage. The more you practice with a handgun, the more comfortable you will be. You do not want to be in an active shooter situation while you are trying to remember how to use the safety on your own gun. There is no substitute for training and practice.

Unless you are a current or recently trained member of law enforcement or the military, or similarly trained in gun safety and use, resist any urge to pursue an attacker. Escape, as always, should be the objective. An active shooter is likely to outgun you, and is determined to die in the effort. However, if caught with no chance of escape and no hiding, then the weapon should be used to stop the attacker who is coming after you.

Owning any firearm that is kept in the home carries with it the responsibility to secure the weapon(s) in such a manner that they cannot injure or kill others either in the heat of anger, a suicide, or accidentally. In a recent *Pediatrics* journal article, it was noted that each year, approximately 1,300 children die and 5,790 are treated for gunshot wounds.[5] Home gun safety, as well as gun safety at all times, is tied to gun ownership.

Before I was born, I had a great uncle Manuel. Both my father and I share his name. He was 12 years old and was walking up the country house front steps when his 12-year-old cousin opened the front door to scare him, as kids do. He pointed what he thought was an unloaded 12-gauge shotgun at Uncle Manuel's abdomen and said, "Bang, you're dead." At the same time, he pulled the trigger. At point blank range, Uncle Manuel was killed instantly by the horrific effects of the shotgun blast. My brother and I grew up being instructed frequently by my father that "More people are killed by unloaded guns than loaded guns." The obviously incorrect statement makes a salient point. Always treat a gun as if it is loaded even if you assume it is not loaded—mistakes happen. Although you remember leaving the gun unloaded, you may have forgotten or someone else could have left it loaded. If guns are not secured properly, accidents can happen, and they do. Keep all weapons at home locked to ensure safety of all family.

When are concealed carry guns most likely to be useful for saving your life? If the attack is a bombing or vehicle run-over, the concealed carry gun is less likely to be effective. It is highly unlikely that shooting at a fast vehicle coming your way and running down victims can be stopped with gunshots. Again, this is not the movies, where someone stops a vehicle rapidly by shooting out tires or hitting the radiator. It just doesn't work that way. If a bombing, the event is over almost instantaneously, and the attacker is either dead from being part of a suicide bombing or has fled the scene. However, if the attack is a stabbing event or one in which attackers are armed and shooting, the gun as a last resort can be useful and effective.

Lethal Weapon: Knives

A knife can be a terrifying and lethal weapon in the hands of a determined and motivated attacker. They are easy to obtain essentially anywhere, and it is legal to carry a knife—if the right kind of knife. Knives can also be a lethal weapon for the person who is put in a situation where he or she is a targeted victim of a mass attacker and has absolutely no choice but to attack back. Knives can cause extremely grave wounds. In one study conducted by the University of Pennsylvania's Perelman School of Medicine there was no significant difference in adjusted overall survival rates between gunshot and stabbing (so-called penetrating trauma injuries) victims whether transported to the emergency room by police or emergency medical services (EMS).[6]

Knife wounds can penetrate deeply, sever multiple internal organs, and cause profuse bleeding (out-of-control bleeding without immediate treatment). As with guns, the lethality goes both ways. The attacker depends on the lethality that is caused by sharp-edged weapons such as knives. Plus, they may use machetes or long knives. This illustrates one major difference between sharp-edged weapons used by attackers and knives carried for self-protection: Protection is not likely to include machetes, hatchets, or long knives. However, it is not just the length of the blade that dictates the effectiveness, it is the skill with which the object is used. Make no mistake, a knife can provide effective protection IF used as a last resort and you absolutely do not have any other option for escape or hiding.

There is a large variety of knives available for sale in every state. They range from long-blade hunting knives to small pocketknives. Different states have different regulations for carrying knives in a concealed manner. Looking across state regulations, you can be almost certain that if you carry a small knife with a three-inch blade that must be opened manually, you are OK. Opened manually means that the blade is folded into a handle and must be pulled open. Many states do not allow gravity-feed knives—those where, if held in a certain way, gravity pulls out the blade. Switchblade knives are basically illegal. Most likely to be seen in the movies, a switchblade knife springs open when a button on the side of the knife is pushed.

If you have interest in carrying a knife for protection, please see the specific regulations for concealed knife carry in your state and any state you might travel in with a concealed knife. There are many sites with interactive maps. You can click on the state of interest and you are automatically directed to that state's concealed knife carry regulations.[7, 8]

Continuing with the overriding message that escape is the primary objective and hiding to escape is second, a knife would be used as a last report, particularly if the attacker is a stabber. It is difficult to imagine a scenario where a concealed carry knife would be useful to fight back against an attacker if the attack was a bombing, active shooting attack, or a vehicle run-over. This book does not discuss how to use a knife. I recommend searching for any number of training videos and instructions for use of a small concealed knife as an effective weapon. However, I will say that if caught by a stabber with no escape and you have no other recourse, use the knife on very vulnerable spots such as the neck, face, and eyes. As gruesome as it sounds, it could be a life-and-death situation, and your objective is to stop the attacker so that you can escape before he achieves his objective of killing you.

Personal Protection Devices

I offer the following definition of a personal protection device (PPD) from the perspective of defense against a mass victim attacker.

A personal protection device (PPD) is a nonlethal object that may be used to temporarily incapacitate an attacker to actively defend yourself as a means to aid escape from a threatening assault.

To be clear, a PPD is not designed to kill; it is designed to stop an attacker through a variety of severely unpleasant means, depending on the device. Because they are nonlethal by design, they require fewer regulations than guns. The purpose of a PPD is to stop the attacker so that you, and perhaps others, can escape from a location where you could be harmed or killed.

PPDs include a variety of devices. For the purposes of protecting yourself against a mass victim attacker as a last resort, I will focus on a few effective devices. These include pepper spray and tear gas, as well as electrical shock/stun devices. There are numerous websites that focus on PPDs, with some focusing on protection for women.[9, 10] However, these useful and portable devices are suited to all. Most importantly, they can be carried at all times in a purse or pocket and can provide a degree of protection and escape across a variety of situations.

PPDs are clearly not devices used for offense; from a mass victim attack perspective, they provide a last resort when there is no escape opportunity, no place to hide, and you are going to be confronted by the attacker. Using a PPD like pepper spray can effectively incapacitate the attacker temporarily to allow the possibility of an escape. One advantage of many PPDs is that they provide some distance so that you are not face-to-face. This is particularly important if caught in a stabbing spree. For example, a typical small handheld container of pepper spray has a range of 8 to 20 feet. If used correctly, such as sprayed at the face, the target can become disoriented, experience great discomfort and pain, and temporarily not be able to function.

Like guns and knives, there are a variety of PPDs suitable for different purposes. However, I will focus on the devices relevant for mass victim attacks—although these devices can be used for basic self-protection purposes. My focus is based on the following criteria:

- Portable (can easily be carried)
- Effective (can debilitate an attacker)
- Legal
- Easily obtained

These devices fall into the following categories: (1) sprays (pepper gas and tear gas), and (2) electrical shock/stun (taser and stun gun)

The purpose of sprays is to provide a noxious and debilitating gas in a small container, much like the size of a lipstick tube, which can deliver multiple shots at a minimum distance of 8 to 15 feet. I have experienced both pepper spray and tear gas. I can attest to the noxious effects. If delivered properly to the face, it is possible to escape while the attacker is temporarily incapacitated.

Pepper Spray: The Method of Choice

There is often confusion among the terms pepper spray, tear gas, and Mace. The original Mace is no longer available commercially but was an irritant more like tear gas than pepper spray. In fact, today's commercial version of Mace is actually a pepper spray.

Tear gas is very different from pepper spray. Where tear gas is an irritant, pepper spray is inflammatory. Pepper spray is more effective and can result in temporarily incapacitating the target, allowing valuable time to escape. Tear gas affects the eyes and the nasal cavity and is irritating. However, it does not cause inflammation of the eye capillaries as does pepper spray. Most importantly, the original Mace was discontinued because law enforcement officers were being injured when using it. It appeared that it was not effective with those under the influence of drugs or alcohol.

The active ingredient in pepper spray is technically labeled Oleoresin Capsicum (OC), an extract of cayenne pepper. Commercially available pepper sprays are available in small containers approximately the size of a large tube of lipstick. A fully charged cylinder is capable of multiple sprays with a range of 8 to 20 feet. The debilitating effects can last as long as 20 to 90 minutes. The spray is inflammatory and effective when the OC spray makes contact with the mucous membranes, such as eyes, nose, throat, and lungs. Debilitating symptoms are immediate on contact. Immediate and temporary blindness can occur and breathing becomes difficult, although possible.[11]

There are several advantages of pepper spray:

- Significant effects are immediate;
- Results in immediate and temporary blindness and difficulty in breathing—it is not likely that an attacker would function after receiving a full spray to the face;
- Effects are so debilitating that there is at least an increased chance of escape while the attacker is suffering from the spray effects;
- The spray works just as well or better than tear gas or Mace if the attacker is under the influence of alcohol and/or drugs;
- It comes in a portable container that easily fits into the pocket or purse;
- Has a minimum range of 8 to 20 feet;
- Legal in all 50 states (although check each state for regulations).

There are a few things to know about the use of pepper spray. You must be 18 years of age to purchase it, and it cannot be taken on a commercial airliner. If you carry it on an airliner, you are subject to a hefty $25,000 fine. You are not likely to be able to take pepper spray through a security checkpoint. Although you can purchase pepper spray online, you can't purchase it through the mail or through the Internet from Hawaii, Indiana, Massachusetts, Michigan, New Jersey, New York, Pennsylvania, Rhode Island, or Wisconsin. This information, as well as state regulations, can be found at: https://www.cabelas.com/assets/product_files/pdf/pepperspray_lawsregulation.pdf

Electrical Shock/Stun Devices

There are two basic types of electrical devices relevant for mass victim attacks: (1) the stun gun, and (2) the Taser. First, for clarification, the word Taser is not a technical acronym. It was inspired by a novel describing Tom Swift's adventures, including his invention of an electric rifle. Hence the interesting name of the device, "Thomas A. Swift's Electric Rifle, or TASER." The name was given by one of the developers of the device, John H. "Jack" Cover, an aerospace scientist who worked on the Apollo program. Among Cover's favorite young adult books were the adventures of Tom Swift. One book, *Tom Swift and His Electric Rifle*, provided the nontechnical acronym for the device once Cover added an "A" to the name.[12]

The stun gun and the Taser are similar in that high-voltage, non-life-threatening electricity is delivered to a target to incapacitate him. In law enforcement, the time the target cannot act is used to handcuff the person, or otherwise move to the next step of capture while incapacitation is in effect. From a mass victim attack perspective, both types of device are used to incapacitate the assailant, to allow time for escape.

Although the stun gun and Taser are similar in that they both are handheld and used by the person who is threatened, there are differences. The stun gun has two metal contacts, or prongs, on the end. The user reaches out with the device and touches the assailant with the metal contacts. This causes a strong electrical current to pass through the assailant, which can incapacitate him immediately. The Taser shoots two probes, which are connected with wires to the handheld shocking device as far as 8 to 20 feet away. It is aimed at the assailant and the trigger is pulled. The probes hit the assailant and can embed in the skin. The electrical shock is automatically delivered on contact. The Taser has the advantage of also being used as a stun gun by touching the assailant with the contacts if the probes did not hit the target properly when fired.

If you search the Internet for stun guns and Tasers you will notice that often the terms are used interchangeably. For the purposes of this book, stun gun is defined as a handheld device that is held against a target to deliver the electrical charge, while a Taser can shoot prongs with wires attached an average distance of about 15 feet to deliver the electrical charge.

The first thing to know about stun guns is that different types have distinct characteristics. Check the specifications carefully and use only as directed. Regardless of the specifications, they all have one thing in common: You must touch the device to the skin of the target. As a general description for use, the following is provided by one manufacturer. I am not endorsing any single product, but the following is a clear and concise description for use.

To use the stun gun, hold the contact probes firmly against the attacker. The best target areas to aim for are on the neck and torso, particularly the underarm, upper shoulders, groin, and upper hip (below the rib cage). These areas are nerve centers and the electrical current will affect the whole body when struck here; however, the stun gun will work when touched to any body part. Hold it against the attacker for three to five seconds, maybe longer if the person is large or is continuing to pursue you. This should repel your attacker, giving you enough time to get away. If you touch the attacker, the current will not pass back into your body.[13]

The following brief summary is provided as an overall general guide on how to use a Taser.[14] Detailed instructions are provided when purchased.

The Taser is a real weapon and is used by law enforcement officers for control of unruly individuals. You should know the device well, how it works, and how to use it. It comes with a user's manual, so use that as a reference. It is not an object to be used without studying the user's manual. A Taser works if the needles or prongs that are projected when the trigger is pulled contact the skin of the target and remain there for the brief time it takes for the electrical shock to be delivered. Although civilian Tasers can work for up to 15 feet, the user should fire at an ideal distance of 7 feet. This improves accuracy and functionality.

If you are planning to take the Taser with you, check it. Follow the instructions provided by the manufacturer for checking the device. Basically, you pull the trigger with the cartridge removed and see if there are sparks. If so, it is ready for use once you replace the cartridge and make sure the safety is on. Refer specifically to the owner's manual on how to aim and shoot your particular device. If laser aiming is used, a red dot falls on the target where the prongs are to hit.

One convenient factor of the Taser is that if you shoot and miss the target, you still have a functional stun gun in your hand. The contacts at the end of the handheld device work as effectively as a stun gun if held against the target's skin. Last, and very important, make sure the use of a Taser is legal in your state. If it is legal, then make sure you follow any and all restrictions. If interested, please visit http://www.stungunbuyersguide.com/stun-gun-laws to obtain an overview of laws covering stun guns / Tasers in states, cities, and, in some cases, counties. The site is an excellent source of information for the use of electrical shock devices, including travel restrictions. Regardless of state regulations that you find on the Internet, always make sure you check with your local law enforcement to ensure the most up-to-date information.

Weapons of Opportunity

The following can be a real scenario. There is a mass victim attack in progress. You do not have the opportunity to escape or hide, you do not have a concealed weapon carry permit and no gun and no knife, you do not have a PPD such as pepper gas, and it looks like you are cornered at arm's length. What do you do? Hopefully, seeing that you are likely to be face-to-face with an attacker and your life is going to be at risk, you grabbed a weapon or weapons of opportunity to protect yourself to the degree that you could, still hoping for an escape.

What is a weapon of opportunity? As it relates to mass victim attacks, I define a weapon of opportunity in the following way.

A weapon of opportunity is an object obtained at the scene of an attack that can be used as a weapon if you have to defend yourself in an arm's-length confrontation. The object is likely not considered a weapon, but it is "weaponized" by use to hurt, stop, or kill the attacker.

Why use any form of weapon to defend and protect yourself? A mass victim attacker is well armed and may even have body armor. He is there to kill, is determined, and adrenalin is flowing. He is likely strong and fit, and determined to kill. You find yourself in a situation of no escape and no hiding, and are not armed with a weapon or any form of PPD. You do not want a hand-to-weapon struggle. The odds of surviving are low, at best. However, any form of device that can be used as a weapon can increase the probability of survival.

This is not a book that provides self-protection strategies. There are courses that are likely taught near you as well as online training. I believe we now live in a time that we need to know the basics of self-protection. We likely do not expect to be in public with some form of weapon, although some are armed for protection. But, we are not helpless. There are many things we can do.

You can debilitate an attacker with no object, but this is more likely to be successful only if you are trained to know the vulnerable spots and how to strike. However, grabbing any object that could help you to attack the attacker when you have no other choice is better than not using harmful objects. This section will just introduce the basics that hopefully motivate you to find detailed information describing self-protection methods.

The attacker has vulnerabilities. He may wear protective gear, have superior weaponry, and be determined to kill, but he can't cover eyes, ears, nose, and mouth. He must see, hear, and breathe. You may not have much of a chance against a stabber or active shooter without some form of object to help. Bombings and vehicle run-downs are different. A weapon of opportunity simply may not be available or relevant in these forms of attack.

Objects used for weapons of opportunity depend on the location in which an attack occurs. Eating establishments are similar, as well as bars, lounges, and nightclubs. Sporting events and malls are in a class of their own, as are schools. At the most basic level, literally anything thrown at the eyes of an attacker will cause an automatic reflex of momentarily closing his eyes or ducking for protection. There is not time for the attacker to figure out what is coming at him, even if relatively harmless. However, unless the object is physically harmful to the attacker, only a second or two delay may be gained. But that may be time to move.

Picking up any hard, and hopefully sharp or pointed, object and throwing it at the attacker's face with force may have an effect and may cause severe injury, increasing the time to escape. For example, a bottle, a broken bottle, drinking glasses, knives, forks, bowls, chairs, serving dishes, or any similar hard or sharp object can be grabbed, even if on the way to hiding or escape. Absent any other options, the only objective is to kill the attacker to save your own life.

III

HOW TO SET UP YOUR PERSONAL PROTECTION PLAN

7

The Need for a Personal Protection Plan

This is a book about survival. It is not about listing all the mass victim attacks—there are many sources that do that. Instead, my focus is on how people have survived across bombings, active shooting attacks, stabbings, and vehicle run-downs. There are commonalities across all forms of attacks, whether perpetrated by international terrorists, domestic terrorists, self-radicalized terrorists, those with serious mental health issues, and those with hate for a group so deep that they risk all to kill multiple individuals of that group. After a career focusing on threat and anticipation of threat, I have realized some key factors to survival. This chapter focuses on these key points.

First, LUCK! Yes, it is possible to be at the right place at the right time. Call it what you will, the attacker approaches you, he aims, you cower, and the gun jams—you escape successfully while he reloads! It has happened, and it has been captured on video (the referenced video link is the definition of luck!).[1] Likewise, an active shooter enters a location, you happen to be near an exit and escape through it successfully before the shooter reaches you. There are those who just happened to be fortunate at the beginning or during a mass victim attack. Can you explain it, can you duplicate it, or can it be converted to an actual strategy for survival?

We tend to think of having good luck or bad luck as beyond our control, primarily because it appears to be random. For all practical purposes, we see chance as randomness. For example, we realize that buying a lottery ticket and taking an assigned number is a random process. We are hoping for good luck, or a lucky win. Being a victim of a freak accident, such as a vehicle sliding in the snow and ice and hitting a pedestrian who just happens to be in the path, is viewed as bad luck. Such occurrences reinforce our views of the randomness of luck.

Mirriam-Webster's Learner's Dictionary defines luck as "the things that happen to a person because of chance: the accidental way things happen without being planned."[2] There are some philosophical differences between the terms luck and chance, but for all practical purposes they both have the same common element of events happening without our design. For example, the Merriam-Webster's Learner's Dictionary defines chance as "something that happens unpredictably without discernible human intention or observable cause. Which cards you are dealt is simply a matter of chance."[3]

It was a normal Sunday evening in Orlando, Florida, on June 12, 2016. Ricardo Negron, a frequent patron of Pulse nightclub in Orlando, Florida, finished work for the day. He decided to go to the nightclub and have a few drinks. People were having a good time, drinks were to be had, and music was playing. Ricardo was near an exit that led to the adjacent patio when he first heard the sounds. After first thinking the sounds were part of the music, it became clear that it was gunfire. The sound stopped briefly, which allowed Ricardo to escape through the exit immediately next to where he was standing.[4]

Whatever we choose to call this, "good luck," "good fortune," or "lucky," there is no doubting the fact that Ricardo being near an exit when Omar Mateen started shooting was likely the foundation for his survival. Not fortunate were the 49 who were killed. In addition, 53 others were wounded but did survive. As a separate topic, the wounded, injured, and those who escaped without physical harm still suffered, and likely still do, psychologically and emotionally. This topic is so important that chapter 10 is devoted to the psychological effects of surviving the trauma associated with being caught in a mass victim attack.

On the morning of April 16, 2007, Derek O'Dell, a student at Virginia Polytechnic Institute (Virginia Tech), was attending German class. It seemed like a normal morning. The students in the class noticed a student peering into the room from the door twice, but did not think much about it. The student was Seung-Hui Cho. Then it sounded like a nail gun was being used across the hall. It wasn't; it was a 9mm Glock pistol. Cho was shooting—wounding and killing—fellow students.

Cho came back to the German class and fired scores of rounds into the classroom aiming at the teacher and students. First killing the teacher, he walked calmly around the room shooting students at point-blank range, typically in the head. He emptied the gun, reloaded, and resumed his shooting spree as some of the shocked students moved around desks cowering, while others headed toward the back of the room. Derek went to the floor as Cho left the room. Derek noticed he was bleeding. Of the 15 students in the class, 5 were left conscious, including Derek. He had been shot in the shoulder. Cho was continuing his killing spree down the hall and had left the classroom door open.

Climbing over desks, students, and blood, Derek and another student who was still conscious closed the door to keep Cho out, just in case Cho came back. Cho did return and tried aggressively to enter through the closed door. He managed to open it a few inches, but the two students were lying on the floor holding the door closed with their feet. Cho started shooting at the 2-inch-thick wooden door. Bullets were getting through at point-blank range. Cho finally left, continued his killing spree, then eventually took his own life.

Later Derek was interviewed by journalist Matt Rogers.[5] Derek showed the interviewer the jacket he was wearing during the attack. He was shot once in the left bicep, but there were three bullet holes in the jacket. In addition to the bullet hole that hit him in the left bicep, one was in the right shoulder area, and one was near the zipper directly above the heart area. He was not hit in these two areas. The jacket over the right shoulder, to his reasoning, was slack when the bullet sliced through it, missing his flesh. He also reasoned the bullet must have pierced the jacket in the area near the heart when he was lying on the floor holding the door shut with his foot. The bullet came through the door and sliced through the raised jacket. What is the probability of having three bullet holes in a jacket with only one connecting with the body? We don't know, but I have never heard of this happening before. One could say Derek was lucky.

At the conclusion of the attack, Cho had managed to kill 32 students, with an additional 15 wounded and sent to local hospitals. There were actually two Cho attacks that morning. The first attack occurred in a coeducational dormitory. In that attack, Cho killed a woman and man. An email from school administrators warning teachers and students was written but, unfortunately and for whatever reason, was not released immediately. Two hours later the email was released, but Cho had just entered Norris Hall and was already shooting and killing teachers and students in classrooms. The heartless slaughter continued until Cho ended his own life.[6]

On October 1, 2017, an outdoor country music concert near the Mandalay Bay Resort in Las Vegas was wrapping up late on a Sunday night. An estimated 22,000 attendees were shoulder to shoulder in an area of about two acres. Jason Aldean, country music star, was finishing the concert with his finale song. Suddenly, rapid bursts of gunfire could be heard over the music.

Witnesses reported that at first they thought the sounds were fireworks, or part of the show. However, with the incessant repeated and long bursts, attendees started falling, bleeding, and dying. It had become clear the sounds were automatic gunfire, or machine-gun sounds. In fact, the shooter had modified 12 semi-automatic rifles by attaching bump stocks—devices that can make a semi-automatic rifle fire continuously. He fired over a thousand rounds during the 11-minute massacre.

Panic and chaos spread throughout the crowd as the shooting occurred. Some victims dropped and remained still, and others ran, almost as a stampede. The bump-stock fire continued for at least 10 minutes. Blood was everywhere as bodies went limp, people dead or in need of immediate critical care. Stephen Paddock, the 64-year-old self-appointed sole executioner, had set up the headquarters of his killing field on the 32nd floor of the Mandalay Bay Resort, breaking out two windows pointing at different angles overlooking the concert field 400 yards away to give him maximum killing venues.

Paddock had constructed a platform in front of each window. On each table was an AR-15 rifle with scope and modified to be automatic—in other words, the rifles could keep firing as long as he held the trigger. The rapid, continuing, and indiscriminate shooting can be heard on many videos taken during the concert. Paddock had at least 19 weapons in that room with ample ammunition. Eventually, the smoke from the rapid firing set off the fire alarm in his hidden vantage point, betraying his location. However, at the time of writing this book, there are still many mysteries surrounding the events leading up to this attack and the underlying motivation that fueled Paddock to commit such a horrific act.

SWAT focused on the room. Paddock had installed cameras so that he could tell when law enforcement would discover him. SWAT exploded the door open, and found Paddock dead apparently by his own hand. Hundreds of sirens were screaming. Some attendees were dead already, some were dying, some were escaping, and some remained to give aid to the wounded, even driving them to hospitals themselves. By the end of that early morning when some of the confusion was cleared, 58 attendees were dead, and 527 were injured and distributed among five hospitals. The mass victim attack carnage was unparalleled in U.S. history.

These are just examples of the many mass victim attacks we have experienced within the United States. You can pick any attack and point to deaths, severe wounding in which victims were lucky enough to survive, and even those caught in the attack who not only survived but were not injured. However, there is much more to this than luck, or chance.

The important premise of this book is that by analyzing how victims survive in mass victim attacks, we can derive strategies for survival. Although survivors' actions and location at the time may not have been planned, it is precisely the actions and often locations that saved their lives. Accidental survivals can lead to strategies for survival. As mentioned in this book and using Derek O'Dell, the surviving student in the Virginia Tech shooting as an example, you do not want to stand in front of a door to keep an armed attacker out. You certainly want to block the door, but bullets can come through the door. The bullet that pierced Derek's jacket near the heart came through the door when he was holding the door shut by lying on the floor and using his foot, along with another student. The jacket was loose, and the bullet went through the 2-inch-thick wooden door.

This leads to a strategy: To block a door, lie prone on the floor and use your foot. This is a survival behavior that we can learn and use if necessary. Locations are also extremely important. In the Pulse nightclub attack mentioned above, Ricardo Negron just happened to be next to an exit to the patio. When Omar Mateen entered the nightclub shooting, Ricardo was able to escape through the exit next to him. This converts to a strategy: Know the exits in any location you are in. Position yourself as close as you can to the exit, or a window large enough to break and escape through. What may be luck demonstrates how we can develop strategies that work.

Just as we see a lucky example of being near an exit when an attack starts, we can expand to windows, stairs leading up a flight, particularly if there is an exit, or down, again if there is a downstairs exit. Knowing your location and knowing how to act under different circumstances can increase survival rates significantly. This also can provide a strategy to keep yourself updated in the future after reading this book. New methods will no doubt surface. By reading about survivors and how they managed to live, you may note creative ways people survive in future attacks.

To expand upon this concept, you must be very aware of who you are physically, emotionally, and psychologically. Behavioral and location strategies on how to escape, how to hide if you can't escape, how to stay in place, and how to attack the attacker as a last resort depend heavily on who you are. This is why simple articles, bullet-point lists, and short videos are insufficient. You must think about the various contexts and how you would handle each of these. In a sense, you can train yourself by realistically considering how you would respond. Such thought can prepare you in the event that you get caught in a mass victim attack. When an attack occurs, it is not the time to try to determine what to do. Seconds count, and if prepared, your escape can start immediately.

You need to consider what you can, and perhaps cannot, do. You must give scenarios some thought, taking into consideration your potential behavior and location choice, given your own personal characteristics. What can work successfully for a 20-year-old athlete is not going to work for a 65-year-old wheelchair-bound person or a 6-year-old child.

WHAT IS A PERSONAL SECURITY PLAN?

Law enforcement over the years has become more accustomed to mass victim attacks. Response is usually measured in minutes. However, results are mixed on what law enforcement does when they do arrive. The Pulse nightclub attack in Orlando lasted for several hours because Omar Mateen not only killed many but held hostages. In the Columbine school attack, an inordinate amount of time passed before law enforcement entered the school building to intervene. More recently, the automatic fire created by Stephen Paddock at the Mandalay Bay Resort on October 31, 2017, had killed 58 and wounded 527 before he committed suicide in response to being discovered by security. As mentioned, officials are still trying to determine just what happened.

Mass victim attacks are very complex, and to law enforcement's credit, they do an admirable job. They are caught off guard, just like victims. They must respond and then try to determine what is happening before moving to intervention. SWAT may be required, or they may have to go ahead and intervene immediately. However, we must know and fully realize that little intervention is likely to occur for our benefit in the first minutes of an attack. It is fair to say, that the first seconds to minutes are the most critical. The attacker makes use of the startle response, and knows that most will be killed while confused and panicked before victims start scattering for cover. This means, for survival, you must recognize the danger almost immediately and you must react appropriately within seconds.

More than likely, law enforcement will show up on the scene quickly, but most of the damage will have been done. True, they have often stopped an attack from being worse, but the damage is already devastating before they arrive. In some cases, it continues to be devastating even after they arrive. We must always remember that most mass victim attackers are prepared to lose their lives. It is often an all-or-nothing effort on their part. The only concern they have about security and law enforcement arriving is that they pose a threat to them being able to continue their carnage.

What does this mean? It means the first line of defense and security is you! You must know what to look for, and you must know how to react appropriately should the unthinkable happen; that is, you are caught in a mass victim attack. You are not law enforcement, and you have likely had no such training. The whole topic of mass victim attacks may be a mystery to you, or at a minimum, you are not likely an expert in the area.

Most of us take responsibility for all facets of our lives. We pay our bills, hopefully on time. We go to our jobs on time and leave on time. If no job, we seek a new one through a diligent effort. We care for family if we have one, or seek one if we don't. We drive carefully, to avoid a potential accident. But in some cases, responsibility is not taken. Some text while driving—an accident literally waiting to happen. For those who don't pay bills on time, consequences are devastating. We may even ignore, at our own risk, key medical symptoms, resulting in early death.

We can either be prepared for the rare occurrence of mass victim attacks or not. I choose to be prepared. Perhaps it is my history of some close calls, but whatever the reason, I choose to be aware and prepared. I pay my bills, I do preventative medical care, and I am prepared as much as I can be for a mass victim attack. I also know to not stand outside in the lightning, to lock my doors, and turn on the security system at night whether or not I am home. I always wear my seat belt, and I drive defensively. When flying, I even listen to the safety instructions about how to buckle my seat belt! This makes me normal. I prefer to be prepared for all contingencies. This book is for those who want to be prepared.

Why should we be concerned? Frankly, if you live in Herrin, Illinois, a small town in southern Illinois where I was born and lived my younger years, your concern is very different from those living in large cities such as New York City and Washington, D.C., that are targeted by terrorist organizations. I do want to be prepared because I am likely to travel to these big cities, and I will continue travelling internationally. If I want to go to popular destinations like London and Paris, I need to know that many mass victim attacks have occurred in these cities. I need to be aware.

Most importantly, even though an international terrorist may not be interested in small Herrin, Illinois, a bias/hate or mental health issues attack of massive proportions could occur there. Frankly, workplace violence, hate/bias attacks, or attacks fueled by mental health issues could occur anywhere in the United States.

Herrin, a very small town two hours south of St. Louis and 16 miles from Southern Illinois University-Carbondale with a population of around 12,000, would seem to be a most unlikely place for massive killings. But my small hometown has a horrific past, proving that mass attacks can vary from the norm, the usual motivation, and can occur anywhere. On June 22, 1922, the Herrin massacre occurred in what is still the largest killing of strikebreakers in our country's history. On that day, 50 to 60 coal miners transported from Chicago were working in the mine near Herrin, where workers had been striking. Strikebreakers are labeled "scabs." From a union worker's perspective, if there is a strike it must be honored, and you never want to be a scab. The mine entrance was surrounded by striking miners, plus some wives and children.

As the miners congregated at the entrance after finishing their shift, with hands up, they were forced to walk some miles to the Herrin cemetery. There they were lined up along the cemetery fence and suddenly told to run. As they tried to escape, the townspeople opened fire. Dying and wounded, the coal miners were basically slaughtered for being scabs. Twenty-six miners were killed, and some bodies desecrated as they were dying.[7]

I mention this attack to point out that there are many reasons for mass victim attacks. Hate can be just as powerful a motivator as terrorism. Not all mass victim killings fit a set mold. There were legal proceedings following the Herrin slaughter of scabs, but there were no convictions. To this day, very little is spoken of the massacre by townspeople.

I have heard many say that they are not worried about attacks because terrorists are not interested in their small town. The reason I cover attacks driven by bias/hate and mental health issues is that there are many types of attackers, and they are all deadly. The attacks driven by bias/hate and mental health issues can and have occurred in locations that are less interesting to terrorists. Any location is possible if there is a group of people present.

The good news, if there is any, is that there are only so many ways a mass victim attack can occur. Certainly, there must first be a significant gathering of people, whether it be a fast-food restaurant, a nightclub, or a sports gathering like the Boston Marathon. It does not have to be a large-city target.

On July 18, 1984, James Huberty walked into a McDonald's in San Ysidro, California, a town adjacent to San Diego with a population of approximately 28,000, and started shooting outside and in. He had several weapons. He shot people outside the restaurant, including children playing in a park. He turned the guns on the 30 customers and workers inside. Victims ranged from 8 months old to 74 years old.

Huberty showed no mercy in his attack, and anyone present was a target. The attack lasted 77 minutes. A sniper eventually killed him with a single shot. At the end of the attack, Huberty had killed 21 people and wounded an additional 19. There was no apparent motive. However, unusually high levels of cadmium were found in Huberty's autopsy. Cadmium can cause significant health and mental health effects. The mass victim shooting with no apparent motive is characteristic of those more recent attacks fueled by mental disturbance.[8]

Such tragic attacks underscore the need for personal security. If caught in a mass victim attack, there is no guarantee of it stopping quickly. In the case of the McDonald's attack, the shooting persisted for 77 minutes. The much more recent attack at Pulse nightclub in Orlando, Florida, lasted for almost three hours. Those caught in mass victim attacks can only count on their knowledge of what to look for and how to respond to survive.

We are all different. This is especially true when considering how to respond if caught in a mass victim attack. I define a personal security plan in the following way.

A personal security plan is a self-prepared plan that takes into consideration situational awareness and safety practices when in public places modified to fit personal characteristics.

There are several key points to this definition. First, it is a plan, meaning that you are giving serious thought in advance as to how you would respond if caught in an attack. This includes situational awareness—a strong concept. Military and intelligence personnel learn aspects of situational awareness. It basically means that you are aware of your surroundings at all times, including the behavior of others, location specifics, and how to interpret all seen and heard, particularly with regard to any potential or actual danger.

Situational awareness means being tuned into your immediate environment so your senses can assist you to maximum benefit. You need your eyes, ears, and intact thinking ability. This means leaving the smartphone in your pocket or purse and the earphones put away. Many times I have observed pedestrians walking along the street and even through intersections while texting, entirely oblivious to their surroundings.

Recently I was in a packed restaurant in Baltimore, Maryland, and counted the number of people tuned out. Almost 40% of diners were texting on their smartphones. Two youngsters had on earphones and were playing video games. I watched one family of five and a couple using their smartphones for almost the entire meal, with little conversation. If someone had walked in to attack, they would have lost valuable seconds becoming aware of a bad event starting. They were totally distracted.

Terrorist groups such as Al Qaeda and ISIS have called for mass victim attacks using easily obtained tools of death such as knives for stabbing and automobiles and trucks to run over numerous people at one time. We have now seen multiple attacks using both methods, and they are increasing in number. No one should be walking on a street, promenade, or anywhere next to moving traffic while distracted. Again, smartphones should be in the pocket or purse and eyes on the oncoming traffic.

Planning and situational awareness can change being caught off guard to knowing how to respond. It is essential that planning include personal characteristics. Age, physical capability, health, and mobility are different across people. Not one set of steps can work for all. For example, as stressed repeatedly in this book, escape is usually the number-one option to take if an attack begins. If physically challenged or not physically capable of running, how would you escape? Would you have to modify your planning to ensure that you are always adjacent to an exit when in a public place as opposed to just being aware of where exits are located? Would you have to reserve a table near an exit if at a restaurant, bar, or nightclub? These are important considerations.

Location has many aspects. At various levels there is first the consideration of general location. Being in Springfield, Illinois, or in any of the many small-town locations in the Midwest is very different from being in high-target areas such as New York City, Los Angeles, Las Vegas, and, of course, Washington, D.C. Next, the activity becomes very important. Is it a sporting event, restaurant, bar, grill, mall, house of worship, government building, etc.? These require different considerations. Regardless of location, you must think ahead and consider your personal characteristics in the location. Furthermore, if responsible for others, their personal characteristics must be taken into consideration over yours.

WHAT DOES A PERSONAL SECURITY PLAN PROVIDE?

A personal security plan presents a variety of features that better prepare us with tactics of survival in the event of a mass victim attack. Furthermore, it has other effects. The plan works to better prepare us for a variety of threatening situations. Unlike some strategies for dealing with attacks, usually focused on one type of attack, if you go through the personal security plan process in the next chapter you will be better prepared for types of attackers (international terrorist, domestic terrorist, self-radicalized terrorist, hate/prejudice, and mental health issues). Furthermore, you will be better prepared for tactics such as massive shootings, bombings, vehicle run-downs, and stabbings.

One of the best defenses is to be aware of what could happen, so that the element of surprise is not as bewildering. The other part of good defense is to know what to do in any location to minimize the probability of being killed. All of this is before the fact and with situational awareness can make you always prepared. This is not to say that you should worry constantly about being attacked or become afraid of leaving the house. It is simply about increasing awareness and being better prepared. Just as we know where to go and not to go in a big city after dark, a personal security plan can become second nature. Increased awareness, situational awareness without distraction, and the presence of knowledge of how to respond immediately is the objective.

Just as important, and maybe more important, is that if you are the responsible adult with this knowledge and you are accompanied by others, you will be better prepared as a group. You could have family, friends, acquaintances, business colleagues, someone who is physically or mentally challenged or very young or very old with you at any number of events or situations. You could be dining out at a fine restaurant or a fast-food restaurant, at a club or bar, shopping at the mall, attending a concert or sporting event, or just walking down the street as a group. All have been locations that have attracted past mass victim attacks. Being prepared is essential.

There is another added benefit to making your own personal security plan and customizing it to meet your activities. That is, the more aware you are, the more likely you are to recognize early signs that someone observed could be a threat. I often hear that nothing can be done about mass victim attacks. This is blatantly false. Many terrorist attacks have been prevented because someone observed threatening or preparation behavior that was reported to local law enforcement. Just as we need to be aware of what to look for to ensure safety (exits, back doors, etc.) when entering a location, we need to be more aware of what to report and report it. Prevention rests with reporting, even if a family member.

What is a personal security plan? As details are presented in this book, you might think it is a very long document to be carried with you at all times! Not true. The process of completing a personal security plan makes it much easier to remember key principles. From experience, I carry information with me that is always useful. I don't carry an instruction sheet or a field guide. However, I am guided by information that is easily remembered.

When I walk into a restaurant, I know what to look for to maximize safety. I manage to be near either real exits or something that could be made into an exit within seconds. I see stairs, and I may use the facilities just to see what is upstairs or downstairs. I situate myself where I can see or hear entrance activity. There are other key features, easy to remember. I am not 20 years old and not an athlete, so my personal security plan includes the need to be very near an exit because I am not going to be sprinting. Most importantly, I am better prepared.

There are no guarantees, even if you have a concealed carry permit and carry a gun. But being prepared, knowing how to ensure safety, knowing what to observe, and knowing that escape is the number-one consideration all work together to give me an awareness that removes fear of the unknown. I know not to ignore threats and the potential for attacks because they are relatively rare. Getting hit by lightning is very rare, but we seek cover in a storm so as not to get hit. One of the reasons we have fewer fatalities in automobile accidents is because of safety precautions such as wearing our seat belt. Airliners are still statistically the safest way to travel because of the rather large safety features and practices completed before and during a flight. For example, the airliner is checked and rechecked, pilots conduct preflight safety checks, flight attendants provide safety briefings including seat belt usage, location of emergency exists, how to use oxygen masks, and instructions covering when to stay in your seat or move about. Furthermore, all airliners are tracked by radar to provide anti-collision safety, the pilot cabin is locked for safety, and radio contact is maintained with air traffic controllers.

We wear life preservers as a preventative in boats. I insist that anyone on my sailboat wear an inflatable life preserver at all times—even if a champion swimmer. In other words, we follow many safety practices that increase our chances of survival, yet we may not worry about attacks in public places because an attack is rare. The personal security plan is a way to help you have a defense that you put in place before an attack, just like wearing a life preserver or seat belt, and positioning yourself properly in a thunder/rain storm.

What do you need to begin a personal security plan? First, if you skipped to this section or the next chapter, go back and read chapters 1 through 7! The background prepares you for completing a personal security plan. Second, get a tablet or notebook. Jot down anything that seems relevant to you. Perhaps it is a sentence about where to walk on a street, or what could be an exit. As stated in the beginning of the book, the act of taking notes that seem relevant for you is a way of remembering better. This is why we take notes in school.

Think about yourself. What are your strengths? What are your weaknesses? Do you have any challenges? What types of locations do you visit? Does your family go with you, or are you usually alone? What are the differences among international terrorists, self-radicalized terrorists, domestic terrorists, those who attack out of hate/prejudice, and attacks by those with mental disturbance. Background from what has happened in the past helps to anticipate and prepare for the future.

8

Your Personal Security Plan: Generic Information

It is difficult to impossible to list what to look for and how to react with a simple bullet-point list. There are far too many potential locations and potential responses based on the high number of attack modes and types of attackers. Perhaps, most importantly, responses are dictated by personal characteristics. Age, gender, physical ability, presence of physical challenges, presence of mental challenges, prepared or not, or whether alone or the responsible person with family all interact to increase or decrease the probability of survival. It is the purpose of this chapter to help you develop a personal security plan.

Why a personal security plan? Given the complex interaction of attacker type, location, personal characteristics, type of attack, and type of attacker, a plan indicates there has been thought about what you will do under specific situations. For example, if one of the few places you go is to the mall, either alone or with your family, then thinking about being caught in a mass victim attack, identifying exits and hiding places in stores nearest you, how to hide, and how to escape will have prepared you if such an event should occur. Preparation reduces the time lost to startle and bewilderment, and not knowing what to do.

A personal plan provides information on generally what to expect and how to react but doesn't cover every nuance of what could happen. This is especially important as mass victim attacks morph over time. For example, stabbings and vehicle run-overs are more recent. Plans would have to be rewritten often to account for differences over time, while a personal plan you create allows you to interject your own characteristics as part of how to respond. For example, if physically challenged and unable to run or sprint for an exit, this is a constant and should always be considered. Knowing where nearby exits are and how to temporarily hide becomes especially important when in public places.

The most important part of a personal security plan is to know yourself to the greatest extent possible. How well do we know ourselves? It depends. When an 82-pound adult female suffering from anorexia looks in the mirror, she reports seeing a fat person. She wants to continue dieting to lose weight. The perception is so strong that continued dieting can be fatal. We have all seen the person who believes he or she is an expert singer try out on *American Idol* or similar television shows only to be shocked that accolades and applause did not follow their tone-deaf rendition of a song. Are these extremes, or do we have a difficult time trying to know ourselves?

As a psychologist, I know there are extremes in faulty perceptions. For the most part, especially as it relates to how we might respond in a mass victim attack, we can know ourselves well, in particular if we put movies and television shows aside. We must make the reality of possibly being severely wounded or killed in a mass victim attack the center point of our thinking. If we focus on our physical characteristics, age, health, any mental or physical challenges, and ability to focus or not, we have a great start knowing what we need to know and how to respond under different situations. To think about a personal security plan does not mean that we need to know our deepest innermost motivations. However, we do need to have a sense as to how capable we are, and how we might respond.

AGE

Age is a very important consideration in our capacity to respond in a mass victim attack. Whether a toddler or in your 80s or 90s, extremes in ages are a problem requiring special attention.

Newborns and Toddlers

Parents are excited to take their newborn out, and often it is a necessity if unable to find a babysitter at the last minute. Typically, they use a stroller because it makes the outing more comfortable for both the infant and the parent. Stroller types vary as well as their cost. Ranging from hundreds to thousands of dollars, we certainly would be reluctant to leave it in a public place. You could be in a mall, store, restaurant, walking down the street, or in any crowded public place.

If caught in a mass victim attack, forget the stroller. Escaping with the infant in your arms should be the only thought. You can always come back to get the stroller. If gone, it can be replaced. You need freedom of movement to escape, and rolling a stroller is not a viable option. Furthermore, pushing the infant in a stroller to escape makes the infant more vulnerable.

If holding your infant, seek the nearest exit or escape route. When accompanied by helpless infants or toddlers, you should always be aware, regardless of setting. Situational awareness is always important, but is especially important if you have a helpless child or children with you. It is time to put the earphones away, stop texting, and keep calls to a necessary minimum.

This book has focused on escape as the primary option. This is especially true if you have an infant or toddler in your care. The options of hide, stay in place, or attack back are simply not viable options if with infants or young children. Remember, mass victim attackers kill all in their sites—including infants and toddlers and even unborn children when the mother is obviously pregnant. Expect no mercy. Even temporary hiding while seeking escape can be difficult, at best. If an attack occurs, panic and chaos follow. It is normal for a toddler to be frightened and cry hysterically when surrounded by a loud situation. Hiding is unlikely to be successful, and your position will be given away. Having an infant or toddler in your care is the optimal reason for escape in a mass victim attack. Pick them up and escape while shielding them in your arms.

Children

Children between toddler and preteen age are able to run on their own and follow instructions but are not old enough to be left alone in a public place and are in your responsible care. The first thing that you should do if an attack begins is to concentrate on escape while projecting as much calm as possible under the circumstances in front of your child, or children. Children of this age can "freeze" in place if frightened too severely. Hold their hands and lead as quickly as possible to the nearest escape route.

Pre-Teens and Teens

Few would argue with the notion that the world has changed over the past several generations. A survey of teens shows that teens spend time with friends in various locations. Some of these I consider safe from mass victim attacks: for example, spending time in the neighborhood, at a friend's house, and online. Other locations are public and of more concern. The location where most time is spent with friends is school (83%), while 23% report they spend time with friends at such places as coffee shops, malls, or stores, and

21% report time with friends at a place of worship.[1] These locations (schools, malls, houses of worship, and fast food / coffee shops) are of concern because mass victim attacks have occurred in all of these types of locations.

Mass victim attacks have occurred in elementary schools, high schools, and colleges, as described in this book. My recommendation is for taxpayers and parents to push for steel-reinforced doors to classrooms with deadbolt locks so that classroom doors can serve as a barricade if hiding in a classroom. There should be no glass surrounding any door. Most importantly, for the safety of children in school, insist on armed and trained security.

The new hangout for preteens and teens is the local mall. Shops, fast food, and friends abound in the mall, and the inside environment stays the same regardless of the weather outside. Malls often swell with young people when the cold snow is just deep enough to cancel school. Catching up to malls in popularity are the popular coffee shops such as Starbucks. The shop owners are smart, and many have provided Wi-Fi and power outlets, which allow customers to have coffee, meet with friends, and be online. Of course, smartphones are everywhere, which allows teens to be in contact on a continuous basis, and distracts from situational awareness.

Not to alarm teens unnecessarily, but because they are often out on their own, they need to know the principles in this book. They are young, typically healthier and more athletic than adults or the elderly, and may be physically more capable of escaping unless there is the presence of a physical challenge. Knowing what to expect and how to escape or hide can save valuable seconds that can lead to survival. What do they need to know? The following is a brief outline:

- Mass victim attacks are rare, and there is no need for alarm, but all should be prepared.
- Think escape and hide only if escape is not possible. If hiding is a must, try to get behind a door that has been blockaded.
- Know where exits are located in any enclosed location. For example, most mall shops have back doors that lead to the outside or to back passages leading to the outdoors that are much closer than actual mall entrances. On the other hand, smaller stores or shops such as coffee shops may have just one front entrance.
- Be aware! When in a public place, be aware of surroundings and be tuned in to strange behavior that is out of place in that setting. If concerned, leave immediately—you can take your coffee with you!
- If popping sounds are heard, someone with a knife is spotted, or an explosion is heard, leave immediately! Do not wait to see what is happening or to take photos or videos. It is not worth your life.

- If something is causing people to run or scream, leave!
- If in a movie theatre, be aware of exits and use them immediately if something dangerous appears to be starting.
- If in school, and escape is not possible, barricade in the classroom; barricade is very important.
- Once escape is successful, call 911 immediately.

This is a minimum, but important, set of points to remember. If possible, and you have read this book, you can have a more detailed discussion with teens, particularly if there is the presence of physical or mental challenges. If physically challenged, include information from the challenges section of this chapter. Being alert, knowing store exits, knowing that if "popping" sounds are heard, or if a threatening person is actully seen, escape is the first reaction that should occur. For the physically challenged, knowing that many stores and restaurants have back exits is very important.

Adults

One of the major differences between adults and teens/children is that adults can afford to visit many more venues. Restaurants, bars, sporting events, movies, malls, nightclubs, work places, coffee shops, casinos, hotels, and motels, among many options, are all public places containing crowds. Of course, not all crowded public places will experience an attack, but 100% of mass victim attacks have occurred in crowded public places. Therefore, preventative care should be taken in such places. It is less about the specific location and more about a large number of targets assembled in one place. Adults, for the most part, are capable of a hasty escape if reaction is immediate, unless they are physically or mentally challenged.

Adults are often accompanied by small children, the physically or mentally challenged, or elderly. Although capable of fleeing, it is more difficult with the defenseless under your care in a public place. Carry a personal protection device (PPD) such as pepper spray, which is the most effective of sprays. Although legal in all 50 states, be aware of any restrictions in your state. However, in all cases, remember, even if accompanied by the defenseless, escape, if possible, is always the best option.

Elderly

Elderly individuals simply do not react the same as adults or teens. While it is true that some of advanced age may be in great shape, after a certain age this is much more the exception than the rule. We all have seen reports of elderly people finishing a marathon or jumping from a plane. But the typical person of advanced age may have serious health issues, ambulatory problems, have difficulty walking, cognitive deficits such as Alzheimer's or cognitive brain disorder, and could be weak and frail. If in your care, situational awareness is always necessary with an eye kept on potential exits and escape routes.

For the elderly person alone in a public place, the tips in this book are particularly useful, especially if exercising by walking or while shopping in a mall. Being aware, knowing where to exit through stores and restaurants, and knowing physical limitations can help with escape or to hiding if necessary. Because vision and/or hearing could be affected, situational awareness takes on even more importance.

PHYSICALLY CHALLENGED

What are physical challenges? Specifically as they pertain to mass victim attacks, they are *challenges that interfere with mobility, ambulation, or normal sensory functioning used to detect impending danger or severe enough to negatively affect the capability of escaping from a dangerous situation.* Physical challenges often go hand in hand with being elderly. Examples of physical challenges could appear to be endless, but major examples include: poor vision/blindness, hard of hearing/deaf, stroke effects, inability to run or walk fast, dependence on a prosthetic device (e.g., walker, cane, wheelchair, missing limbs, stroke effects, breathing apparatus, special shoes, artificial limbs, and missing limbs, as well as many other physical conditions that impair mobility).

When a mass victim attack begins and as it progresses, it is necessary to detect the danger. This does not mean that the source of the danger must be seen. For example, if loud popping sounds are heard and people are running and screaming, then it is time to act. You do not want to wait to decide for yourself. Hopefully, preventative forethought has been given to being in public places with a specific physical challenge and how best to escape given the challenge. If vision and/or hearing is affected, depend on the observation of others nearby.

The first step of survival is to detect the danger. This does not mean sticking around to identify the source of panic that is occurring. Seeing the direction people are running can provide clues as to the direction of the threat. Certainly, those near the threat are going to try to escape in an opposite direction. Knowing nothing else about the threat, you would not run or move toward those fleeing the scene. It is not necessary to observe the shooter, stabber, bomber, or driver of the vehicle that is running over pedestrians. The sights and sounds of an attack are all you need.

Just as important, if you do not see the sights and do not hear the sounds but see people panicked and running, that is detection, as well. Once the sights and sounds of an attack are present, the second stage of surviving must occur: escape.

Preparation, such as knowing the information in this book, can shorten response time and prevent to some degree the "deer caught in the headlights" response, whereby we freeze in place to determine what is happening. If we see or hear an attacker, or if we see panicked people running, it is time to act immediately, especially if physical challenges are present.

It is especially true for the physically challenged that the best time for anyone to escape is at the beginning of an attack. It simply takes more time to achieve escape to safety if mobility is affected in any way. At the beginning of a mass victim attack, many people are reacting, trying to run away, screaming, and maybe even pushing and shoving. This is a very confusing time, and the attacker must select targets from many. As time progresses quickly, many have sought cover, some have escaped, and the attacker(s) moves into a search-and-kill mode. Targets may be a little more difficult to find, so he moves about searching for those hiding.

Hopefully, thought has been given to escape routes and exits as part of the normal course of visiting public places. Across numerous attacks, people have fled to restrooms. Attackers know these locations do not have exits, and that people try to hide in closed stalls by standing on toilets. If there is no other option, always blockade a door. But be aware that bullets can penetrate a door. Many objects jammed under a closed door can help to prevent the door from being opened. Also, keep in mind, if physically challenged in any way, you are simply not as likely to be able to stand up to the physical stature and capabilities of a young, healthy attacker who is willing to lose his life to succeed in killing others.

Never worry about being embarrassed. If you must dismount a wheelchair and move to the floor to crawl, do what you need to do to get to a safer place. Don't wait in place for anyone to help. You might receive help, but don't wait and depend on it. People may be fleeing for their lives and panicked in the midst of chaos.

In thinking about how you would react with a specific physical challenge, think of how you would escape with no help whatsoever. If you are physically challenged and are accompanied by someone, discuss how you both would escape a dangerous situation. This alerts the other person, and allows him or her to give additional thought to potentially dangerous situations—especially as it relates to assisting with your specific type of physical challenge.

MENTALLY CHALLENGED

The incidence of mental challenges is not insignificant. Many would be surprised to know that there are around 200 forms of mental illness that can be classified. What is a mental challenge? A mental-health-related challenge from the perspective of a mass victim attack is basically *an intellectual or mental disability that affects how one thinks, processes information, or perceives environmental surroundings or reality*. This limits mental challenges to a fraction of those that are present and diagnosable. For the most part, we are concerned with those disorders that adversely affect the ability of a person to accurately assess a dangerous situation and to make sound judgments in such a situation.

It is estimated that there are approximately 3 million Americans who are affected by intellectual disability, formerly known as mental retardation and developmental disability. This disturbance is characterized by significant subaverage intellectual functioning and adaptive behavior.[2] Adequate intellectual functioning is required to properly detect and identify threat from the perspective of mass victim attacks. A failure in adaptive behavior means that an affected individual may not be able to adapt to a unique, dangerous situation never experienced, again from the perspective of a mass victim attack.

The person suffering from a severe degree of low intellectual functioning as compared to others is not likely to be in a public setting alone. Because of the significance of the deficit, he or she is likely to be accompanied by a caretaker. This caretaker could be a family member, or an official caretaker if from a special living situation like a group home. This places special emphasis on the caretaker to be aware of the principles provided in this book if accompanying the affected person to a public setting.

It will be up to the caretaker to be prepared, know what to look for, practice situational awareness at all times, know how to escape, know the exits, and know how to hide if there is absolutely no chance of escape. We cannot depend on the affected person to adapt to a dangerous situation and to escape.

There is no doubt that being a caretaker of a person with a deficit in intellectual functioning carries with it a significant responsibility. Escaping, and even hiding if there is no chance of escape, may be harrowing and slowed down significantly. The caretaker's response must include convincing the affected person that it is time to move—quickly. He or she may want to understand what is happening, and why they should move so quickly.

It may be beneficial to have discussions with the affected individual about dangerous situations in which it is better to follow directions without questions. This is beneficial in cases of fire, floods, tornadoes, earthquakes, and any number of other emergencies. This can be especially beneficial if the unthinkable happens and a mass victim attack occurs. Knowing that this is one of those times to follow without question and escape danger is very important.

I recommend teaching both young children and mentally challenged individuals under your care a code word. Then, with practice, the code word will be interpreted as *let's go hide*. This can be approached as a game in the home. A code word or term such as *let's go* is not threatening or scary. When used in the home, it can be followed by practicing hiding in different places. This helps to remove fear if in a public place and the code word or term must be used.

OVERALL HEALTH

Overall health is an important concept and may be difficult to assess. To accurately assess it, you must be honest! This is difficult to do at times, because we all want to be considered vibrant and healthy. We may not have an accurate view of our own health status. However, it is important to know, again from the perspective of being caught in a mass victim attack, your true capabilities. A person could be suffering from a severe health issue, and it might not be apparent. We are all human, and we engage in wishful thinking and denial. This is normal, and may be a good thing for coping with daily life.

Given that the rare mass victim attack occurs, and you are caught in it, are you capable of escaping? Can you run? If not run, can you walk briskly? How do you handle dangerous situations? These are difficult questions to answer, particularly if you are like many others and have not been in an extremely dangerous situation like a mass victim attack.

One of the complicating factors with overall health is significant obesity. Approximately 30% to 40% of adults in the United States are obese and 1 in 13 morbidly obese.[3] Morbid obesity is a condition whereby the person is at least 100 pounds over ideal weight for their height, with a Body Mass Index (BMI) of 30 or more. The BMI is the ratio of height over weight. This is enough for this discussion, but if interested, there are many BMI calculators available on the Internet. Why concerned? If obesity is high, then the chances of associated health effects are much higher. Heart, diabetes, stroke, and high blood pressure are among health-related issues of great concern.

Again, from the perspective of mass victim attacks, being obese can affect escape and hiding. Stamina for running may not be present, or the ability to run may be absent altogether. Breathing, ability to run, and even ability to hide may be affected. If danger should break out, nearby hiding and escaping take on even more importance. If you cannot move fast, have difficulty breathing, and move slowly, then keep exits in mind at all times, and be near them. The close proximity can help bring peace of mind regardless of the venue, environment, and activity.

Overall health is important. There are those who suffer from mobility issues. They may suffer from severe arthritis. Approximately one in five Americans suffer from some form of arthritis. With symptoms ranging from mild to debilitating pain, there are millions who simply cannot run in an emergency. It is not just the pain, but years of joint involvement may have left them with physical impairments or deformity leading to the inability to run or even walk fast. In fact, walking may be difficult and painful. Overall, they might rate their overall health as good, but we are taking the perspective of surviving mass victim attacks. Mobility is essential. If mobility is missing, then situational awareness, proximity to escape routes and exits, takes on even more importance.

LOCATIONS

Locations and their characteristics are important to consider. Method of attack is associated with weapon choice and attack strategy. For example, if targets are massive in structure, then massive tactics are used, and usually consist of explosives. If targets are smaller, such as a nightclub, movie theatre, restaurant, or a party or celebration, then semi-automatic firearms tend to be used. If pedestrians are targeted, then we are more likely to see vehicle run-downs and stabbings—sometimes combined into a single attack.

International terrorism is most likely to seek big targets that are symbolic in nature that can provide a political message. Such targets as those that have military, government, and economic symbolism have been attacked in the United States. The most devastating international terrorist attack in the United States was the September 11, 2001, or 9/11, attack with hijacked airliners directed against the North and South towers of the World Trade Center and the Pentagon in Washington, D.C. In one attack, Al Qaeda hit both economic and military/government targets with deadly effectiveness.

Al Qaeda's Ramzi Yousef exploded a truck bomb below the North Tower of the World Trade Center on February 26, 1993, foreshadowing the 9/11 attack eight years later. Although there have been many types of domestic terrorism, attacks of this form can also target large structures such as the bombing of the Alfred P. Murrah government building in Oklahoma City on April 19, 1995.

Self-radicalized attacks in the United States have tended to occur in confined, celebratory locations such as a nightclub (Pulse in Orlando, Florida) or celebrations (San Bernardino) and weapons of choice have been semi-automatic weapons. However, as mentioned, Al Qaeda and ISIS both have called for less sophisticated, easy-to-carry-out attacks among the self-radicalized. This includes stabbings and vehicle run-downs, since knives and vehicles can be obtained almost anywhere and special training is not required.

Attacks fueled by hate/bias share characteristics of attacks perpetrated by those with mental health issues. These attacks tend to be focused on a given location that is either the subject of the hate/bias (e.g., African American Christian church, Sikh temple) or simply contains innocent victims with limited escape options (e.g., Sandy Hook Elementary School; Century 16 movie theatre, Aurora, Colorado; Washington, D.C. Navy Yard shooting). What we tend to label as workplace violence fits within the categories of mental health issues and hate/bias and may be a combination due to a grudge or workplace retaliation.

Table 8.1 presents locations that would likely be visited and the likely attack method based on past mass victim attacks.

Mass victim attacks have occurred across a variety of locations. One of the primary reasons for the variety of locations is the preference of attackers. Different types of attackers tend to select different types of targets. For example, international terrorists are not likely to select a mall for a target because

Table 8. 1   Likely Attack for Locations Visited Based on Past Mass Victim Attacks

Outdoors	Likely Attack Method
Street (walking, jogging, bicycling)	Vehicle Run-down, Stabbing
Sporting event	Small portable bomb(s)
Concert	Semi-automatic rifle
Outdoor protest	Semi-automatic rifle, Vehicle run-down
Military/Government installation	Massive bombing
Economic structure	Massive bombing

Indoors	Likely Attack Method
Restaurant	Semi-automatic handgun/rifle, Shotgun
Airport	Semi-automatic handgun, Bombing
Movie theatre	Semi-automatic handgun/rifle
Bar/Nightclub	Semi-automatic handgun/rifle
Mall	Semi-automatic handgun, Stabbing
Workplace	Semi-automatic handgun
Military/Government installation	Semi-automatic handgun/rifle
Party/Celebration	Semi-automatic handgun/rifle
Elementary/High School	Semi-automatic handgun/rifle
College	Semi-automatic handgun/rifle, Vehicle run-down, Stabbing
House of worship	Semi-automatic handgun

it is not symbolic, and not likely to carry a political message. However, an attacker who is suffering from mental health issues may select a mall or a school because it is local, available, and he is not trying to deliver a message. In the latter case, the incentive may be internal, contorted, and wrapped in the need for recognition.

Mass victim attackers tend to select targets and victims based on their own motivations (international terrorist, self-radicalized terrorist, domestic terrorist, those driven by mental health issues, or those driven by hate/bias) that match with locations to attack. For example, international terrorists tend to target locations that are symbolic of United States power, while those driven by hate/bias may target a church, temple, other religious location, or a former employment location. It appears that those with mental health issues tend to target schools, movie theatres, and restaurants. Of course, there are exceptions, but often because there is a crossover between types with some attackers (e.g., combination of mental health issues and hate/bias).

In turn, target selection influences weapon choice. The international terrorist who plans a large-scale attack wishes to kill as many people as possible, while making a major politically based message. This makes a large bomb an attractive method. A bomb, in the loosest sense, does not have to be what we always think of as a bomb. As Al Qaeda demonstrated, it could hijack freshly fueled airliners, gain control through violent means, and crash the planes into symbolic economic, government, and military targets as in the infamous coordinated 9/11 attack. The fully fueled hijacked airliners were converted to a form of high-yield weapons of mass destruction.

We have learned that international terrorism cannot be underestimated. The death toll of 9/11 exceeded the infamous Japanese attack on Pearl Harbor on December 7, 1941. That surprise sneak aerial attack resulted in 2,403 fatalities and 1,143 wounded. It is, perhaps, ironic that our most serious attacks were aerial attacks. The Pearl Harbor attack launched the United States into World War II, and the 9/11 attack launched the country into a war against terrorism.

It must be mentioned that such massive attacks as Pearl Harbor or 9/11 are indeed horrifying. However, the amount of planning to prepare for such attacks is significant. Post-9/11 it appears that mass victim attacks have taken the form of far less planning. Terrorists have learned that the act of killing innocent victims in large numbers has a strong effect on fear. In a similar way, those motivated by hate and bias and those suffering from mental health issues have learned that the key to their success is also based on the slaughter of large numbers of innocent victims.

As I am writing this chapter, and while always watching the news as I write, a special report just announced an attack in New York City. It is October 31, 2017,

Halloween. A driver plowed into pedestrians on a bike path near the 9/11 World Trade Center, was yelling "Allahu Akbar," exited the vehicle brandishing two guns that turned out to be a pellet gun and a paintball gun. He was stopped when an alert police officer shot him. The result of the attack was that 8 innocent victims were killed and 11 seriously injured. One month ago, on October 1, I was writing the previous chapter, and again watching the news. Reports started of the unfolding of the Las Vegas attack in which 58 were killed and over 500 injured at an outdoor concert with "bump stock" automatic weapon fire.

As can be seen in table 8.1, weapons typically include semi-automatic pistols and rifles, the occasional shotgun, vehicles used for run-downs, knives for stabbings, and large-scale and smaller-scale bombs. The weapons are used for different purposes, based on targeting. If we exclude very large-scale attacks such as airliners used as weapons during 9/11, we are faced with smaller-scale bombs, semi-automatic weapons, vehicles, and knives. These are the weapons that should concern you.

For the most part, if visiting enclosed locations, meaning a location that is inside and contained by walls, semi-automatic weapons should be the concern in a mass victim attack. Locations such as restaurants, bars or nightclubs, malls (to include knives for stabbing), parties, conferences, houses of worship, and elementary and high schools, semi-automatic weapons appear to be the weapons of choice. Why?

Semi-automatic handguns and rifles are very effective weapons because they can shoot as fast as the trigger is pulled. Given that an attacker has adequate extra ammunition, which is usually the case, multiple fatalities and serious injuries can be inflicted in just minutes. The firepower can cause devastating tissue damage and death and can occur with multiple shots fired within seconds. This makes aim less important. The attacker does not have to be a trained marksman. He just needs to point at all people and keep pulling the trigger and reloading clips.

An example of how deadly semi-automatic guns can be was the Sunday, November 5, 2017, shooting at the First Baptist Church in Sutherland Springs, Texas. The shooting was the worst in Texas history. Devin Kelley, a mentally disturbed 26-year-old armed with a Ruger AR-556 semi-automatic rifle, started shooting from outside the church. He walked in, sprayed the congregation with bullets, then walked systematically pew-by-pew shooting churchgoers multiple times. He especially targeted small, crying children. Few escaped injuries in the small congregation: 26 were killed and 20 injured.

After the shooting, 15 empty ammunition magazines were found, all capable of holding 30 rounds of ammunition (450 shots). As Kelley left the church, a neighbor, Stephen Willeford, engaged him in gunfire, hitting him in the leg and torso. Kelley drove off but was chased by the neighbor and a passerby driving a truck. They found him, called 911, and Kelley was found dead in his vehicle.[4]

Most attackers use clips for extra ammunition. A clip is a device that holds many rounds (bullets). Once a gun is empty, the attacker just replaces the clip that is empty with a full clip. Although there are many types of clips for different weapons, a typical clip would hold about 17 to 20 rounds. It only takes seconds to change clips, making it possible to shoot as fast as the trigger can be pulled. Seek cover and escape at the first sounds of rapid gunshots. Remember, the attacker's objective is to kill anyone he sees, and he has extra ammunition. There is no favoritism.

Another reason why semi-automatic weapons are a popular choice for attackers is that they are not only powerful but can be concealed easily, especially semi-automatic handguns. Because they are relatively small, more than one weapon can be carried, and this has happened across mass victim attacks. Semi-automatic weapons can jam, and there have been multiple reports of guns jamming during an attack. It is obviously much faster to disregard a jammed weapon and use another than try to repair a jammed weapon. No one should ever expect that an attack will stop if a weapon is jammed. You can be almost certain that there is a loaded replacement ready to go.

Mass victim attacks are not just about guns, although there have been lively disagreements about gun control. Terrorists, those filled with hate/bias, and those with mental health issues who are violent have a single objective: to kill innocent victims. The more innocent the victims are, the better. It is important to mass victim attackers to shock people and leave them in a state of absolute fear, regardless of the type of attacker. Terrorists, in particular, will use any method to achieve the objective of massive numbers killed. Whether it is hijacking fully loaded airliners to crash into massive structures, vehicles to run down innocent pedestrians or bicyclists, knives to stab the innocent, or exploding large or small-scale bombs, methods of killing are numerous.

Locations visited are important because they interact with the type of attacker. To summarize, we have looked at five major types of attackers: (1) international terrorists, (2) domestic terrorists, (3) self-radicalized terrorists, (4) those driven by hate/bias, and (5) those driven by mental health issues. Although there is variation, types of attackers tend to focus on specific categories of location for their type.

International terrorism is most likely to seek big targets that are symbolic in nature that can provide a political message. Such military, government, and economic entities have been targets in the United States. Self-radicalized terrorists tend to select smaller but significant targets, using semi-automatic firearms (San Bernardino and Pulse nightclub in Orlando) or smaller bombs

(Tsarnaev brothers' pressure cooker bombs at the Boston Marathon). These forms of attacks are carried out by those living in the United States who swear allegiance to international terror organizations.

More recently, Al Qaeda and ISIS have suggested that followers use knives to stab individuals and vehicles to run down pedestrians. Followers are typically self-appointed, which is why the category is labeled self-radicalized terrorism. Easy to obtain, such forms of weapons can be devastating. More prevalent in Europe, these types of attacks are starting to occur within the United States, and are more likely to occur in the future. Most importantly, self-radicalized terrorists don't have to travel to a foreign country to receive special training. Instead, they just need to buy sharp weapons or rent a truck.

On November 28, 2016, a self-radicalized student at Ohio State University, Abdul Razak Ali Artan, jumped the curb in his car at high speed and ran down several pedestrians (see chapter 2). Hitting a concrete block, he then exited and stabbed several more students. Eleven were injured before he was shot to death.[5] On September 17, 2016, just seven weeks before the Ohio State University attack, another self-radicalized attack occurred in the Crossroads Center shopping mall in St. Cloud, Minnesota. The attack was a stabbing attack. Dahir Adan walked through the mall stabbing anyone he could reach until he was shot and killed by an off-duty policeman (see chapter 5).

Then on October 31, 2017, 29-year-old self-radicalized Sayfullo Saipov used a rented truck from Home Depot to run down pedestrians along a bike path in Manhattan, killing 8 and injuring 11. He was stopped and apprehended when shot by a police officer. He also had knives in the vehicle.

These newer forms of attack are straight from the Al Qaeda and ISIS playbooks designed to assist self-radicalized terrorists to attack with simple methods. The results of such attacks have broadened locations for attacks to outdoor targets that include common walking and bicycling paths. Table 8.1 displays the common locations targeted by mass victim attackers. This is important, because these need to be kept in mind anytime we visit these or similar locations.

We must know what to look for, how to escape, be prepared, and always be situationally aware when there. We do not want to become fearful or paranoid, we just need to be better prepared to increase our chance of survival. In the next chapter, details of a personal security plan will continue with how best to escape, hide, stay in place, or attack the attacker, given the location and your own personal characteristics.

9

Your Personal Security Plan: Specific Tips

This chapter is provided as a deeper guide on how to develop your own plan on how to react in a mass victim attack, given the location and type of attack combined with personal characteristics. Because attack types vary based on whether the attack occurs outdoors or indoors, the chapter is divided in this manner. Although outdoor and indoor activities share some commonalities of attacker weapon choice, there are significant differences. For example, large-scale bombings and vehicle run-downs occur primarily outside, while semi-automatic to automatic gunfire and stabbings occur both outside and inside.

The use of vehicles can hide very large-scale bombs such as the ones used by Timothy McVeigh in the Oklahoma City Alfred P. Murrah building bombing on April 19, 1995, and the initial World Trade Center bombing, led by Ramzi Yousef on February 26, 1993. Of course, using hijacked airliners as explosive devices directed at the World Trade Center and the Pentagon with almost 3,000 killed still ranks as the worst mass victim high-explosives attack (full airliner fuel tanks) in U.S. history.

Vehicles, more recently, are used outdoors by necessity to run down pedestrians or bicyclists as per Al Qaeda and ISIS instructions. There is an increasing number of examples, but the vehicles range from smaller trucks such as the Home Depot truck rented by Sayfullo Saipov, who ran down multiple victims in Manhattan on October 31, 2017.[1] He killed 8 and injured 11 in his rundown. On a larger scale, Tunisian Mohamed Lahouaiej Bouhlel drove a 20-ton rental truck down a beachfront promenade in Nice, France, on July 14, 2016, killing 86 people and injuring more than 200 in the worst of such attacks to date.

Vehicles are convenient, and can look innocent because they blend with existing traffic until such time as used in an attack. Whether used to run over innocent victims or to conceal an explosive device, vehicles are indiscriminate. If exploded, anyone within close proximity will be killed immediately. If surviving the blast itself, there will be those who die from injuries or must live with disfigurement. If used to run over unaware victims, the effect of a heavy truck running over bodies is obvious. Even if hit and not killed, death can come from injuries sustained during the attack, and like a bombing, one may have to live with some form of permanent disfigurement.

Shootings occurring outside are with semi-automatic weapons and, more recently, have included automatic gunfire from rifles. In some cases, attacks occur from an elevated position, which complicates the attack. For example, the Charles Whitman attack from the top of the Texas Tower at the University of Texas at Austin in 1966 killed 16 people—11 from the top of the tower itself. He used sniper tactics and was an expert marksman. In a similar manner, Stephen Paddock, on October 1, 2017, killed 58 and injured nearly 500 from his elevated position at a hotel window, shooting innocent victims at an outdoor concert within view of the MGM's Mandalay Bay Hotel windows in Las Vegas. Both Paddock and Whitman were killed by authorities stopping their carnage.

Smaller-scale bombs detonated outside can also have devastating effects. The Tsarnaev brothers' two pressure cooker bombs detonated near the finish line of the Boston Marathon on April 15, 2013, killing three and injuring hundreds, with some losing limbs. Attackers know that it is easier to blend in with the crowd when on foot or in a vehicle outdoors. The use of blade weapons (sharp objects used for stabbings and slashing) are also being combined with some vehicle attacks.

Indoor attacks are most commonly perpetrated with semi-automatic guns. Most attacks have involved handguns and assault-like rifles. Attacks indoors present a few challenges for the attacker in that they do not want to be noticed until ready to attack. Therefore, smaller firearms are easier to conceal. However, in most attacks there are multiple weapons and extra ammunition. This equates to a quick entry and a quick attack.

SURVIVAL TIPS BY LOCATION, TYPE OF ATTACK, AND PERSONAL CHARACTERISTICS

- Know how to use your smartphone to make emergency calls. But, first, escape from danger. You can call emergency services once clear.
- Using an iPhone, you can make an emergency call using your phone or

anyone else's phone without password by clicking on the first screen and then clicking on "emergency" on the lower left of the screen. If not clear on how to do this, search on the Internet for your type of phone and look for "how to make emergency calls." This saves you time.

- If you call for emergency services, be specific. Indicate what is happening (e.g., active shooter, bombing, etc.) and give specific location.
- You have four options: Escape, Hide, Stay in Place, and Attack the attacker. Always be thinking escape! Hiding is only to be used if escape is simply not possible, and then take the first chance to escape from hiding.
- Carry a personal protection device (PPD) such as portable pepper spray that can fit in your pocket or purse and can spray at a distance of up to 15 feet. Use it as a last resort, especially if in a situation of being trapped by a stabber; the spray can debilitate an attacker. Aim for the eyes. Also, check with your state about specific regulations for carrying a PPD. Pepper spray is legal in all states, but the regulations vary. Do not try to take pepper spray on an airliner!
- If you hear "popping" sounds, especially while inside, don't wait but react immediately and leave (escape). Survivors of mass attacks report they first thought sounds were fireworks, busting balloons, or some other explanation of such sounds before realizing they were gunfire shots.
- Many mall stores have back exits to the outside or to a back corridor leading to the outside. In case of attack, run to the nearest store on the outside perimeter and exit through the back door; don't run to the few entrances that may be far away.
- If outside and an attack begins, this is one occasion in which you escape from the outside to the inside to ensure safety. Duck into the closest building that removes you from an attacker's view.
- If escape is not an option and only the possibility of hiding is present, then pick a hiding location with a door and barricade the door. Hiding must include barricade to increase safety.
- Don't stand directly behind a door to barricade; bullets penetrate doors and you could be injured or killed.
- Know first aid and how to use a tourniquet, directing pressure to slow or stop blood loss, as well as CPR. Take a course. This can save your life, as well as the life of anyone that is accompanying you with benefits far beyond mass victim attack preparation.
- Be aware that if you are under the influence, your judgment may be impaired.
- A number of medium- to large-size houses of worship now have internal

guards with concealed carry permits. If planning to attend a small house of worship and you are not protected, ask if they provide armed protection.

- If you see something suspicious that could be preparation for an attack, report it immediately to local law enforcement. If you see that it could be the beginning of an actual attack, contact 911 immediately.
- Wherever you go, know where the exits are and remain as close to exits as possible.
- When a mass victim attack occurs amidst a high density of people with limited escape routes, be careful of stampedes and panic. To avoid injury, try to stay on the sides of the crowd rushing to escape.

TIPS BY LOCATION, TYPE OF ATTACK, AND PERSONAL CHARACTERISTICS (OUTDOORS)

Street (Walking/Bicycling)

- As much as possible, walk facing traffic so that any fast approaching vehicle can be spotted and immediately escape to the other side of the street.
- Don't run in the same direction as the approaching vehicle—they accelerate during the attack, and you are not going to outrun an accelerating vehicle.
- If bicycling in the same direction as traffic, make sure you have a rear-view mirror on your helmet or bicycle handle and use it often, just as you do in an automobile.
- There are rearview mirrors that can be placed on the inside of glasses or sunglasses that can allow you to see what is occurring behind you if walking or jogging.
- Maintain situational awareness at all time—no earphones or any other device that could diminish your sight or hearing.
- If walking among buildings or on walkways, move to the farthest spot from traffic (e.g., alongside buildings, far side of bike or walking paths).
- If oncoming danger is noted, duck into alleys or stores if among buildings or immediately move off paths in the opposite direction of traffic.
- Always walk or bicycle as far as possible from actual traffic.
- Be aware that vehicle run-downs may be completed with the driver and/ or passengers exiting with knives or other types of blade weapons to stab or slash bystanders.
- If caught in a bombing attack and not injured, it may be safer to stay put

and provide assistance to others until first responders and emergency medical care arrives.

- If caught in a smaller scale bombing and injured, stay put and immediately apply first aid. Know how to limit or stop serious bleeding with first aid measures such as the use of a tourniquet and direct pressure. If seriously injured and bleeding, attempting to run will only increase blood loss.
- Perhaps the only time to stay in place is during a small scale bombing. Because it is immediate, the imminent threat diminishes quickly, and fatalities, serious injuries, and less serious injuries must receive immediate attention.

Sporting Event

Any gathering of people is a potential target for mass victim attackers. Sporting events are no exception. The Boston Marathon attack on April 15, 2013, consisted of two pressure cooker bombs placed among bystanders and then detonated approximately 12 seconds apart (time differences vary slightly). Highlighted in this book, the bombing killed 3 and injured more than 200. Numerous victims lost limbs. We have witnessed attacks across a variety of sporting events worldwide. Sporting events are crowded, and escape can be difficult because of the density of the crowd. Often there are injuries caused by escape itself, on occasion taking on stampede proportions such as during the Stephen Paddock attack in Las Vegas.

Such attacks during sports event date back to at least 1972. In that year, nine Palestinian militants of the Black September group killed two Israeli athletes and took nine Israelis hostage at the Munich Olympic Games. Sometime later, the remaining nine athletes were killed along with a German officer—five of the Palestinians were killed at that time. Just to list a few more examples:[2]

- On July 27, 1996, Eric Rudolf placed a bomb at Centennial Olympic Park during the Olympics held in Atlanta, Georgia. Two people were killed and over 100 injured.
- On May 1, 2002, the Basque separatist group ETA exploded a car bomb near the Santiago Bernabéu Stadium in Madrid, Spain, just prior to a major final soccer game to be held between Real Madrid and Barcelona. A half hour later, a second bomb was detonated. Miraculously no one was killed, but 17 were injured.
- On April 6, 2008, at the start of the marathon race in Sri Lanka, a suicide bomber most likely from the Liberation Tigers of Tamil Eelam detonated his bomb, killing 15 people and injuring nearly 100.

Tips for Sporting Events

- Although there have been different types of mass victim attacks at sporting events, most have been bombings or shootings. Follow preparation guidelines for both.
- Sporting events, whether indoors or outdoors, typically have very high-density crowds. This can lead to stampedes as people try to escape when a mass victim attack occurs. Many injuries, including fractures and even death, can occur from getting caught in a stampede—especially if physically challenged, very young, or very old. Stay to the sidelines and avoid the middle of a shoving crowd as all try to escape, which can include pushing, shoving, and trampling.
- Sporting events tend to have security presence, but keep on the lookout for any suspicious behavior. Trust your instincts. Security may not be sufficient to thoroughly observe and check all attendees properly. As always, you are your own first line of defense. If something feels out of place and could be threatening, report it immediately. If security is not immediately seen, then call local law enforcement or, if the threat is immediate, call 911.
- Sports events can become very loud and could mask harmful sounds. Be aware of crowd behavior. If you suddenly see one section exiting quickly in a panic or there is growing chaos in one section, you should assume something harmful is either happening or about to happen.

Concert/Performance

- Concerts and performances are presented in two different venues: outdoors and indoors. Concert type is a factor. For example, the decibel level (loudness) is much higher at a rock-type concert than at a classical music event. Like an exciting sporting event, concerts can get loud, whether outdoors or indoors. Because background concert sounds can mask the beginning of an attack or add to confusion, be aware of crowd behavior for indicators of something wrong (e.g., panic, running as a group in one area, etc.).
- Be aware of exits when entering an outdoor concert. Ensure that exits aren't blocked to discourage attendees from sneaking in—this also prevents attendees from exiting in an emergency. Be aware that many performances have an inadequate number of emergency exits. Being near an exit may be more important than being in the front.
- If at an indoor concert or performance, check where exits are before the event begins.

- Check for alternate paths of escape other than designated exits.
- If physically challenged, arrange for seating near an exit.

Protest

Protests range from mild and calm complaints outdoors and indoors to heated arguments and violence. Given that a protest setting is based on built-up anger over specific complaints, tempers can flare rapidly. Even peaceful protests can lead to violent, mass victim attacks. For example, on July 7, 2016, Micah Johnson targeted police as he shot from an elevated position near the end of a peaceful protest in Dallas, Texas. Five officers were killed and six wounded by Johnson, who was eventually stopped by a robot laden with a bomb that was guided to his position by police. Once close, the shootings were stopped when the police remotely detonated the bomb attached to the robot. Johnson was killed.[3]

On August 12, 2017, during a "Unite the Right" rally in Charlottesville, Virginia, counterprotestors from the left clashed with those rallying. Several violent situations broke out between the two sides. At the end of the rally and after much violent outbursts, 20-year-old James Fields Jr. was arrested for driving a car at high speed into another vehicle at a crosswalk. The crash resulted in 1 woman being killed and 20 injured.[4]

- If you attend a protest and one side has clubs, helmets, and other protective gear, it is time to leave—even before it starts. The use of protective gear and handheld weapons are indicators of impending violence. The protest is likely to be disrupted and not beneficial. Whether protesters or counterprotesters are wearing protective gear and have shields and or clubs doesn't matter. These are indicators of violence waiting to happen. Leave immediately.
- Security and law enforcement should not condone protestors with shields, helmets, clubs, or any other protective gear; they are there to do more than protest or counterprotest.
- If attending a protest, keep situational awareness in the forefront at all times, continually checking to see escape routes should violence break out.
- Be especially careful near roadways and crosswalks—be aware of traffic at all times. Do not be part of a crowd in the street or at an intersection.
- If attending an indoor protest, determine if security presence is adequate and know where all exits are located—make sure exits are unobstructed.
- Do not wait during violence to take photos or videos, you are likely to get injured.

TIPS BY LOCATION, TYPE OF ATTACK, AND
PERSONAL CHARACTERISTICS (INDOORS)

Restaurant

When dining at a restaurant, whether fast food or fine dining, it is relatively easy to get distracted, especially if you are with others. You are there to enjoy the food, may be engrossed in conversation, and relaxed as opposed to being alert. Again, situational awareness is a key to survival.

- Know the dining establishment you will be attending. Know where the exits are and if there is a back door or kitchen door that can be used as an exit.
- Depending on the restaurant (fast food or fine dining), know what could be gathered as a weapon. Drinking glasses, bottles, knives, forks, and even some chairs can be used as a weapon of convenience, if necessary.
- Weapons of convenience can be important if you must first hide prior to escaping. If a stabber, throw anything at the face/eyes, which are vulnerable targets. We all flinch if something is coming toward our face.
- Don't stay in the open if an attack begins. In fast-food restaurants, remember that escape in the confusion of the beginning of an attack is far better than staying in place.
- If an exit is blocked by an attacker, one avenue may be to crawl behind the counter and to the back door.
- Don't pick hiding in a restroom over an escape to an exit. Restrooms can be a dead end with no chance of escape. They should be used as a last resort only and the door must be blocked if there is a door. Jam anything of substance under the door—even a wallet shoved under a door can discourage forced entry.
- Remember bullets can go through doors. As a last resort, lie prone on the floor and hold the door shut with your feet reducing your target size.

Airport and Airliner

This section must start with myths that should be dispelled to encourage your situational awareness at all times while in an airport or an airliner before, during, and after flight. An airport is a unique type of target. Travelers are in a hurry, some may be waiting for their plane, eating, or even sleeping. A mass victim attack would not likely be on the mind. However, being aware and alert are absolutely necessary. Airports cover a large land area, and are difficult to protect at all times. There have been mass shootings and bombings in airports.

First, are Federal Air Marshalls (FAMs) on every flight? In discussions I have had for years, I have often heard the statement that "thank goodness we have air marshals on board." The presence of air marshals on board all flights is a myth.

- Although there are no official statistics released by the Transportation Security Administration (TSA), informed officials estimate that only .5% of flights have a FAM aboard. This means over 99% of flights are not protected.
- There are approximately 30,000 U.S. flights per day and approximately 3,300 FAMs. Of these, 34% perform office duties (called "chair marshals"), leaving 2,178 FAMS who have days off, holidays, shifts, etc. Currently, it is virtually impossible to adequately cover flights with available FAMs.
- When on board, the FAM's primary duty is to guard the cockpit doors. This stems from 9/11 when Al Qaeda hijackers gained control of cockpits to guide airliners into the World Trade Center, Pentagon, and the field in Pennsylvania, killing almost 3,000 people.
- Assignment of FAMs to flights is not random. A threat matrix that uses route and location vulnerability, as well as other factors, is used to determine which flights will be covered.
- On November 1, 2013, 23-year-old Paul Ciancia entered the Los Angeles airport in military-style clothing, carrying a bag. He pulled an assault rifle out of his bag and shot three TSA officers, killing Gerardo Hernandez and wounding two others. Ciancia was wounded by police officers and taken into custody. He was found to have five fully loaded ammunition magazines in his bag plus notes saying the TSA officials were pigs and fascists.[5]
- Clay Biles, a former Navy Seal and a FAM for years, stated that a team of FAMs were less than 100 yards from Hernandez's bleeding body for 30 minutes but, policy bound, did not respond; Hernandez died.[6] Given the vast majority of flights do not have FAM protection and given past attacks by a variety of tactics including bombings and semi-automatic guns, we should not let our guard down in an airport or airliner and assume we are protected.
- If you see an unattended package, luggage, backpack, or any type of unattended package, tell those nearby to move away and report it immediately.
- If you see someone put down a package of any type and walk away, immediately notice the characteristics of the person in terms of dress,

height, etc.; report it immediately with a description of the individual as well as the exact location of the package.

- If you hear loud popping sounds or see people running, seek cover and escape.
- Flying remains the safest form of travel and we should not be afraid to fly.
- It is important to stay alert when boarding and awaiting takeoff. If something threatening happens, law enforcement can be contacted immediately and can board the plane very quickly.

The solution of staying at home should not guide our lives. However, we should maintain situational awareness in airports, while boarding and during flights. We have had attacks at all levels and a number of mass victim attacks have been prevented on airliners and in airports. We must realize how thin resources really are and play our parts by reporting immediately anything we see that is suspicious. We can help by extending security's eyes and ears.

Movie Theatre

Movie theatres, as well as other types of performance theatres, are dark and draw our eyes and ears to the screen or stage. That is why we are there. We may be totally unaware what is happening around us. Therefore, we do our preventative homework when entering.

- When entering the theatre, take note of all exits as well as back exits/ entrances.
- Although you are there to be entertained, pay partial attention to what is going on around you. Note any suspicious behavior, and if you see any, walk out and report it.
- Be especially aware if you see anyone in tactical gear. Those with mental health issues seem to be attracted to these types of locations (i.e., James Holmes, Aurora, Colorado, Century 16 movie theatre attacker). Be concerned about anyone entering through a back exit.

Bar/Nightclub

Bars and nightclubs are noted by alcohol consumption. This ranges from someone having a casual drink to those who have difficulty controlling their intake. Again, customers are there to enjoy the surroundings. There may be parties, good friends celebrating, and those who are there just to drink. Judgment and awareness are impaired more than in other locations frequented.

These locations can also be loud, making it more difficult to be situationally aware.

- When entering the location, note the exits, including back exits.
- Pick a seating location as near as possible to an exit.
- Be aware of anyone entering who looks out of place, such as someone wearing a long coat that could be hiding firearms and ammunition, especially if the weather does not warrant this type of dress.
- Be observant if you see someone wearing a backpack or carrying a bag. You can tell if it is heavier than you would expect by the way it is being carried. If it appears too heavy for the situation, report it.
- If you hear popping sounds outside the entrance, leave immediately. Be aware that gunfire may not sound like what we think gunfire would sound like. In the Pulse nightclub attack in Orlando, Florida, Omar Mateen had a shoot-out with outside security before entering the club.
- Suspend disbelief. Many survivors have reported that they thought the beginning of an attack was not real or could not be happening. Often, according to reports, many valuable seconds are lost at the beginning of an attack because there is such disbelief that what they are actually seeing is happening. Assume it is not part of the performance. At the first sound or sight of anything suspicious, move immediately, with escape the focus—you can always reenter if in error. It is better to be safe than sorry.

Mall/Shopping Center

Although online shopping is becoming very popular because of ease and the ability to find what you want at the best prices, Americans still enjoy malls and shopping centers immensely. The mall has become entertainment and a social-gathering location as much as a place to shop. Whether young or old, or challenged in some way, the malls remain a top location, as do strip malls. When visiting our local malls, it is common to see wheelchairs, motorized wheelchairs, canes, blind people, infants and children, and the frail elderly. Of course, we also see healthy looking athletic types and normal looking people. Malls also tend to attract the occasional mass victim attacker who may choose stabbing as a method or semi-automatic gunfire.

Physical barriers prevent vehicle run-downs, and the manner in which people are dispersed throughout a mall is not attractive to the bomber who wants densely packed crowds. Malls do have some advantages.

- Know the exits that could be used as escape. These exits go beyond the typical entrances, although they too can be used in an emergency.

- Malls have an almost unlimited opportunity for hiding if danger is imminent and nearby. It is easier for the attacker to target those easy to see. However, the purpose of hiding should be temporary only while waiting for a better time to escape—then escape!
- As mentioned, almost all mall stores have a back exit or, if in a center location with no back outside exit, typically they open to an internal corridor that in turn leads to an external exit.
- Many mall stores have a security gate that closes during off hours—if running to a nearby store to avoid being a target, tell a store clerk immediately what is happening (e.g., someone is stabbing others, or there's an active shooter) and mention closing the gate.
- Turn your cellphone ringer off if hiding—you don't want your position given away by a ringing phone.
- Call 911 at the first opportunity—law enforcement can respond quickly. Give the precise location of the attacker when calling and state specifically what he/she/they are doing (e.g., stabbing, shooting, etc.). However, don't stand in place exposed while calling—escape if possible or hide while waiting to escape and then call.
- The mall is a very big space with ample places to escape and hide—there is no reason to attack the attacker when such options are available, unless the attack begins within a few feet of you and it is clear you are the target.
- If you are responsible for others because of their age or if they are physically or mentally challenged, seek the first hiding place to get out of the attacker's view on the way to fully escaping.

Workplace

Workplaces are a bit different from other locations we may visit because we have spent many hours there and typically know every nook and cranny. We know escape routes, and we likely know where to hide temporarily. If you don't, then take the time to walk around and know more about your workplace from a mass victim attack perspective.

- If you see a former employee in the workplace or approaching the workplace who was previously terminated and could be disgruntled, report them immediately to security if there is a security presence. Don't be afraid to call local law enforcement if there is no security presence. Report the demeanor of the person, especially if there is anger or any threatening activity or language.

- Don't engage with a former employee who was terminated—if seen, avoid him or her.
- Most workplace mass victim attackers use semi-automatic weapons. If it looks like a disgruntled employee is carrying a heavy bag when they typically do not carry a bag and is obviously angry, leave and report immediately.
- Be aware of current employees if bitter, openly vocal about the faults of coworkers and vocalize threats.
- If shots are heard (loud popping sounds), try to avoid going to your office. If you are a target then you would be going to the one location where you would be expected to be, resulting in being easily located. Concentrate on escape and exits not hiding unless absolutely necessary.
- If you are in a multilevel building, escape to the stairwell from the second floor or above and go down steps to the ground level to escape from the building. Do not hide in the stairwell. Call 911 immediately once safe. *Do not* assume that someone else has called 911!
- Don't hide in a trapped space such as an office, especially if you know the attacker and are not on good terms.
- Forget the notion that "this can't be happening" and move quickly to escape, especially as an attack starts—this is a time of multiple targeting as opposed to hunt and shoot.

Military/Hardened Government Installation

Military and hardened government installations are considered to be secure locations. They have secure perimeters with security geared toward keeping nonapproved individuals off the base. However, insiders (approved personnel) present a different type of threat. They are "badged" and are officially allowed to be present within the confines of the guarded installation. Therefore, behavior and statements must be relied on for indicators of impending threat of a mass victim attack. There have been a surprising number of mass victim attacks committed by employees within a workplace setting.

Although military installations are secure, we have seen insider attacks even within such secure facilities. On November 5, 2009, self-radicalized major Nidal Hasan walked into a military processing center at Fort Hood, Texas, yelled, "Allahu Akbar," and then started shooting unarmed soldiers. A military psychiatrist, Hasan had a history of dressing in Islamic-inspired clothing, exhibiting radical Islamic anti-U.S. behavior, and making anti-U.S. statements on base and during official duties. He killed 12 soldiers and 1 Department of Defense employee and wounded 30 others. Civilian police stopped the 10-minute attack by shooting him, leaving him paralyzed from the waist down. He has been sentenced to death.[7] There was a multitude of warning signs prior to this attack.

On April 2, 2014, again at Fort Hood, Texas, army specialist Ivan Lopez pulled out a .45-caliber pistol he had recently purchased and opened fire on fellow soldiers. He killed one by shooting through a closed and barricaded door. He then killed 2 other soldiers in addition to wounding 12 others. At the beginning of the shooting, Lopez asked that he be killed. The shooting ended when Lopez shot himself in the head. There was not a clear motive. However, Lopez had suffered from and complained of undisclosed "behavioral health" disorders.[8]

- Be aware of behavior or anti-U.S. statements that are radical Islamic-inspired or praises for radical Islamic terrorism. This includes wearing clothes that are supportive of Islam when on duty and not a part of any approved uniform (e.g., Major Hasan), or wearing shirts with radical pro-Islamic messages.
- Be aware of strong, stated, and any repeated disgruntlement that is focused against the U.S. government/military. React if you hear "Allahu Akbar."
- If a shooting or stabbing attack occurs, remember escape is the first option if unarmed. Do not stay in place. If armed, follow your training for what to do to counter and neutralize the threat.
- Be aware of unusual behavior, such as shouting, yelling, or threatening statements near an entrance of the base or installation; report it immediately.

Elementary School//High School

It is difficult to understand how any person or persons can attack a group of innocent victims in any mass victim attack. But, perhaps, the least understandable is when children in an elementary school or teens in high school are targeted and killed. Mental health issues are typically present in such attackers, which is one reason why such attacks defy logic. Although there have been stabbing attacks in elementary and high schools, the number of fatalities tend to be much lower than attacks in the same type of locations with semi-automatic weapons—the weapon of choice in the United States.

Table 9.1 was compiled by CNN from a list of 72 attacks directed at elementary school and high school children in the United States.[9] The table depicts the 12 attacks that met the criterion of mass victim attacks used for this book: a minimum of three fatalities in one event. Several points should be highlighted. Most attacks were orchestrated using guns as weapons. All

Table 9.1 U.S. Elementary School and High School Mass Victim Attacks (Minimum of 3 Killed)

Date	Attack	Attacker	Age	Location	Fatalities	Consequence
February 14, 2018	Shooting	Nikolas Cruz	19	Marjory Stoneman Douglas High School, Parkland, FL	17	Apprehended
December 14, 2012	Shooting	Adam Lanza	20	Sandy Hook Elementary School, Newtown, CT	27	Suicide
October 2, 2006	Shooting	Charles Roberts IV	32	West Nickel Mines Amish School, Nickel Mines, PA	5	Suicide
March 21, 2005	Shooting	Jeff Weise	16	Red Lake High School, Red Lake, MN	9	Suicide
April 20, 1999	Shooting	Eric Harris & Dylan Klebold	18/17	Columbine High School, Littleton, CO	13	Suicide
March 24, 1998	Shooting	Andrew Golden & Mitchell Johnson	11/13	Westside Middle School, Jonesboro, AR	5	Jailed 8 & 10 years
December 1, 1997	Shooting	Michael Carneal	14	Heath High School, Paducah, KY	3	Life in prison
February 2, 1996	Shooting	Barry Loukaitis	14	Frontier Junior High School, Moses Lake, WA	3	Life in prison
May 1, 1992	Shooting	Eric Houston	20	Lindhurst High School, Olivehurst, CA	4	Death row
January 17, 1989	Shooting	Patrick Purdy	24	Cleveland Elementary School, Stockton, CA	5	Suicide
September 15, 1959	1 Bomb	Paul Orgeron	49	Edgar Allen Poe Elementary School, Houston, TX	5	Suicide
May 18, 1927	2 Bombs	Andrew Kehoe	55	Bath Consolidated School, Bath, MI	44	Suicide

perpetrators of mass victim attacks listed were committed by or led by a male. Two of the 72 incidents included a female accomplice. Seven of the 11 mass victim attacks ended in suicide.

Attackers targeting schools will attack even if guns are not available. China has very strict gun laws, so attacks in schools are with knives, cleavers, or machetes. There have been many such attacks in China with fatalities and many injuries. Just as one example, on December 14, 2012, in Chenpeng Village, China, mentally ill Min Yingjun first stabbed an 85-year-old woman and then attacked children at the front of a school, injuring 22. By chance, this was the same day as the Sandy Hook Elementary School attack in Newtown, Connecticut, in which Adam Lanza shot to death 20 children and 6 adult staff at the school.[10]

- All schools need to have an immediate lockdown policy and training for all staff on what to do if threat approaches.
- If an attack begins, have an immediate alert to all classrooms and throughout the school and specify clearly (e.g., "Shooter! Lock Down!").
- All doors should be heavy reinforced doors with deadbolt locks on the inside. There should be no glass around any entrance door or any classroom. A shooter can gain entrance simply by shooting through the glass (e.g., Adam Lanza, Sandy Hook Elementary School, shot his way in through front-door glass panels).
- Parents should pressure the school board to ensure security features are high-priority expenditures.
- To the extent possible, have security who watches the perimeter for oncoming threat to initiate a lockdown.
- Escape if possible and if not possible because of the nearness of the threat stay in place in classrooms, blockaded behind reinforced doors with dead bolt locks. Do not stand behind the door.
- Recommendation: In new school construction, each room should have a second door leading to the outside to aid escape. Parents should insist on safety features.
- Have mandatory first aid training for all staff.[11]

College

Compared to elementary schools and high schools, colleges and universities are obviously different. It is the next step, but a very big next step. There is much more freedom. Classes are not held in one enclosed building and almost all have an open campus. Schedules can be divided into various times of the day, and can even include evening classes. Students may drive, and classes may be distributed across campus.

Of the types of attacks observed across types of terrorism, hate attacks, and mental health issues, anything is fair game. In elementary and high schools, we are not likely to see vehicle run-downs, but we have seen stabbings, shootings, and even rare bombings. However, any form of mass victim attack could occur in the college setting.

Given a much more open environment with multiple structures, security has additional challenges. Conducting a lock-down at an elementary school or high school is frankly easier than at a college. An intercom announcement of threat, although possible depending on the campus, is more challenging. Security presence is also more challenging.

- College students need to be more situationally aware, being in an open environment; be aware of the behavior of others walking on campus.
- Follow guidelines in this book for walking if along a street where a vehicle could veer into pedestrians.
- At any sign of a weapon (e.g., blade weapon, gun, someone leaving an unattended package/bag or an already unattended package/bag) leave immediately and report exactly what you saw and give the specific location.
- Colleges need to establish an emergency communications system even if limited to sending emergency tweets, with all students following.
- If popping sounds are heard in a classroom building, immediately blockade behind the classroom door. Don't stand directly behind the door holding it. Remember, gunfire may sound different from what you might expect and direction may be hard to determine.
- When checking out a campus, walk through classroom buildings and check availability of exits, determine if classrooms have doors that can be blocked, determine the status of campus security, ask about campus preparations for emergencies, and ask how emergency situations are communicated to students.

House of Worship

Multiple mass victim attacks have occurred in or at houses of worship. Primarily fueled by hate/bias, attackers have been merciless. Although the weapons of choice have been firearms, the method of attacks have been different.

- Attacks can occur outside near the entrance or inside; security for houses of worship need to patrol perimeter, as well as inside the structure.

- Houses of worship of all sizes need to have someone available with a concealed carry permit who is trained properly in the use of firearms.
- Off-duty police are excellent choices for security.
- Be alert to anyone who enters a congregation who is not known and exhibits any type of negative behavior or statements.
- Make sure structures have multiple exits available—a house of worship with a single entrance/exit is not safe.
- If an attack occurs from the outside and bullets are coming through window(s), lie prone on the floor and let assigned security intervene.
- Ensure security presence at each service or special activity.

10

Surviving with Psychological Trauma

Survival is not a simple concept. After a mass victim attack, we see the number of victims killed and the number physically injured. It often seems these two numbers are the primary focus—that and the absolute horror associated with the slaughter. Fatalities are the most unfortunate aspect of an attack, and then we tend to see the number injured as fortunate survivors. On the face of it, this is definitely true. However, there are levels of survival.

If we dissect an attack we see victims falling into the following categories:

- Killed instantly or on the scene of the attack
- Those who die in treatment that was not successful because of the severity of injury
- Severely wounded with lifelong physical damage
- Severely wounded with eventual full physical recovery
- Injured but not by the attacker (i.e., injuries from escaping)
- No physical injuries
- Severe psychological trauma effects resulting in Acute Stress Disorder (ASD) or longer-term Post-Traumatic Stress Disorder (PTSD)
- Mild psychological trauma not reaching the levels of ASD or PTSD

Although an attack may only last a minute to a few hours, the effect on victims, even if they are survivors, can be devastating. Life for almost all surviving victims will never be the same. The terror and fear resulting from an attack typically changes a victim for a lifetime. Certainly, the attack will be replayed in memory innumerable times, involuntarily. There could be bad thoughts and nightmares that keep the attack fresh in the mind for years.

Those sustaining physical damage that can last a lifetime may have to learn how to use an artificial limb or cope with disfigurement. They may have to cope with not being able to run or play sports. The effects of a mass victim attack can, in turn, have a strong impact on the family. Spouses, children, other family members, and friends are part of the victims' struggles to cope with both physical and psychological recovery. In many cases, the psychological effects can outweigh and outlast the physical effects of the attack.

On September 11, 2001, the United States was attacked by international terrorists. The coordinated attack began when four airliners were hijacked by 19 terrorists working in four interconnected cells. In New Yok City, the attack began when an airliner flew into the North Tower of the World Trade Center. Shortly after this attack, a second airliner flew into the WTC's South Tower. Another airliner flew into the Pentagon, and one crashed into a field in Pennsylvania, due to passengers attempting to gain control.

In New York City, 2,753 were killed, including first responders (343 firemen, 27 policemen, and 37 Port Authority officers). The airliner making a direct hit on the Pentagon killed 184, including those in the airliner and in the destruction area of the Pentagon. In the fourth attempted attack, the downing of the airliner, likely headed for the U.S. capital, resulted in 40 deaths, as passengers tried in vain to retake control of the aircraft.

At the time, I managed a threat team in the Pentagon. I was headed for my external office that day when the airliner struck the Pentagon. One of my staff members was leaving the Pentagon front doors when the impact occurred. She met me at my office in Georgetown in D.C. and we watched the smoke billowing from the Pentagon. When she arrived, I asked if she was OK. She immediately said, "Yes." I asked again, "Are you sure"? She then broke down crying. This was normal behavior, given the trauma of a mass victim attack. Realizing that we could have been victims weighed heavily, especially because we worked in the Pentagon the next day. Amidst the still smoking structure, I was impressed that life in the Pentagon life had already resumed. The dedication of staff was remarkable.

It was a day that those old enough to remember will never forget. It was a day of shock, loss, and tears. Most of us know someone who was directly involved in one way or another, and when almost 3,000 people died, all with family and friends, untold numbers were directly and indirectly affected. However, with the repeated television coverage showing the horror of the event as we watched the towers collapse and the Pentagon being struck on rerun after rerun, many were psychologically affected.

The worst mass victim attack committed by international terrorists had an immediate and long-lasting traumatic effect. One of my close colleagues had a cousin who was a fireman first responder at the World Trade Center towers.

All they ever found of his remains was part of his helmet. The attack succeeded in changing the response to terrorism. The psychological pain from such events affects far more people than the victims themselves.

POST-TRAUMATIC STRESS DISORDER (PTSD)

Many think of PTSD being caused by war. This is certainly true, and many veterans are affected by this disorder. Known as "shell shock" in WWI and "combat fatigue" in WWII, the disorder can have many causes.

> *Post-Traumatic Stress Disorder, known by its acronym, PTSD, is a psychiatric disorder that can occur in people who have experienced or witnessed a traumatic event such as a natural disaster, a serious accident, a terrorist act, war/combat, rape or other violent personal assault.*[1]

Affecting over 3 million people in the United States, effects of the anxiety disorder can be debilitating. Most importantly, you do not have to be directly exposed to the traumatic event to suffer from PTSD. Repeated exposure to the event on television, or losing a family member or friend to the trauma, can result in PTSD. How long do the effects last? This depends on the person, the event, and treatment.

Most of us have likely heard the term PTSD and probably have some sense of what the term means because of its heavy use. However, Acute Stress Disorder (ASD) is also very important. ASD symptoms are highly similar to PTSD but are short-lived compared to PTSD. ASD may start right after a traumatic event or within several days at the most. However, although very similar to PTSD, the effects do not last more than a month. If the symptoms persist, a qualified mental health professional may move the diagnosis from ASD to PTSD.

Many people exposed to traumatic events do not develop PTSD or ASD. But some do. It is also possible to suffer from ASD after a traumatic event that does not progress to full-blown PTSD. We are all different and respond in our own ways if caught in a traumatic event. For sure, we will feel the effects of the trauma, although the depth of the effects and the length of time the effects last are highly individualistic. PTSD and ASD are relevant to those who experience symptoms so severe that life is disrupted at home and even at work. The effects of the trauma become a problem that interferes with the normal daily routine and quality of life.

The diagnosis of PTSD and ASD requires assessment by a psychiatrist or psychologist with the appropriate clinical training and experience. Diagnoses such as these involve a process of determining symptoms, the context of the traumatic event, when symptoms began, how many symptoms of different types exist, how long they have persisted, and if they are severe enough to interfere with daily life with family and/or work. If you are interested in the clinical details, the specific diagnostic process used by professionals can be found in the *Diagnostic and Statistical Manual of Mental Disorders*, 5th edition (DSM-5), published by the American Psychiatric Association. However, I caution against self-diagnosis. Professional assessment is required. If you are concerned that you may be affected by a stress-related, anxiety-based disorder, seek the services of a qualified professional.

WHAT CAUSES SERIOUS STRESS DISORDERS?

There are indicators of stress disorders. If the indicators are present, it is not a given that a stress disorder will result. However, working backwards, if a person is affected and the symptoms suggest ASD or PTSD, then these indicators were likely present.

(1) The person is caught in the traumatic event or was physically close to the event;
(2) The person was injured during the traumatic event;
(3) The person was close to someone who was a victim of the traumatic event;
(4) The person watched a significant amount of media coverage of the traumatic event.

Notice that the person did not have to be directly affected by the event in question. Knowing someone or watching repeated coverage can lead to stress effects.[2] This is very important. In my opinion, there are those who suffer from severe PTSD and try to discount it because they were not actually present during the traumatic event.

Children deserve special concern as related to stress effects. There is some evidence that shows that three to five days after the 9/11 attacks in 2001, 35% of parents surveyed nationally reported their children presented at least one stress-related symptom. Two years after the 1995 Timothy McVeigh / Oklahoma City bombing, 16% of children living within 100 miles of the bombing still exhibited stress-related symptoms. Risk factors were reported to include:

- Higher levels of television viewing of the event
- Higher parent distress

Again, these findings are very important because the children were not related to any of the victims, and were not directly involved with the attack.[3]

Such findings place focus on parents and the home environment. Given that a child, and an adult for that matter, can suffer from ASD or PTSD without being present at the traumatic event and can be influenced by repeated exposure to an event on television, we must think about how such topics are covered in the home. Parents can pass their dismay and horror of such events to their children inadvertently by actions and words.

An overfocus on discussing how the world has changed for the worse, including open discussions about violence, killings, gangs, attacks, etc., can frighten children. We may be presenting a picture of a frightening world that is new to them, and one that will be their future. It is not unusual for children to fear the loss of a parent. There are many other things that a child could be doing other than watching repeated replays of mass victim attacks. Parents need to be aware of what children see and of the words they use to describe horrific events. Remember, you, as parents, are the most important people in your children's lives, and they trust what you are saying.

WHAT ARE PTSD SYMPTOMS?[4]

DSM-5 criteria describe symptoms in groups. For example, there are symptoms that have the overall term of "re-experiencing." This means that thoughts of the specific traumatic event causing the distress to occur repeatedly. Re-experiencing should have at least one of the following present:

- Intrusive thoughts (thoughts occurring without personal control)
- Nightmares
- Flashbacks (vivid images of the traumatic event suddenly occur)
- Emotional distress after exposure to traumatic reminders (heightened, stressful feelings following reminders of the traumatic event)
- Physical reactivity after exposure to traumatic reminders (physical reactions when reminded of the traumatic event)

There is also effortful avoidance of reminders of the trauma in one of the two following ways:

- Trauma-related thoughts or feelings (required effort to avoid recurring thoughts of the trauma)
- Trauma-related reminders (e.g., avoiding discussions, reruns, etc.)

Also, there is the presence of negative thoughts/feelings that become worse after the trauma. These negative thoughts include:

- Inability to recall or remember key features of the traumatic event
- Presence of strong and negative thoughts and assumptions about self or the world
- Exaggerated blame of self or others for causing the trauma
- Negative affect (appearing in an overall negative manner and appearance)
- Decreased interest in activities (loss of interest)
- Feeling isolated (feelings of being alone)
- Difficulty experiencing positive affect (difficulty in appearing and acting in a positive manner)

In addition, the following started to occur, or if present worsened, after the traumatic event occurred:

- Irritability or aggression (e.g., bad or short tempered, striking out verbally or physically)
- Risky or destructive behavior (increased risk-taking behavior that appears not to serve the person well)
- Hypervigilance (increased sensitivity to danger and energy identifying it)
- Heightened startle reaction (easily startled when new noises, movements, or touch occurs)
- Difficulty concentrating (person experiences difficulty in focusing thoughts as needed for the situation)
- Difficulty sleeping (not able to sleep well)

Finally, there are symptoms clinically labeled as "dissociative." This means that the affected person feels detached as it relates to the trauma. This occurs in one of two ways:

- Depersonalization (the person experiences feelings that he was outside the event observing himself or herself, instead of being in the event itself. It may have a dreamlike quality)
- Derealization (the feeling that the event was not real)

To be eligible for a diagnosis of PTSD, symptoms must be present for more than a month and be severe enough that life is disrupted. For example, family life or work may be disrupted because of the presence of PTSD symptoms. The effects observed should not result from the effects of drugs or other causes.

It is important to note that it is not only victims of mass victim attacks that can suffer from ASD or longer-lasting effects of PTSD in a mass victim attack. Our first responders deserve a special note of appreciation for their efforts to save the lives of others. The overwhelming consideration of any victim caught in a mass victim attack is to escape. The remaining options of hide, stay in place, or attack the attacker are far removed from the first option of escape. The obvious advantage of escape is that you are leaving a situation of imminent danger to go to a location that is safer and more secure. As victims concentrate on escape, rightfully so, first responders are running to danger. The law enforcement officer, security staff member, fireman, SWAT team member, and emergency medical staff rush to a scene to provide assistance in many ways. First and foremost, the attack must be stopped. This is accomplished by confronting the attacker(s) either through direct and forceful action or by adding so much pressure that the attacker stops the attack by ending his or her own life.

Second, injured victims need immediate assistance, especially if multiple victims have received life-threatening injuries, which is often the case. First responders put their lives on the line by placing their own survival secondary to saving others. This is not to say they are not careful and well trained. It simply means they are running into danger as we focus on escaping.

First responders experience situations similar to a battle. They must face the enemy and may be working under fire. As brave as they are, they also face the prospects of ASD and PTSD. Arriving on the scene of a mass victim attack can be particularly horrifying. Multiple victims killed, many suffering, many bleeding profusely, some already dead, and the sight of severely wounded or dead children can leave its toll on the first responder. They are no strangers to stress-related disorders. The same symptoms that impact the victim of an attack can be experienced by first responders.

Imagine for a minute a mass victim attack, and you have signed on to rush into danger. First responders are human, and they experience fear the same way we all experience it. They may be better prepared, but when they rush into what appears to be a mass victim attack, they know they can be severely injured, disfigured, or killed and families could experience a severe loss. Even if the event is resolved, that very act of rushing into danger and absorbing risk to well-being, life, and family happiness is a recipe for ASD and PTSD. First responders are special people, and they deserve our admiration. *I take this opportunity to thank first responders for risking their lives so that we can survive.*

There is one major difference between first responders and victims caught off guard in a mass victim attack. First responders have been trained to know what to expect, to know they are responding at a specific location, and to know how to marshal a first response to the attack. This preparation may help. In a similar way, the purpose of this book is to make you more aware, provide strategies for survival, and reduce the response time when such a tragic event starts. Knowing the details of how to escape, what to expect, and knowing to move immediately can help develop the sense of being prepared. This does not reduce the nature of a horrifying attack and the unfortunate sights and sounds of a vicious attack, but can help psychologically.

HOW DO YOU MANAGE ASD OR PTSD?

The most important statement I can make about ASD or PTSD is that if you experience symptoms presented in this chapter, please seek qualified medical assistance. Stress effects associated with ASD or PTSD require the assessment and diagnosis of a qualified professional. Even if you do seek help, there are still things you can do to assist in your treatment and recovery.

In an excellent post by the Mayo Clinic staff on the topic of self-management, they provide the advice that I have paraphrased in this section to make it specific to the topic of mass victim attacks.[5] I encourage readers to check the referenced site.

The first step is that if you have followed advice and have sought medical advice, do what the doctor has told you to do. In other words, follow the treatment plan. This is very important. The plan could involve medication, therapy, counseling, and tasks to follow at home—yes, homework. Treatment professionals know what to suggest based on individual needs and symptoms. *Trust your doctor and follow the advice.*

Second, you need to know the details underlying ASD and PTSD. This is important in treatment. It also removes much of the mystery of why you may be suffering. However, be careful of the source. I have referenced the U.S. Department of Veteran Affairs publications on PTSD, as well as those of the Mayo Clinic, in this chapter. These are reputable choices. You can check them out and the references they mention. The American Psychiatric Association and the American Psychological Association (of which I am a lifelong member) are authoritative sources. Reputable knowledge removes mystery.

As a third point, it is time to focus on your health. If suffering from a strong anxiety disorder stemming from a mass victim attack or any traumatic event for that matter, proper sleep, eating well, exercise, relaxation, getting outdoors, and engaging in activities with family or friends can help. There may be a tendency to increase smoking, if you are a smoker, or to drink more coffee—don't. This does not help an anxiety disorder, even if temporary. Most importantly, although this moves into another major point, do not self-medicate and do not drink too much!

What is self-medicating? In times of trouble or increased stress some people turn to drugs or alcohol, or both, to reduce pain. I might add that drugs can include increasing the dosage of prescribed medication on your own without the advice of your physician. Avoid this urge if it is there. Furthermore, there are no over-the-counter drugs at the pharmacy to help you: avoid over-the-counter self-medicating. There are powerful drugs at the local pharmacy that one can buy without a prescription and they can harm you: Avoid this urge.

Drugs and alcohol cannot help ASD or PTSD. Medication prescribed by a trained physician or psychiatrist can help tremendously but, as said earlier, only if taken as prescribed and followed as directed. Many self-medicate, and many suffer or make the situation worse by doing so.

Don't isolate yourself and don't focus on being alone with thoughts of the traumatic event. Seek out those who are supportive. By supportive, I mean those who do not dwell on the details of the traumatic event. You need to associate with those family members or friends that can honestly help to get your mind off the event. Movies, bicycling, fishing, long drives, swimming, boating, playing chess, playing monopoly, a poker game—it doesn't matter. If you are spending quality time with family and friends, it will be to your benefit. If you are a person of faith, then getting more involved with your church, temple, or synagogue can be of great benefit. It is a support group, regardless of the faith.

The highly respected Mayo Clinic staff make a very important suggestion, in my opinion. There is a tendency to isolate oneself and dwell on thoughts of the traumatic event. It is possible the person does not have extended family or friends that are close enough to depend on for regular activities. In this case, or even if you are flooded with supportive friends and family, ask your professional if he or she can recommend a support group for ASD or PTSD. If they can't, I recommend visiting your local mental health clinic and explaining your situation. They will likely be able to assist.

HOW COMMON IS PTSD?

Estimates suggest that about 25% of those experiencing a severe traumatic event will experience PTSD. On an individual basis, the intensity of the experience, the type of traumatic event, and the degree of *individual resilience* makes a difference.[6, 7] Resilience basically means the ability to recover quickly. Research has been carried out to try to understand why some develop ASD or PTSD symptoms and some don't, following exposure to the same traumatic event. It is beyond the scope of this book to delve deeply into these findings, but I will say that much more research needs to be completed. For sure, ASD or PTSD result from individual reactions to traumatic events. Active research is being conducted in three major areas.

(1) Can ASD and PTSD be diminished before a traumatic event?
(2) Can ASD and PTSD be diminished after a traumatic event?
(3) What are the most effective treatments and treatment plans for ASD and PTSD?

This is such a major topic that I suggest if you are interested in the medical and psychological details across all three questions or any of the three questions then conduct your own research on the Internet. However, care should be taken to ensure that the sources are legitimate. These stress-related disorders go far beyond mass victim attacks. It is important to realize that these effects can occur as a result of exposure to basically any form of extreme traumatic event.

The following is a strong statement, but justified. There are two ways that a mass victim attack can kill you. The first way is obvious. You are caught in the attack and are killed outright or as a result of severe physical injury that could not be treated successfully whether short term or longer term. The second way is also unfortunate and is, perhaps, more preventable. That is, some victims suffer so severely that suicide appears to be the only option, and that option is taken. *It is very important to know how to deal with stress related to mass victim attacks. The assaults are extremely traumatic.* While many go through such attacks and do not develop ASD or PTSD, their lives can be changed forever. For those who do suffer, there are many approaches that can be effective.

The association between PTSD and suicide is present and real. The correlation is higher between PTSD and suicide and the incidence of suicide in the general population. Certainly, traumatic events can have an impact. However, there can be many causes of PTSD. For example, many may find it shocking that in 2014, 7,400 veterans took their own lives. To repeat, because it needs to sink in, *in 2014, 7,400 veterans took their own lives!* This is an average of around 20 dedicated veterans per day. We also must keep in mind that some suicides are not reported as suicides. Certainly, depression and PTSD were in play. It is a complex issue to understand and makes it difficult to even gather accurate statistics. Regardless, the symptoms following traumatic events can be devastating. Where is the treatment? I leave that as a question.

This is not meant to be a distressing report but is meant to impress upon all of us that symptoms of depression, anxiety, ASD, and PTSD should be taken very seriously. Extreme trauma can have extreme effects on many of us and can even be deadly. Before we go further, the following is the national suicide hotline. If you know of someone suffering to a significant degree, make sure they have this number. **The National Suicide Prevention Hotline number is: 1-800-273-8255.** It is available 24 hours a day, seven days a week, 365 days a year. The website[8] presents the following as warning signs:

- Talking about wanting to die or killing themselves
- Looking for a way to kill themselves, like searching online or buying a gun
- Talking about feeling hopeless or having no reason to live
- Talking about feeling trapped or in unbearable pain
- Talking about being a burden to others
- Increasing the use of alcohol or drugs
- Acting anxious or agitated; behaving recklessly
- Sleeping too little or too much
- Withdrawing or isolating themselves
- Showing rage or talking about seeking revenge
- Extreme mood swings

To quote from the site:

Some warning signs may help you determine if a loved one is at risk for suicide, especially if the behavior is new, has increased, or seems related to a painful event, loss, or change. If you or someone you know exhibits any of these, seek help by calling the Lifeline.

To repeat: If you are in trouble or you know someone who needs help, call the National Suicide Prevention Hotline at 1-800-273-8255. Help is available 24/7.

SURVIVING WITH STRESS-RELATED ISSUES
AND PHYSICAL DAMAGE

Stress-related effects following a mass victim attack can range from mild to extreme. All humans caught in a mass victim attack are going to react from a psychological perspective. The effects may be mild to severe to the point where serious treatment is required. Much is based on how you are caught up in the attack, what you have actually witnessed, the severity of injuries, and the realization that you could have been killed. There are those who don't have the choice to dwell on the memories—they are just there and disturbing. Just as real as physical injuries and disabilities, psychological effects can be debilitating.

It was April 15, 2013. Jeff Bauman was near the finish line of the Boston Marathon to support and cheer on his girlfriend who was running in the race. In a split second, his life was changed forever by the nearby pressure cooker bomb exploding. It was one of two bombs that exploded some seconds apart. Both of his legs below the knee were damaged beyond repair and were amputated within hours of the bombings.

Just a short moment before the explosion, Jeff saw a hooded man place a backpack on the ground, look him in the eye, and leave. Then the explosion came. As time passed in intensive care, critically injured, Jeff woke up and wrote a brief note to the FBI that he had seen the person. This was the beginning of identification of the Tsarnaev brothers, who had placed both bombs that exploded in the crowd.[9]

Jeff had to cope with several aspects of his horrifying injury. He had the bad memory of the event; he had seen one of the attackers; he lost his legs and was critically injured; and now he had to fight his way back to some sense of normalcy. His struggles were so challenging that, with Bret Witter, he wrote the *New York Times* bestselling book *Stronger*, highlighting his struggle and recovery.[10] This led to the movie of the same name, starring Jake Gyllenhaal as Jeff. I recommend seeing this movie, not just because it was well played by Gyllenhaal, but to see how an attack like this can present such challenges in recovery.

It was September 16, 2013, and work at the Washington Navy Yard in Washington, D.C., started like most other days. Workers in the large complex were going about their early morning duties. Thirty-four-year-old Aaron Alexis, a contractor, used his pass to enter the building. However, he was concealing a Remington 870 shotgun—a weapon capable of highly destructive damage and instant death to anyone targeted. The gun was sawed off and broken down so it could be concealed in a bag over his shoulder. By 8:16 a.m. he had assembled the gun and started firing at his targets.

Alexis was not unknown to authorities, having come to the attention of law enforcement on several occasions, including an incident the preceding month. There had been indications of mental illness issues.[11] He had reported to police that people were talking to him through the floor and walls and were following him. He further indicated they were using some sort of microwave machine. However, the severity of these symptoms appear not to have been acted on. His active shooting ended when he was killed by a police officer. Alexis had killed 12 people and wounded three others.

One of the wounded, 57-year-old Jennifer Bennet, received an extreme wound from Alexis's shotgun blast. As described, her left shoulder and top of her arm were "blown to bits." An eight-inch scar now crosses her chest and runs down her arm. The arm is connected by a metal plate held in place with 10 metal screws. Jennifer has been vocal about the incident and has become an inspiration, much like Jeff Bauman. When friends heard that a bossy woman survivor was in the hospital telling people what to do, they knew it was her. She escaped the effects of PTSD. Determined to recover, and after much physical therapy, she can use her arm more than may have seemed possible after such a devastating wound.[12]

The Boston Marathon bombings and the Washington Navy Yard attack were totally different. The bombings were a result of self-radicalization and the Navy Yard attack the result of a single shooter with mental health issues. But there are similarities shared by Jeff Bauman and Jennifer Bennet, survivors of two very different attacks: strong character, bonding with other victims, and the unstoppable determination to recover and move on. These characteristics tend to inoculate against the extreme psychological effects that can be debilitating.

HOW TO MANAGE LIFE WITH PTSD AND/OR
PHYSICAL DAMAGE FROM MASS VICTIM ATTACKS

It is normal for any survivor of a mass victim attack to feel emotional and psychological effects following the attack. The sights and sounds are relived to various degrees, and pain and physical damage may be present. This is not the type of trauma that carries with it an expectation of bouncing back to normal the next day. It can take some time, even if not developing ASD or PTSD.

If weeks have passed since the attack and the effects are getting worse, if you have not already done so, seek immediate medical help. For many, there is a stigma attached to seeking help from a mental health professional. Forget the stigma and seek help—it is important. There should be no stigma attached to surviving a horrific, mass victim attack. Trust me, people will understand, if they know.

The number of those who suffer PTSD effects after mass victim attacks is very high, and it is not uncommon for many to need assistance. In a systematic review of 35 research studies focusing on the prevalence of PTSD following terrorist attacks, it was reported in *Psychological Reports*[13] that 33% to 39% of direct victims developed PTSD, while the incidence was lower for those who experienced the event indirectly (4% of the affected community, 5%-6% of emergency, rescue, and recovery staff, and 17%–29% among relatives and friends of the directly affected injured or killed victims).

If we suffer a bombing injury, have been shot, have been hurt in a vehicle run-down, or have been stabbed, we rush to receive medical services. If we are incapacitated due to injuries, first responders rush us to the emergency room with medical treatment beginning immediately. Psychological injury is just as real. The injury may progress more slowly than a direct physical injury to the body, but it is not unusual for psychological/psychiatric assistance to be required.

When you seek medical attention for symptoms associated with PTSD, you can expect the following:

- The physician will conduct a physical exam to identify any medical problems that could be causing the symptoms experienced. This should always be done, and it should be the first thing to expect.
- A psychological examination is likely to follow that includes a focus on symptoms, experience, and details of personal involvement in the traumatic event.
- The criteria stated in the Diagnostic and Statistical Manual of Mental Disorders (DSM-5) mentioned previously in this chapter will be used as the guide to determine the presence or absence of PTSD.

If medical attention is sought early, it is possible that ASD may be diagnosed, unless the symptoms have directly affected your life at home and work and have lasted more than 30 days. Following the diagnostics, there will likely be a specific treatment course your physician or medical team will take, depending on the severity of the symptoms, the details of how much trauma was experienced, the length of time symptoms have persisted, and if the symptoms appear to be getting worse.

Chapter 11 is devoted to summaries of major survival points raised in this book. These include how best to survive the attack itself, as well as how to survive psychologically. Although medical attention is often absolutely necessary and should always be sought if symptoms worsen or continue, there are many things we can do to help cope with the psychological effects.

11

How to Prevent Mass Victim Attacks

The best way to survive mass victim attacks is to prevent them from occurring. The largest successes of all have been when such attacks were stopped prior to being carried out. *See Something, Say Something* has worked to stop attacks that could have killed numerous innocent victims. Behavior does not occur in a vacuum. There are always indicators prior to a mass victim attack. There are antecedent events and situations encountered by a would-be attacker that serve to fuel the desire and drive of a would-be attacker. Others may encounter the same events and situations but respond in a very different and nonviolent manner.

Attacks require preparation, thought, and the decision to attack mass victims. It is not just about the attack itself. There are events and situations that occur that serve as antecedents to an attacker that serve to fuel the drive to attack. It is possible that a single behavior or statement may not be as disturbing as observing a series of behaviors or statements that appear to be getting worse.

Successful mass victim attacks are the result of many actions to prepare for an attack that either were not observed by others or not acted on. We have all seen on television or have read in the media the interviews of neighbors, friends, or family members after a mass victim attack. For the most part, preparation and concern were present but not reported. Just as important, when reports are actually made, officials need to investigate and act on the concerns that are being relayed. I would change *See Something, Say Something* to: *See Something, Say Something,* **Do** *Something.*

Prior to the 9/11 attack, the worst attack on U.S. soil, killing almost 3,000 people, the U.S. government knew of the threat for years. It had been reported that Osama bin Laden had ordered his followers to take pilot training in the United States and in other countries. There were mixed reasons given for this training, but all involved hijacking, and several included intelligence that airliners would be used to crash into structures.[1, 2, 3] Although investigation was underway, it did not result in preventative action prior to the 9/11 attack.

Some mass victim attackers have sought help. James Holmes, the Aurora, Colorado, Century 16 movie theatre attacker who killed 12 and injured 70, had sought psychiatric treatment. He had been brought to the attention of mental health services at the University of Colorado in Denver. His psychiatrist, Dr. Lynne Fenton, during Holmes's trial, indicated that Holmes had mentioned killing people several times a day and the thoughts were getting worse over time.

Although Holmes was acquiring weapons and checking out movie theatres, Dr. Fenton mentioned she could not do anything and place him in psychiatric hold because he had not mentioned specifics of a target. He had never mentioned suicide. His ex-girlfriend recounted how she had received messages from Holmes that he wanted to kill people. Just hours before the attack, Holmes mailed a notebook to his psychiatrist detailing his plans for the attack. Some victims' families are suing Dr. Fenton and the university for failure to intervene.[4]

Aaron Alexis, the Washington, D.C., Navy Yard attacker who killed 12 people and injured three (chapter 10), had brought himself to the attention of police a month before the incident. He self-reported that people were talking to him by microwaves through the floors and walls and were following him. There were clear indications of mental illness that should have been of concern. In some cases, the attacker himself recognized there was a problem and sought help.

Sometimes, it is just too late. Charles Whitman who killed 16 at the University of Texas, Austin, attack, and who was killed by a police officer, had left a diary requesting that his brain be checked after death. This was done, and he had a brain tumor that could have contributed to his worsening mental health condition. We need to ensure that those individuals who have mixed feelings about the thoughts that are driving them to a potential attack know how to seek mental health services and that mental health services intervene when necessary. The best person to prevent an attack is the attacker himself.

Prevention means acting on indicators, behaviors, thoughts, situations, and any other potential precursors that precede an attack. Those who are in the best position to see something threatening include family, friends, acquaintances, teachers, and neighbors. Because preparation for an attack could take months to years, there are often multiple occasions to observe behavior that may be cause for concern. As an example, Adam Lanza, the Sandy Hook

Elementary School killer, exhibited numerous signs that should have been reported by his mother. This could have prevented her from being killed, as well as the 20 children and six adults he shot to death (chapter 2).

Lanza's mother was aware of the level of disturbance of her son and had confided the issues to friends. His school work was accompanied by violent depictions and disturbing accounts of death and killings. When his mother searched his room, she found drawings of mutilated children and violent deaths drawn by him as his disturbance became worse.[5] Lanza eventually totally withdrew into a world of violent thoughts and target practice with the weapons purchased by his mother.

THE ROLES OF ANTECEDENTS AND BEHAVIORS

Over the past decades, I have led the development of scores of applications to predict threat. Having invented Automated Behavior Analysis (AuBA), the underlying approach is useful for anticipating threat and knowing what to observe that could be an indication of attacks without the automation tools.[6] AuBA, based on the foundations of applied behavior analysis, a field in psychology, stresses that behavior does not stand alone. There are antecedents (A) that precede behavior (B) and the behavior has consequences (C). Antecedents and consequences have profound effects on the behavior in question.

My definitions as related to mass victim attacks are as follows:

Antecedent
An antecedent is any event or situation that precedes a behavior that is logically associated with multiple occurrences of that behavior over time.

Behavior
The behavior is the specific act of an individual, group, or country that follows antecedents.

Consequence
The consequence is the effect of the behavior when it occurs. If the consequence is beneficial to the actor, then the behavior is more likely to occur when the antecedents or highly similar antecedents are present in the future.

The method I have used for prediction is to identify antecedents of past attacks that repeat and are associated with consequences that are beneficial to the attacker from the attacker's perspective. Then, monitor for these antecedents in the future. If a constellation of antecedents occur that were associated with past attacks or are highly similar, the probability that an attack will follow is increased.

Antecedents associated with past mass victim attacks can include such things as time of day, specifics of the location (e.g., nightclub, sporting event, house of worship, statements made, parades, shopping specials, school opening, etc.), or U.S. government actions against a favored group, among many others. These are events and situations that "attract" attacks based on the motivators of potential mass victim attackers. For example, the objective of a mass victim attack is to kill as many people as possible in the shortest amount of time. In the case of the Pulse nightclub attack in Orlando, Omar Mateen attacked late in the evening when the maximum number of people was partying. Four o'clock in the afternoon would not have been a good time because far fewer customers would be present.

For any location, the antecedents of interest can be determined prior to attack. What is the maximum crowd time of a public place? Are there few exits available? Is security absent? When is security not available? Business owners, security, and law enforcement need to understand the vulnerabilities of any locations surveyed. Vulnerabilities can be readily identified and rectified to make a location more secure. For example, a location may only have one entrance/exit, no windows, and no visible security, among other weaknesses.

Although vulnerabilities and how to strengthen locations is not the topic of this book, it should be said that it is not difficult to make locations more secure. Obvious changes could convince an attacker to go elsewhere, much like the obvious presence of an alarm system/cameras at a home can persuade a burglar to move on to another location.

Why are known antecedents valuable? Because when they occur in the future, we know we should be more careful, increase security, and ramp up vigilance and situational awareness. As one important example, we know that an attacker seeks maximum crowd density for his attack. The actual presence of the crowd may be more important that the event itself. For self-radicalized terrorists such as brothers Dzhokhar and Tamerlan Tsarnaev, their interest was not likely the marathon but a nearby gathering of a large crowd with a symbolic target that was an all-American activity. This means that such events as the Macy's Thanksgiving Day Parade, which was listed by ISIS as a target in 2017, and other public events are likely targets. They are symbolic and attract large crowds.

Antecedents set the stage for an imminent attack while actual attacker behaviors prior to an attack are present as preparation. Security and law enforcement, as well as everyone else, should be aware of both. If we observe a neighbor renting a moving truck that is parked in front of the house for a week and not used, this is enough to report to law enforcement, especially if accompanied by any other suspicious behavior. On October 31, 2017, 29-year-old Sayfullo Saipov, drove a rental truck from Home Depot down a bike path near the World Trade Center site, killing eight, before crashing into a bus and exiting. He was captured after being shot by a police officer (chapter 9).

The following tables (11.1 and 11.2) are provided as examples of two attacks showing antecedents versus preparation behaviors. The attacks are shown because they were very different approaches to killing multiple people.

Table 11.1 shows a breakdown of antecedents and preparation behaviors for the Boston Marathon attack. This type of analysis can be completed across all mass victim attacks and leads to characteristics included in this book. As can be seen, the fact that a symbolic, all-American event such as the Boston Marathon was scheduled to occur near the Tsarnaev brothers' residence near Boston made it a logical anti-U.S. target of convenience. In

Table 11. 1   Key Points Associated with the Boston Marathon Bombings

Antecedents	*Preparation Behaviors*	*The Attack*
Who, Where	*How, What: Bombing*	*When*
Boston: symbolic event	Locate plans for bombs: Internet	Time of race
Scheduled Boston Marathon	Purchase pressure cookers	Place two bombs
Finish line: maximum density	Purchase black powder	Detonate
Observers: distracted	Construct bombs/detonators	
U.S. actions in Iraq and Afghanistan	Fill with nails/ball bearings	

Table 11. 2   Key Points Associated with Sutherland Springs First Baptist Church Attack

Antecedents	*Preparation Behaviors*	*The Attack*
Who, Where	*How, What: Shooting*	*When*
Local church	Purchase weapons	Sunday morning service
Ex-wife family church	Purchase ammunition	Time of maximum density
Conflict with ex-wife family No security	Practice shooting at home	

addition, the large crowds, especially near the finish line, added to the attractiveness of the target, including the presence of innocent victims. As antecedents that drove motive, the Tsarnaev brothers were upset with U.S. actions in Afghanistan and Iraq that resulted in deaths of Muslims.

Bombings are indiscriminate, and explosives can be detonated once the attacker has left the scene of bomb placement. This is why reporting unattended packages is essential, especially if at any event or situation where there is a crowd. The pressure cooker bombs were straight out of the Al Qaeda magazine available on the Internet. The timing of the detonations was based on the brothers successfully leaving the scene after planting the backpacks that hid the loaded bombs.

Table 11.2 shows the breakdown of antecedents and behaviors associated with the mentally disturbed 26-year-old Devin Kelley's semi-automatic rifle attack on the First Baptist Church in Sutherland Springs, Texas (chapter 8). Antecedents for target selection included the church being local to him and the strong, threatening conflict with his ex-wife's family. The grandmother-in-law was present during the attack and was killed. The remainder of the family did not attend that day. Kelley had threatened the family repeatedly. Preparation included purchasing weapons and ammunition.

Attack timing was based on Sunday morning service time, which is the service of maximum attendance at small churches. My father, a Christian pastor, always worked to obtain maximum attendance at Sunday morning services.

It is important to note that officials can be lacking in their responsibility to report. Kelley's violent behavior was well known, even when he was in the air force. He received one year in jail for crushing his young stepson's skull and repeatedly beating his wife, and there were other crimes and serious threats. The result was a "bad conduct" discharge from the U.S. Air Force, yet the service did not report the conviction to the FBI. Such a report would have prevented Kelley from acquiring the firearms he openly purchased to commit the church massacre—an unfortunate breakdown of responsibility.

Targets for mass victim attacks are not random. Target selection is basically antecedent based. Given the common journalistic questions—who what, where, when, why, and how—the items are divided among antecedents and behavior. *Who* and *where* are antecedent based. A potential attacker must determine the target (who) and the location of the attack (where). Based on the motivations of the potential attacker, these are important considerations. *Who* may be innocent victims at a symbolic location. Innocent victims are more horrifying, and location is to amplify fear.

How and *what* are more method-based and tend to be associated with preparation behaviors. *What* type of attack? We have observed vehicle run-downs, stabbings, shootings, and bombings, as well as hybrids. Given what type of attack, *how* will it occur? *When* is obviously the timing of the attack itself. When is antecedent based as well. What are common attack antecedents? The time for maximum density of targets present is key.

The type of victims may be very important. In hate/bias attacks, the consideration is when the maximum density of hated targets will be present in one place. If workplace motivated, it is work hours. If a house of worship, it is worship time. If international, domestic, or self-radicalized terrorism, it is when a crowd is assembled at the target location. Mass victim attacks care much less about structure damage—the purpose is to kill people of all ages and physical capability literally ranging from the unborn and infants to the elderly. All are fair game. In most cases, these characteristics become the *why*.

It is important to realize that we could observe antecedents as well as actual threatening behaviors. We should be on the lookout for antecedents that lead to attacks, as well as the behaviors required to prepare for an attack.

INTERNATIONAL TERRORISM

Antecedents
- Increased U.S. efforts to counter Al Qaeda, ISIS, fringe elements, Taliban, or other known international adversaries
- Economic progress
- Recent military enhancements on global basis
- Anti-international terrorism rhetoric from U.S. leadership

Behaviors of Concern
- Anti-U.S. rhetoric
- Calls for attack
- Suggestions of targets
- Weapons of mass destruction preparation (bomb construction, pilot training)
- Practice with weapons
- Acquisition of guns, ammunition, and clips, with behavior not consistent with the activity

SELF-RADICALIZED TERRORISM

Antecedents
- U.S. efforts to identify self-radicalized (SR) elements in the U.S.
- U.S. efforts to decrease international terrorism influence

- U.S. provocative statements against radical Islam
- Anti-radical Islam behavior/statements among private groups

Behaviors of Concern
- U.S.-based person(s) preoccupied with anti-U.S. radical Islamic social media, blogs, or websites
- Communication with foreign international terrorism contacts
- Bomb preparation
- Rental of large vehicles without apparent use
- Acquiring blade weapons (e.g., knives, machetes, axes)
- Acquiring guns, particularly semi-automatic rifles and pistols
- Excessive home target practice

DOMESTIC TERRORISM

Antecedents
- U.S.-based law enforcement or military efforts directed against U.S. persons opposed to government activities or actions

Behaviors of Concern
- Expressed disgruntlement in the work setting
- Threats made to coworkers
- Acquiring bomb-making supplies (e.g., ammonium nitrate fertilizer, military-grade explosives)
- Acquiring homemade materials for bombs (e.g., pressure cookers, timers, pipes)
- Acquiring guns, ammunition, and clips, with behavior not consistent with the activity

HATE/BIAS

Antecedents
- Location of the hated group becomes apparent, such as a church that contains only member of the hated group (e.g., [in past attacks] African Americans, Sikhs, Jews)
- Time of hated-group gatherings

Behaviors of Concern
- Acquiring weapons, primarily semi-automatic weapons
- Weapons practice

- Wearing hate clothing (e.g., presence of swastikas, anti-group clothing statements/images)
- Stalking protests
- Wearing protective gear and carrying weapons at protests
- Preoccupation with harsh, anti-group bias or hate rhetoric in public or on blogs, websites, or other forms of social media (e.g., white supremacy, anti-religious, anti-race, anti-gender)

MENTAL HEALTH ISSUES

Antecedents and Behaviors of Concern

Antecedents to those suffering from mental health issues may be very different than for other, more rational mass victim attackers such as international terrorists, domestic terrorists, self-radicalized terrorists, and those driven by hate/bias. We certainly disagree with the motivators that drive these attackers, but, given their perceptions, they are easier to understand. Those suffering from mental health issues may respond to antecedents that are self-generated based on the level of disturbance they may be experiencing. In reality, antecedents may be internal and be fantasized and imagined.

Those suffering from mental health issues may hear voices, hallucinate events, situations, and actions that did not occur, or see events and behaviors that actually occurred in a much different way than actually happened (illusions). We cannot know what is going on in the heads of those suffering, but it may be obvious they are seeing and hearing things that are simply not there.

We may observe the affected person talking to himself or others who are not there, acting in such a way that simply is not appropriate for the situation, or reacting in strange ways to normal events. We must infer that the person is suffering, and use what is said and done as indicators that he is responding to events that are not based in reality. This can be a real concern if threatening statements or behaviors are being made in response to what they believe they are seeing and hearing.

- The person makes threatening statements or reacts to events that did not happen.
- The person, to us, is speaking nonsense, is angry, and has weapons (e.g., guns) or attempts to acquire weapons.
- The person makes threats toward others that are not based on reality.
- The person threatens suicide.

WHAT SHOULD BE OF CONCERN TO REPORT?

There are multiple types of people who can report when they see something of concern. There is self-reporting, family, friends, neighbors, employees, service people at work, and strangers. All are slightly different and afford different opportunities where one may see something of concern. These times range from many years with a family member to perhaps just a few seconds for a stranger or bystander. But first, what might you see that should raise concern to the point that it should be reported? In other words, when should you "say something"?

Any behavior that reveals:

- Special and repeated interest in violent, dangerous actions of others whereby innocent victims were stabbed, shot, bombed, or run down by a vehicle
- Interest includes collecting past news articles and other material focusing on mass victim attacks, killings, or any gruesome attacks,
- Frequenting anti-U.S. or racial/hate/bias websites or social media
- Posting anti-U.S. or racial/hate/bias content
- Writing a journal or manifesto with anti-U.S. or hate/bias content
- Repeated instances of violent or threatening behavior
- Ongoing criminal activity
- Appearance of purchasing guns and ammunition or blade weapons (knives, machetes, hatchets) and any practice with weapons combined with threatening behavior or actions
- Renting a truck that sits for days or weeks without obvious use
- Any appearance of acquiring or using bomb materials or explosives, including black powder, ammonium nitrate fertilizer, dynamite, or weapons-grade explosives, especially combined with threatening behavior or actions
- Any verbal or written stated plans or threats to hurt or kill others
- An obvious obsession with killing others
- Person is speaking nonsense and making threatening statements against a specific group that are not based on reality
- Suicide statements combined with threatening behavior, statements, or demeanor

SEE SOMETHING, SAY NOTHING?

In my review of past mass victim attacks, it was rare to review an attack where unusual behavior of concern was not witnessed by someone prior to an attack—almost always discovered on interview after the fact. It is clear that when attacks have been prevented, behaviors of concern were noted, leading to prevention and apprehension. This underscores a basic question, if unusual, threatening behaviors of concern combined with antecedents that force a concern, why don't those who *see something, say something?* Why not report?

See something, say something does not mean to say something to a friend, colleague, or family member. *Say something* means to report it to the proper authorities so that intervention will be be forthcoming. If it looks like preparation for an attack, call law enforcement. If it looks like an attack is ready to happen, call 911. Although I have not seen hard data to answer why more frequent reporting does not occur, I believe it is fair to say that most non-reporters fear revenge, retribution, discovery, or simply being disliked by the potential attacker if a family member. This creates *see something, say nothing.*

In private conversations, when I ask people if they believe they can make an anonymous phone call to tip off law enforcement, the answer is more often *no.* In these days of national security surveillance, wiretapping, reverse-look ups (available capabilities to obtain name and address from a phone number), and known lack of security on cell phones and social media, there is a basic distrust that makes anonymity appear to be elusive, at best. While I believe full information provided is the best, there are times when one would prefer to be anonymous. It is far better to be anonymous than to *say nothing*! *You can make an anonymous call to law enforcement!* This is how to ensure anonymity:

- There is a code for most countries that if dialed before you dial the number you want to call can block your number from being seen by the person called. For example, in the United States, if you dial *67 and then the number you want to call, including the "1" if long distance, your number will be blocked and the recipient will be unable to see your number. There are variations across countries. Rather than listing codes here that could change for any specific country, you can find this code for any specific country by searching on the Internet for "codes to block a phone number from being seen when making a call" or a variation of this search.

- There is an increasing number of law enforcement anonymous-tip telephone lines and websites. As one example, *We Tip* (https://wetip.com/submit-anonymous-tip-2) and anonymous telephone number (1-800-78-CRIME or 1-800-782-7463) are national tip lines.
- For some types of phone, you can go into settings and disable the feature that shows your phone number when you call. However, I recommend finding the specific code for your country and use it on a call-by-call basis.
- Don't use your phone—call from a public phone. Yes, they still exist. Use a hotel pay phone and cash only.
- Purchase a cheap disposable phone, or *burner* phone as they are called, make your call, and then dispose of the phone. Both can be prepaid with cash, and the number is for temporary use only. Disposables may be used a little longer than burner phones, with the latter purchased typically for a one-time call and then tossed along with the number.
- If not an emergency, type it, print it, and mail it to local law enforcement. Leave off the return address and don't sign it.
- Be aware that anonymous tips may not be taken as seriously as those with identification, but they do matter. If anonymous, be specific about what the concern is, and if the actions/behaviors are getting worse.

WHO IS REPORTED?

Who is reported and who is doing the reporting can make a difference. If the person heading down the path of violent behavior is a son or daughter, it may be more difficult to report than if the person is an unknown neighbor. This is why anonymous reporting must be an option. An anonymous call or anonymous tip on an anonymous law enforcement website, could literally save the life of the person heading for an attack, as well as the lives of many potential innocent victims. It could also save the potential attacker from a life in prison. A family member may be much more willing to provide an anonymous tip, and this should be respected by local and federal law enforcement.

SELF-REPORTING

Some mass victim attackers have attempted to proclaim their plans to kill others prior to the attack. The reasons are mixed and can range from bragging to a need to be stopped of an obsession that cannot be controlled and a compulsion to kill many people. For the braggart, it is to gain respect from like-minded individuals in his circle of friends or to gain the attention of an organized group such as international terrorists. The person suffering from severe mental health issues may very well complete the act, although reluctant and wanting to be stopped. I have gone by the assumption in my career that if it doesn't make sense at any level, then mental health issues are likely at play.

The following are some guidelines for anyone wanting intervention from carrying out a vicious act. If you are that person, follow the advice. If you know someone, copy the page and leave it for them anonymously. If an attack appears imminent, then call 911, and if in the planning stages, contact local law enforcement, even if trying to get the person to self-report.

- If you are experiencing feelings of being driven beyond self-control, seek help at a local mental health clinic or hospital. However, do not stop here. Also report yourself to local law enforcement. This provides two avenues to help prevent a horrible act.
- If you are contemplating killing multiple people at one time and you are ready to attack, report yourself to 911 and request immediate assistance. Explain that you can't stop yourself from attacking. Give specifics of the target and your exact location.
- If you are reporting yourself, present staff and law enforcement officers with any written plans, journals, or manifestos that you have prepared. Describe the plan, including weapon type and planned timing of the attack.
- If you have been treated for mental health issues and have been prescribed medication, do not miss medication. Take all medications as directed by your physician. Give your physician or therapist/counselor a call and tell them you need immediate help. Go to the emergency room or local law enforcement office—they will help you.
- If you feel suicidal, seek assistance immediately at a local mental health clinic or hospital. Don't just call, but actually go there.

FAMILY MEMBER

Family members have repeated opportunities over a considerable amount of time to observe a family member who may be having issues, may be converting to radical Islamic terrorism, or harboring strong hate/bias, or growing anti-U.S. sentiment. They also could be suffering from severe mental health issues. If this is happening, you will know it. If combined with obsession to obtain weapons, threats, and repeated examples of violent behavior, there should be raised concern.

As a family member, we often feel protective and hope for the best. We are willing to overlook threatening behavior, violent statements, suicidal talk, repeated violence, criminal activity, and even physical or mental abuse, because the offender is family. It is easy to overlook violent behavior as a "stage" and things will get better. Change your way of thinking. Assume it will get worse, not better.

A family member typically does not want to report on another family member. There may be much wishful thinking that all will be OK, the person doing the reporting fears he or she will never be forgiven. However, if behaviors and statements are threatening and there are expressed plans to harm others, the fact that the person is a family member is not the primary consideration. If concern is raised, it is far better to intervene before an act occurs than to be sorry that many were killed and maybe the family member was killed or took his own life. Intervention is better than the alternative for all concerned.

It is OK to express concern directly to the family member of concern if you feel safe to do so. If you do not feel safe, call local law enforcement and explain the concern specifically or provide an anonymous tip. If you report a family member, indicate the behavior of concern, any writings or statements of concern, social media or website postings of concern, criminal behavior, and any verbal or physical abuse.

How do you know what should be reported? My answer: You will know. We all have a lifetime of experience learning the good from the bad, the comfortable from the frightening, and fear from safety. Trust your senses. If you feel concerned, then there is likely a very good reason. Are we always correct—no! That is all the more reason why we should be specific when we report something we have seen that concerns us. Law enforcement is experienced in recognizing threat from descriptions of behavior. This is what they do for a living. If you believe that you have observed something that may be threatening, then report, even if anonymously. Let law enforcement pursue it. Importantly, if you do not see action from authorities, report again and inquire why something is not being done. If still no action, then call 911 or federal law authorities (e.g., the FBI). Remember, you are trying to save lives and do not accept inaction.

Family members have many opportunities to observe disturbing behavior. However, the concerned family member may not know what to do. All states in the United States have laws that provide forced observation in an approved setting if there is evidence of danger to self or others. Both are important.

Call law enforcement if the family member is making threats toward others or expressing suicidal thoughts.

In many cases, those with suicidal thoughts and actions force others to kill them. This is true with mass victim attacks, as well. *Suicide by cop* is an expression that means a person commits an act that forces law enforcement to stop the act by killing the perpetrator. Threats combined with suicidal behavior and statements is a dangerous combination, even if a family member.

FRIENDS

Friends are very special. Sometimes friends are closer than actual family. We are born into family with no choice, but friends are family we select. This can make it very difficult to report a friend, even if on an anonymous basis.

So, you now have concerns. Your friend is not the same anymore. He has become more isolated, and his behavior and statements are more extreme. Although your friend has been loyal for many years, and you have shared many interests, you have noticed that he has become more extreme. He expresses hate for the United States, allegiance for international terrorists, expresses strong bias against racial, religious, or ethnic groups, or seems to be becoming increasingly irrational, and your concern has grown. Now you see some behaviors of concern. He is posting hate or anti-U.S. posts on social media, and is being outspoken, expressing hate for all U.S.-supported groups and associations. Perhaps he is suddenly acquiring weapons and/or ammunition. Trust your instincts. If your friend is heading down the wrong path, you need to intervene.

NEIGHBORS

Because of close proximity, neighbors have numerous opportunities to observe behaviors of those who live in proximity to them. You may know your neighbors well, or not know them at all. But their comings and goings and behaviors within the neighborhood and around the house, apartment, townhouse, or condominium are difficult to miss.

Prior to the Sayfullo Saipov October 31, 2017, rented truck run-down of victims in Manhattan, Saipov's neighbors reported after the attack that they were suspicious of his and the family's behavior for weeks to months prior to the attack. The family kept to themselves and the wife was rarely seen. When she was seen, she wore a *niqab*, the Muslim veil that covers the face except for the eyes. This was unusual because other Muslim women in the neighborhood were not as conservative.

Saipov also rented trucks like the one later used in the attack. The rented vehicles would sit in the street for many days without being used except for an occasional outing with the same two friends. Neighbors reported after the event that Saipov was practicing. It is difficult for neighbors to not give something away if planning a major attack. According to one neighbor, Saipov rented the type of trucks from Home Depot that are used for construction, but never did any construction work.[7]

Again, if there is concern for safety, you can report through any of a number of anonymous methods. One way to determine if there is enough cause for reporting is that if you see multiple behaviors that appear not to be right or suspicious, then it is best to report. For example, Saipov rented trucks that sat in the street unused in a climate where sympathizers have been asked by ISIS and Al Qaeda to conduct run-downs; the family appeared to be devout Muslim; and the same suspicious friends would come and go mysteriously. Any single behavior could be of less concern, but when taken together, concern increases. However, even a single instance of a threatening behavior can raise enough concern to be reported. For example, if three pressure cooker boxes are seen in a neighbor's trash, given the current climate, I would report it anonymously.

Don't worry about being politically correct if it appears there is real threat. Don't let the fact that the suspected person is a member of a particular racial, religious, or ethnic group deter you. If you reported on this fact alone, then that would not be warranted. However, if threatening actions and behaviors are present, do not let group membership prevent you from reporting.

WORK

The workplace is unique. We may spend as much time or more with coworkers than family members. We become familiar with our workplace and coworkers. However, how we don't truly get to know all coworkers. Unless we socialize with coworkers, we may not know their interests, hobbies, pastimes, or even political leanings. In many workplaces, coworkers are reluctant to voice political leanings unless they are very close to one and other.

In short, we know coworkers well enough to determine what would be called normal behavior over time. This means that anomalous behavior, or behavior that is not typical, stands out. Although there can be many reasons for unusual behavior, the focus here is on potential mass victim attack preparation.

It is also important to realize that some mass victim attacks are hybrids. In other words, the person observed may not fit neatly into a single category such as international terrorism, domestic terrorism, self-radicalized terrorism, hate/bias, or mental health issues. For example, Major Nidal Hassan's attack at Fort Hood, Texas, was a mixture of self-radicalized terrorism, workplace violence (hate/bias), and domestic terrorism. Regardless of "type," Hassan walked into a room at Fort Hood, killed 13 people and injured 30 others. This is definitely an example of *see something, say nothing.* Although a U.S. Army major (psychiatrist), he wore Muslim dress on base, made strong anti-U.S. statements, and exhibited multiple examples of radical Islam leanings.

What Should Concern Us in the Workplace?

We should be aware of changes in coworkers in the workplace, That is, changes that should be of concern. The following are among the most significant changes that should be of concern to us:

- The coworker is expressing strong disagreement with the organization or specific managers that includes threatening statements (e.g., I wish he/she was dead, I could kill him/her, etc.).
- The coworker is increasingly disgruntled and unhappy, with emotional charges made against specific staff.
- The coworker expresses desire to purchase or has stated that he/she has purchased a weapon.
- The coworker appears to be self-radicalized, expressing strong radical Islamic statements against the United States or specific managers or employees.
- The person starts wearing Muslim dress while at the same time expressing strong anti-U.S. or anti-organization statements.
- The person makes repeated threats of harm directed against other employees or management.
- The person has quit employment at the organization or has been terminated based on disgruntlement or threats being made and shows up at work unannounced.
- The person, whether currently employed or formerly employed, uses social media to make threats directed toward other employees.
- Any evidence that an employee might have a weapon at work.
- You feel personally threatened by a coworker.

To report, immediately go to human resources (HR) to file a complaint if you have trust that all will be held in confidence. If you do not have trust in

HR (some may be "leaky"), then file an anonymous law enforcement report detailing what specifically is of concern. Does your place of employment have security? You can also report to security, but again make sure all will be in confidence.

Disgruntled coworkers, if upset with you, can harbor grudges or want to seek revenge if they know that you reported them.

IMMINENT THREAT

Imminent threat is different. If you believe that a threat is present, and an attack is about to happen, call 911 and report immediately. Local law enforcement should always be called if behaviors are observed that could lead to a mass victim attack.

The following will provide examples of when you should call 911.

- Someone has placed a package on the ground, leaving it unattended. Immediately tell those around the unattended package, backpack, suitcase, or any other unattended container to move far away and call 911.
- You have witnessed someone having a weapon where a weapon is not allowed (e.g., airport, movie theatre, mall, sporting event, performance, etc.); immediately call 911 and report the exact location and what you have observed. Be as specific as you can.
- The suspected person has left with a concealed weapon or backpack after making such statements as "I will fix everything now," "people will now be sorry," or any threatening statement.

CROWD AWARENESS

The number-one consideration in mass victim attacks is the attacker's requirement that there be a crowd of potential victims gathered in one location. A crowd increases the number of people that can be killed at one time if a bombing or if the attacker is using semi-automatic guns. If the attack is a stabbing or a vehicle run-down, a crowd provides more opportunity for fatalities and injuries. This means that you should have increased situational awareness in any crowded location. Awareness can pay off, especially if suspicious or threatening behavior is spotted prior to an attack.

The crowd is more important than the actual location. We have seen mass victim attacks in fast-food restaurants, bars, clubs, sporting events, malls, movie theatres, the Pentagon, the World Trade Center, government building/

offices, workplaces, military bases and installations, elementary schools, high schools, colleges/universities, houses of worship, and streets with pedestrians. Although there may be a reason for picking an exact location, there would not be an attack without a crowd.

When in a crowd of any type or location, put away the smartphone and stop texting or listening to music. You need your senses functioning and focused on the crowd and situation. It is important to immediately report suspicious behavior. Prevention is our number-one way to survive mass victim attacks.

12

Successful Prevention

Watching and reading the news can lead us to believe that we are helpless when it comes to protecting against mass victim attacks. The descriptions, videos, and survivor accounts are horrifying. The attacks are without mercy, and anyone from the unborn to infants to the helpless are killed or severely injured. Women, children, men, the physically and mentally challenged have been unfortunate fatalities and survivors with lifelong disabilities. However, we are not as aware of the many successes in preventing mass victim attacks. Successful prevention is not as sensational for media to cover. Therefore, we tend to know less about attacks being prevented than actual attacks.

To keep all in perspective, in the time since the 9/11 Al Qaeda attack, many mass victim attacks have been prevented in the United States, as well as in other countries. There have been successes, and we are getting better at prevention. To continue improving success rates in preventing mass victim attacks, we must first understand the reasons why we have had successes. Was it *See Something, Say Something*, increased personal security, more rapid law enforcement response, or improved pre-attack intelligence and investigation?

We must remember the underlying reasons for mass victim attacks. As this book has presented, international terrorism, domestic terrorism, self-radicalized terrorism, hate/bias, and mental health issues are all evident. Because we have not solved many of the various underlying issues that feed these types of attacks, we cannot expect significant reductions in their occurrences. But, with improved methods, prevention can be successful, and we can learn how to better survive.

As an example of making strides against international terrorism, at the time of writing this book, the ISIS (ISIL) caliphate has been destroyed in

Syria. The caliphate was a Jihadi-declared state, with Raqqa, Syria, being the center. This caliphate lasted for over three years and was a breeding ground for attacks against non-Jihadists, including the fueling of ISIS mass victim attacks. U.S. military and U.S.-backed forces have been successful with this mission. However, Al Qaeda and ISIS organizations are still alive and capable of mass victim attacks, as well as strong recruitment and encouragement of self-radicalized followers.

SUCCESSFUL PREVENTION OF MASS VICTIM ATTACKS AND FATALITIES

Successful prevention of mass victim attacks has, no doubt, saved countless fatalities and injuries. There are lists of successfully prevented plots and attacks. For example, the Heritage Foundation tracks such successes with international terrorism that is radical Islamic-inspired. This can include self-radicalized terrorism as well. In one such report, they listed 60 successes since 9/11.[1] Although it is beyond the scope of this book to highlight all successes, they fall into categories which will be highlighted here to demonstrate how successful prevention has been.

Categories of successes have included: (1) prevention of attacks from occurring, and (2) decreasing loss of life and injuries at the time of attack. First, through law enforcement investigative methods, including informants and infiltration, plots have been discovered and attacks prevented from occurring. As a second category of effectiveness, an attack has started but through quick intervention by affected citizens or rapid law enforcement response, additional fatalities and injuries were prevented from occurring.

By far the most successful prevention has been the methods and diligence of local and federal law enforcement. A detailed list of successful prevention, such as the one referenced, as well as additional research, demonstrates the value of discovery of plots to engage in mass victim attacks. Discovery has occurred in several ways, including the use of informants, monitoring social media such as chat rooms, and the successful covert infiltration of anti-U.S. groups and organizations.

There have been multiple examples of sting operations. For example, once a plot, such as a bombing, is discovered, law enforcement infiltrators may help the group acquire the materials for the planned bomb and follow through with attempted detonation at a target site. However, the group does not know the bomb is an ineffective dud. However, for legal purposes, there is no doubt of the intent to engage in an attack with a weapon of mass destruction. As a result of such methods, there are scores of would-be attackers serving lengthy sentences in prison, including life sentences, for their attempts to engage in mass victim attacks.

The most effective prevention has occurred in the categories of terrorism. Hate/bias and mental health disorder–based attacks have been more difficult to prevent. Why? Attacks born out of hate/bias and mental health issues are more private and depend little on others. In hate/bias attacks, the focus is to hit a hated group. This can include workplace violence in which a disgruntled member of the organization returns to seek revenge against a hated group of employees. Attacks born out of mental health issues or disorders may be the result of living out fantasies divorced from reality or seeking much-needed recognition. It is essential that family, friends, acquaintances, or neighbors report suspicious activities of those fitting into these two categories.

Hate/bias and mental health disorders still have pre-incident antecedents and behaviors that are present. Social media postings, website searching for liked-minded individuals, sharing violent plans on social media, surveillance, and personal communications with others motivated by the same drivers all exist.

See Something, Say Something has resulted in many reports. However, such reports are from untrained individuals and overall have not been that useful. For example, it has been reported that the number of suspicious package reports in New York grew from 814 in 2002 to 37,614 in 2006. The *See Something, Say Something* slogan, created by Allen Kay, an advertising executive, has been adopted by multiple agencies, including the Department of Homeland Security.[2] Although there have been rare cases in which reports led to prevention, the reports have been far less effective than law enforcement and investigative efforts.

See Something, Say Something has contradictions. On one hand, reports of effectiveness indicate that there are many "Say Somethings" per day, while other reports indicate that the public is afraid to report. Political correctness has become an overriding concern. To quote from the Department of Homeland Security site that encourages *See Something, Say something*:

> *Protecting Citizens' Civil Rights & Civil Liberties*
> The "If You See Something, Say Something™" campaign respects citizens' privacy, civil rights, and civil liberties by emphasizing behavior, rather than appearance, in identifying suspicious activity.
> Factors such as race, ethnicity, and/or religious affiliation are not suspicious. The public should only report suspicious behavior and situations (e.g., an unattended backpack or package, or someone breaking into a restricted area). Only reports that document behavior that is reasonably indicative of criminal activity related to terrorism will be shared with federal partners.[3]

The intent here is to try to focus reporting on suspicious behavior and not simply on ethnicity or appearance. However, if suspicious behavior is present and you have concerns, you should never let ethnicity, religious affiliation, or appearance prevent you from reporting—just emphasize the suspicious behavior. It is OK if emphasizing behavior to mention ethnicity, religious affiliation, or appearance.

Although *See Something, Say Something* is a valuable concept if used correctly, this is not the overwhelming reason why attacks have been prevented. The overriding reason attacks have been prevented is simple: improved and effective law enforcement intervention. We have learned much since the 9/11 attack. It was a wake-up call for law enforcement and intelligence services. The attack resulted in the formation of the Department of Homeland Security. Law enforcement agencies are working together more now than at the time of 9/11.

EXAMPLES: CITIZENS AND SUCCESSFUL PREVENTION

Citizen prevention can be viewed in two ways: (1) prevention of mass victim attacks, and (2) prevention of additional loss of life during an attack as a result of intervention. As previously presented, the vast majority of attacks prevented from occurring has been the result of official law enforcement actions. However, citizens have assisted in prevention as well. Although fewer than law enforcement successes, citizens have provided significant assistance in thwarting either an attack or reducing the number of deaths and injuries during an attack. There are a few examples.

- Khalid Ali-M Aldawsari was a Saudi Arabian citizen living in Texas. He had ordered phenol (carbolic acid), which is a dangerous and highly toxic substance that is also used to make improvised explosive devices (IED). *The commercial supplier and shipping company staff were suspicious and reported the order to the authorities (i.e., See Something, Say Something).* The FBI arrested Aldawsari after surveillance showed online searching on how to construct an IED and search for suitable targets. He had acquired most of the materials required.[4] He was sentenced to life in prison.

  The following examples illustrate how citizens not acting in an official law enforcement or security role have assisted in decreasing the number of fatalities and injuries:
- Perhaps the most well-known example of citizen involvement in attempting to prevent a mass victim attack from taking multiple lives is the attempt on the part of passengers aboard United Airlines flight 93 to

prevent a successful hijacking from ending in tragedy. On September 1, 2001, four airliners were hijacked by Al Qaeda terrorists working in concert and using the hijacked airliners as weapons of mass destruction. As all likely know, two planes were flown into the North and South towers of the World Trade Center in Manhattan and a third was flown into the Pentagon. However, the fourth did not make it to its target.

Through cell phone calls, passengers on the flight discovered that the planes were being used to crash into targets. There was a vote, and three passengers, after saying their goodbyes to family on cell phones and aided by flight attendants, rushed to the front of the plane to gain control of the hijackers. The hijacker pilot, in response to the attempted intervention, violently tilted the plane back and forth and then finally turned it upside down and crashed it into the ground near Shanksville, Pennsylvania, at over 500 miles per hour and loaded with 7,000 gallons of fuel. All aboard perished. It appears the target was the White House, the Capitol, a nuclear power plant, or Camp David presidential retreat. Due to these brave individuals, and credit to all passengers lost on that flight, the target was not reached.

- In December 2001 Richard Reid had a significant impact on air travel that is still being felt today. In a flight from Paris to Miami, Florida, Reid had placed explosives inside his shoes. He attempted to light the fuses to the explosives while the plane was in the air, but was denied an explosion when passengers and flight attendants subdued him. The airliner made an emergency landing and he was arrested. He is serving a life sentence. We are still removing our shoes prior to boarding today.

  In a similar manner, in December 2009 Umar Farouk Abdulmutallab attempted to detonate an explosive he had hidden in his underwear on a flight from Amsterdam to Detroit, Michigan. He had acquired two chemicals, pentaerythritol tetranitrate (PETN) and acetone peroxide (TATP). PETN is similar to the more known nitroglycerin and TATP is used because it is difficult to detect. Although the substance caught fire, passengers and flight attendants quickly tackled and subdued Abdulmutallab and extinguished the fire. He was apprehended on landing and was later sentenced to life imprisonment.[5]

- At the Sunday, November 5, 2017, Sunday service at the First Baptist Church in Sutherland Springs, Texas, Devin Kelley approached the church and started shooting. He then entered the small church, targeting the congregation. He killed 26 and injured 20. As he was leaving the church, a nearby neighbor, Stephen Willeford, starting shooting at Kelley to stop him. Willeford's gunfire hit Kelley in the leg and torso. Kelley was able to make it to his vehicle and left. Willeford, with the assistance of a nearby driver, Johnnie Langendorff, in his own vehicle, took pursuit. Kelley's vehicle eventually crashed, and he was found with a self-inflicted gunshot wound that ended his life (see chapter 8).

- On September 17, 2016, self-radicalized Dahir Adan committed a hit-and-run of a bicyclist and then approached the Crossroads Center mall in St. Cloud, Minnesota (see chapter 5), with two long knives and started a stabbing attack directed at innocent victims. Jason Falconer, an off-duty policeman who was armed, pursued Adan. It was a confusing situation in that Adan was in a security uniform and Falconer, the plainclothes off-duty officer, was pursuing Adan with a raised gun. Falconer kept showing bystanders his badge, explaining he was the police. Adan approached Falconer twice in a threatening manner and Falconer shot Adan six times, killing him.

Although there are few examples of citizen reporting resulting in actual prevention of a mass victim attack, we see that citizens have assisted during attacks. It should be noted that guns were used by some citizens in preventing additional deaths and injuries. It is difficult to stop an active shooter without the use of force. In the case of the attempted bombings, passengers sprang to action and were able to manually overpower the attackers.

KNOW THE FUTURE THREAT

To date, mass victim attacks have included guns, blade objects for stabbings, vehicles for run-downs, bombs, and even hijacked airliners used as weapons of mass destruction (e.g., 9/11 attack). My work on terrorism and other mass victim types of threat began 32 years ago. In this time, I have witnessed a change in tactics and planning, as well as in the attacks themselves. We even see a difference between the massive 9/11 attack, in which nearly 3,000 people died and many thousands were injured, and those of more recent years. The new trend is to recruit or use self-radicalized zealots in low technology attacks against *soft* targets. A soft target for mass victim attacks is basically a group of innocent, vulnerable, and unprotected individuals.

Low technology attacks follow the Al Qaeda and ISIS instructions and communications. It is easy for a self-radicalized individual to use a rented vehicle or sharp blade weapons to attack, kill, and injure multiple victims. They do not require training or funding, or need to visit a terrorist organization in a foreign country. The attacks are simple, horrifying, and serve the purpose of terrorizing others.

However, we must keep alert and be aware of potential large-scale attacks using weapons of mass destruction. The new trend in vehicle run-downs and stabbings does not mean there is not planning for a massive 9/11 type of attack. Before the 9/11 attack, there was little to suggest an attack whereby multiple airliners could be hijacked almost simultaneously and essentially be used as guided suicide missiles. But, it happened. This type of threat still exists, although I would expect a different method. Today, if a small group of terrorists threatened a plane full of passengers with a box cutter or knife, I believe they would immediately be overpowered. *My suggestion to airlines is to arm all staff on board with pepper spray and other nonlethal defensive weapons such as Tasers.*

To successfully prevent mass victim attacks in the future, we must be aware of much more than how events in the past unfolded. The past is important, and we are likely to see much more of the same in the future. However, there are new threats, new bad actors, and more advanced ways of killing innocent people. Prevention and survival in the future requires understanding of both past threats and methods and what *could* be coming in the future.

CHEMICAL, BIOLOGICAL, RADIOLOGICAL, NUCLEAR, AND HIGH-YIELD EXPLOSIVE (CBRNE)

The referenced list provides dangerous chemical, biological, radiological, and nuclear agents (CBRN) available today to terrorists who have attacked the United States.[6] Many add high-yield explosives (CBRN*E*) to this list because they can be obtained or created from scratch (e.g., ANFO, made from readily available ammonium nitrate fertilizer and fuel oil).

Why should we be concerned about such weapons of mass destruction? Because they are well within the reach and current capabilities of terrorist organizations, particularly if they have support and resources provided by nation states (e.g., Iran among others). In the following section, I highlight these risks. We should make no mistake that such organizations as Al Qaeda and ISIS still desire mass victim attacks of even more massive proportions than those we have seen.

Chemical Weapons

On March 20, 1995, five Aum Shinrikyo cult teams of two terrorists per team boarded separate subways from a Tokyo, Japan, subway hub, and in a coordinated manner released toxic Sarin gas. The attack killed 12 passengers with 5,500 treated in hospitals. Many were in a coma when treated, and some suffered permanent damage to eyes, lungs, or digestive systems. Although the effects of the attack were devastating, the delivery of the poisonous gas was not efficient. A U.S. Senate committee that investigated the attack later estimated that if delivered properly, the Sarin gas might have resulted in the death of tens of thousands.[7]

Toxic substances are indiscriminate and will affect all who come into contact with them. The purpose of chemical substances is to kill massive numbers of people and, unfortunately, there is no shortage of such substances. The following are examples.

Cyanides

Sodium or potassium cyanides: white to pale chemical that can be easily used to poison food or drinks.

Hydrogen cyanide (HCN) and cyanogen chloride (CICN): colorless to pale liquids that turn into gas at room temperature.

Symptoms

Symptoms can include nausea, heart palpitations, vomiting, mental confusion, and heavy and rapid breathing. If not treated immediately, exposure can progress to total confusion, extreme irritability, coma (passing out), and ultimately death. High doses can cause immediate breakdown of body systems resulting in collapse.

Survival

- Do not touch wet or greasy surfaces associated with foods, especially under suspicious conditions (sodium or potassium cyanides).
- HCN has an odor of bitter almonds, and CICN has a choking odor.
- Both HCN and CICN must be highly concentrated in an enclosed area to be lethal. Ventilate immediately and leave. Time is of the essence.

Mustard Agent

To dispel any misconception, this is NOT mustard that goes on a hamburger. In its toxic form, it can be clear to dark brown with a garlic-like smell. It is labeled as a blister agent because exposure results in just that— harmful and extensive blisters both external, on skin, and/or internally. It can occur as a liquid (room temperature) or as a gas. Both are exceedingly harmful, if not deadly. Mustard gas is not commercially available, but instructions are available on how to develop this toxic chemical.

Symptoms

Noted as a slower acting agent, the first contact may result in mild skin irritation which becomes more severe with fluid-filled blisters yellow in color. If inhaled, the lungs can be damaged, which results in labored breathing. In severe cases, death may result from actual suffocation due to water in the lungs and the inability to receive enough oxygen to sustain life. Symptoms might take 6 to 24 hours to appear. Unfortunately, there are few medical remedies once the process has started.

Survival

- Be aware of strong smelling substances such as garlic under unusual or suspect circumstances. Leave. Escape.
- If in an enclosed space such as a building or subway and strong noxious smells are noticed, escape at the first opportunity. If in a subway, you can always get the next ride if mistaken. Better safe than sorry.
- Seek medical assistance at any first signs of skin irritation or any form of blistering after being in an enclosed, crowded, space. If the irritation appears to be getting worse, drop everything and seek emergency medical services at once.
- Concern is raised if in a high-target area such as New York City, Washington, D.C., or high population subway or transportation hub.

Military-Grade Chemicals

Sarin, Tabun, and VX are military-grade chemicals that are nerve agents. This means that if a person comes in contact with them, the nervous system is attacked. Because Sarin, Tabun, and VX are not available commercially, possession alone is cause for concern. The only purpose of a person not in an appropriate research or clinical setting to have any of these substances would be to weaponize any of the agents to cause death and injuries—at least that should be the assumption.

Symptoms

Sarin, Tabun, and VX are extremely toxic, and it takes relatively small amounts to achieve the wanted malicious effects. However, there are other substances that are less toxic but reach lethal levels if used in larger amounts. These other substances, according to the CIA site listed, are labeled as toxic industrial chemicals.

Toxic Industrial Chemicals

Two examples of these substances include Chlorine and Phosgene. Sarin, Tabun, and VX must be prepared by an expert. As mentioned, they are not commercially available. Although Chlorine and Phosgene are less toxic, they are present in large enough amounts to rival the commercially unavailable toxic chemicals. Perhaps one of the more significant vulnerabilities posed by Chlorine and Phosgene is that they are often shipped by truck or rail in very large quantities—large enough to be severely toxic, if released. Explosive detonation at the right location could be devastating. If tanks are ruptured by an explosion at the right time and at the right place, the effects could be highly similar to the release of a mustard agent.

Organophosphate pesticides include many different products but have highly similar actions. Products such as Parathion act as nerve agents if released in large quantities. They are not only highly toxic to insects, but also to humans. In fact, that is how they work against pest insects. Unfortunately, they also have the same nerve agent effect on humans even if less toxic than typically unavailable nerve agents. The solution for those with malicious intent to kill others is to ensure the release of large amounts of the substance. The agricultural pesticide can be purchased by the ton without raising concern if it appears the purchase is for agricultural pest control.

Symptoms

There are a number of symptoms related to nerve agent exposure, as well as other substances listed in this section. If interested, detailed information may be found on the Centers for Disease Control (CDC) website.[8] However, primary symptoms of nerve agent exposure consist of pupils contracting to pinpoint size, more salivation than normal, and convulsions. All can progress to the point of death.

Survival

- Leave the scene immediately, and try not to breathe in deeply—cover mouth and nose with shirt or other form of clothing or material when leaving and slowly breathe through the material only.
- Seek emergency medical treatment immediately. The speed of acquiring medical assistance is very important to survival.

Biological Agents

Biological agents are substances that are living or capable of replicating. There are well over 1,000 that are capable of infecting humans. However, there are several that are of extreme concern that can be used to cause mass fatalities. Anthrax, Botulinum toxin, and Ricin are among the top of the list of substances that can be weaponized and used against a target of a massive number of innocent people.

Anthrax

Perhaps the number one biological agent of concern is Anthrax. It can be found in nature, and cultivated, it is highly toxic, and has been used in attacks before. It occurs as spores, and can be weaponized as a spray (aerosol) or used to contaminate food. Less than a month after the 9/11 attack, reports of individuals contracting Anthrax delivered as a fine powder in mail started to surface. Letters were mailed to a news anchor, major politicians, and New York post offices—all mailed from Trenton, New Jersey.

The series of mailings resulted in five deaths, including two postal workers. Seventeen lived, but became ill.[9] After much investigation, and given there was a suspect, no arrests were ever made. The suspect was Dr. Bruce Ivins, a microbiologist researcher at Fort Detrick, Maryland, who committed suicide by overdose after learning that criminal charges were going to be made. The series of events underscore the harsh reality of how Anthrax can be weaponized and how deadly the substance can be. Anthrax is typically fatal unless treatment is started within hours of exposure.

Of increasing concern is the potential for a foreign country–supported attack against U.S. citizens. Recent reports have indicated that North Korea is testing the use of ICBMs loaded with a warhead containing Anthrax. To date, the missiles are capable of reaching any spot in the United States from North Korea.[10]

Symptoms

- Symptoms can occur within a day up to a week.
- Symptoms can include fever, extreme fatigue, malaise (general uneasiness or discomfort), and shortness of breath.

Survival

- If exposure is suspected or known, immediately seek emergency treatment. Immediate treatment within hours of exposure is necessary for survival.
- If symptoms occur hours to days after exposure, still seek immediate medical treatment. There is a form of Anthrax that can occur with skin contact that usually is not fatal.

- If food or drink is suspect, avoid it at all costs.
- FDA-approved BioThrax Anthrax vaccine is now available and may be used if exposure is anticipated or after exposure (especially for first responders, law enforcement, and military—not yet publicly available).[11]

Ricin

Ricin is extremely toxic, being many times more deadly than military grade VX by weight. A dangerous substance, it can be easily extracted from common castor beans. Because it is slightly off-white in color and odorless, Ricin is extremely difficult to detect. Unfortunately, there is not a known treatment if it enters the bloodstream. Fortunately, it would take a significant amount, if inhaled, to be fatal. The substance breaks down in food if heated. It can be delivered by food, air, or water.

Symptoms

- If inhaled, within 4 to 24 hours, symptoms would include increasing difficulty in breathing, fever, cough, nausea, tightness in the chest, and heavy sweating. Because of difficulty in breathing and fluid buildup in the lungs, skin may turn blue.
- If ingested, symptoms will occur within 10 hours and include vomiting and diarrhea.

Survival

Survival depends on how Ricin enters the body.
- If exposure occurs inside, then go outside immediately to get fresh air, and if expected exposure outside, immediately leave that area.
- Remove clothing and wash your entire body—don't pull clothing over the head but cut it off to avoid getting the substance on the face.
- Seek immediate medical attention at first suspicion of contact, regardless of method of contact.[12]

Botulinum toxin

Botulinum toxin is a naturally occurring substance found in soil. It is one of the most toxic substances known and is among the top agents as a potential weapon of mass destruction. Instructions to produce this toxin have been found in terrorist training manuals. However, it is difficult to weaponize but likely to be effective in small, enclosed spaces (such as a movie theatre).[13]

Symptoms

- Symptoms can occur 24 to 36 hours after exposure to the agent or up to several days if dosage is small.
- Symptoms include abdominal issues, vomiting, muscular weakness, vision problems, and as it progresses, progressing paralysis.

Survival

- Seek immediate medical treatment.
- Wash hair and skin thoroughly.

Radiation and Nuclear Bombs

A radiological dispersal device (RDD) is also referred to as a "dirty bomb." It is not a nuclear bomb. The RDD is comprised of radioactive materials wrapped with a conventional explosive. When detonated, the radioactive material is spread throughout the area with the objective of contamination. There are two threats rolled into one: the explosion itself, and the spreading of radioactive material. If the material is placed without any explosive material it is referred to as a passive RDD. A small amount of radioactive material even with an explosive can be easily carried. If spread, the radioactive material can cause significant contamination.

The radioactive materials that could be used in a dirty bomb are readily available. For example, hospital diagnostic/treatment devices incorporate radioactive materials. Research laboratories may also have radioactive materials in enough amounts to result in significant threat, if used. There are other local organizations/companies that may use radioactive materials that could be stolen or purchased from an unethical employee.

There is also a risk of a true low-yield nuclear weapon that could be detonated. Such a device is known as an improvised nuclear device (IND). It is possible to construct such a device by modifying stolen weaponry or even constructing from scratch.

Symptoms

The use of an RDD or IND would be recognized more by the explosion than by symptoms. There would first be an explosion that would result in radioactivity being released, as well as having to deal with the effects of the explosion. In the case of an RDD, the explosion is not a nuclear explosion. In the case of an IND, the explosion would likely be greater and be a true nuclear explosion. The significance of the latter cataclysmic explosion would be obvious and immediate action would be warranted.

Typical symptoms at first would include nausea and vomiting. The speed at which such symptoms appear is directly related to how much radiation exposure occurred. For example, nausea and vomiting could occur within 6 hours for mild exposure and 10 minutes for severe exposure. After initial exposure, symptoms can continue to develop. I refer you to the Mayo Clinic website for a very good description of radiation sickness and amount of exposure.[14]

Survival

- If an explosion occurs and there is reason to believe it could be a radiological dispersal device (dirty bomb), immediately go outside if inside, or leave the area immediately if outside.
- If the explosion is significant and large and an improvised nuclear device (IND) is suspected, continue with the following as you would with an RDD:
- Immediately breathe through an item of clothing to prevent breathing the potentially contaminated air. The radiation cannot be seen, so act is if it is there.
- Seek medical attention so that the presence of radiation to the body may be detected and follow medical advice.
- Watch for new symptoms to occur after treatment.

Drones

We have likely all seen a drone of one type or another. Perhaps we see the toy-like versions in the mall stores, or videos of drones used by the military. We may even see an occasional drone where it should not be—sporting events, near airports, or near businesses or schools. Because they are popular, recreational, and increasing in popularity, we will see more in the future. Yet they are new enough to require regulation if we are to protect ourselves from an attack from the air from drones operated by those who want to kill and harm us.

Drones have been weaponized and used by ISIS in battle to drop bombs. Claiming multiple deaths with the use of unmanned drones, ISIS and other terrorist groups certainly have the technology, means, equipment, and desire to kill others.[15] This concern includes the U.S. efforts focused on mass victim attacks. It is also important to note that attackers do not have to be international terrorists. Certainly, domestic terrorists, self-radicalized terrorists, those fueled by hate/bias, and those with mental health issues can easily obtain drones commercially. Also, drones do not have to be used as a single drone attack. Multiple drones used simultaneously increase the chances of success.

If an explosive, or some form of chemical, biological, or radiological material is attached and dropped, there is little chance the perpetrator will be even noticed. The drone can be controlled from a distance. Certainly, remote-controlled devices carrying explosives is nothing new, but what was missing in the past was commercially available, unmanned vehicles, at relatively low cost. It does not take much ingenuity to attach a harmful payload.

Drones are here to stay. It is only a matter of time until we see a more serious, drone-based attack in the United States. It is one of those topics to know about from a mass victim attack perspective. The above section on chemical, biological, and radiological threats should be enough to know the types of payloads that could be attached to multiple drones attacking at the same time.

Survival

- If at a crowded event and you spot a drone overhead, keep alert and be prepared to leave the area.
- If multiple drones are flying together over a crowded area, concern should be raised, and you should leave that area immediately.

PUTTING IT ALL TOGETHER

- One of the best ways to detect approaching or imminent danger is to become accustomed to observing others. If people in one area start expressing alarm, shouting, coughing, or begin to run, it is clear that a group of people have all observed or have experienced something alarming. Escape in the opposite direction.
- If you will be traveling out of the country, do your homework. Check the U.S. Department of State travel advisory site (travel.state.gov).[16] The State Department issues regular warning for current threats if traveling to foreign countries. Also search on current terrorist threat for any specific country/city you may be ready to visit (e.g., "London England current terrorist threat").
- Be aware of future threats and not just what has happened in the past. Reports of outbreaks of illness in one area should be heeded for many reasons.

SUMMARY

Unfortunately, mass victim attacks are here to stay. Such attacks allow those with malicious intent and limited resources to commit horrible acts of slaughter that will certainly result in massive media coverage. Such coverage guarantees attention for an attacker's message if an international terrorist, domestic terrorist, or a self-radicalized terrorist. It can also highlight a person seeking recognition if suffering from mental health issues and highlight the cause against a specific hated group if the attacker is motivated by hate/bias. In short, a successful mass victim attack provides the results to complete the act of targeting, planning, attack preparation, and committing the attack itself.

Local law enforcement, security, and federal law enforcement have learned much since the infamous 9/11 attack. They have been successful in actually foiling plots and stopping scores of attacks. We now need to ensure that citizens know the risks, know how to recognize threat when it occurs, how to report it, and how to survive if caught in a mass victim attack. This book was written to fill that gap. My last words: Practice situational awareness, recognize threat when it is there, and escape, if possible. If not, then hide until an escape is possible. Know when to stay in place, and know how to attack back if ever caught with no other alternatives.

Share knowledge with families, and keep alert if you are the responsible person with children, elderly, or physically/mentally challenged family, friends, or acquaintances in public places. Most importantly, don't stay home. Live your lives and enjoy the many public places available within the United States. But times have changed. Just make sure you are knowledgeable and capable of acting out your self-protection planning.

Notes

INTRODUCTION

1. Gary M. Jackson, *Predicting Malicious Behavior: Tools and Techniques for Ensuring Global Security*, Hoboken, NJ: John Wiley & Sons, 2012.

CHAPTER 1

1. Bob Frost, "Ten Misquotations and Misattributions from History," History Access.com, 2010. http://www.historyaccess.com/tenmisquotationa.html
2. Azmat Khan, "The Magazine That 'Inspired' the Boston Bombers," PBS, Frontline, April 30, 2013. https://www.pbs.org/wgbh/frontline/article/the-magazine-that-inspired-the-boston-bombers
3. Elizabeth Walsh, Alec Buchanan, and Thomas Fahy, "Violence and Schizophrenia: Examining the Evidence," *British Journal of Psychiatry*, June 2002, 180 (6): 490–95. http://bjp.rcpsych.org/content/180/6/490
4. Steve Almasy, "In Notebook Read to Jury, James Holmes Wrote of 'Obsession,'" CNN, May 27, 2015. http://www.cnn.com/2015/05/26/us/james-holmes-trial-notebook/index.html

CHAPTER 2

1. Steven Bucci, James Carafano, and Jessica Zuckerman, "60 Terrorist Plots Since 9/11: Continued Lessons in Domestic Counterterrorism," Heritage Foundation, 2013. http://www.heritage.org/terrorism/report/60-terrorist-plots-911-continued-lessons-domestic-counterterrorism
2. Zachary Cohen, "DHS Chief: Terror Risk as High as on 9/11," CNN Politics, April

197

18, 2017. http://www.cnn.com/2017/04/18/politics/john-kelly-dhs-terrorism-isis-threat/index.html

3. "If You See Something, Say Something," Department of Homeland Security. https://www.dhs.gov/see-something-say-something

4. https://www.merriam-webster.com/dictionary/anomaly

5. Carol Kuruvilla and Vera Chinese, "Families of Newtown Victims Say Adam Lanza's Mom Shares Blame for Raising a Murderer," *New York Daily News*, November 29, 2013. http://www.nydailynews.com/news/national/newtown-families-blame-adam-lanza-mom-raising-murderer-article-1.1531903

6. Richard Fausset and Serge Kovaleski, "Nikolas Cruz, Florida Shooting Suspect, Showed 'Every Red Flag,'" *New York Times*, February 15, 2018. https://www.nytimes.com/2018/02/15/us/nikolas-cruz-florida-shooting.html

7. Patrick Sauer, "The Story of the First Mass Murder in U.S. History," Smithsonian.com, October 14, 2015. https://www.smithsonianmag.com/history/story-first-mass-murder-us-history-180956927/

8. Jeff Wallenfeldt, "Texas Tower Shooting of 1966," *Encyclopædia Britannica*, 2017. https://www.britiannica.com/event/Tesax-Tower-shooting-of-1966

9. Luis Martinez, Matthew Mosk, and Karen Travers, "Fort Hood Shooting Report: Warning Signs Were 'Missed' and 'Ignored,'" ABC News, January 15, 2010. http://abcnews.go.com/Blotter/fort-hood-warning-signs-missed/story?id=9572844

10. Ray Sanchez and Ben Brumfield, "Fort Hood Shooter Was Iraq Vet Being Treated for Mental Health Issues," CNN, April 2, 2014. http://www.cnn.com/2014/04/02/us/fort-hood-shooter-profile/index.html

11. Dan Frosch and Kirk Johnson, "Gunman Kills 12 in Colorado, Reviving Gun Debate," *New York Times*, July 20, 2012. http://www.nytimes.com/2012/07/21/us/shooting-at-colorado-theater-showing-batman-movie.html

12. Ray Sanchez and Laura Smith-Spark, "Who Is the Charleston Church Shooting Suspect?," CNN, June 18, 2015. www.cnn.com/2015/06/18/us/charleston-church-shooting-suspect

13. Timothy M. Phelps, "Dylann Roof Tried to Kill Himself during Attack, Victim's Son Says," *Los Angeles Times*, June 20, 2015. www.latimes.com/nation/nationnow/la-na-dylann-roof-suicide-attempt-20150620-story.html

14. Gal Tziperman Lotan, Charles Minshew, Mike Lafferty, and Andrew Gibson, "Orlando Nightclub Shooting Timeline: Four Hours of Terror Unfold," *Orlando Sentinel*, May 31, 2017. http://wwworlandosentinel.com/news/pulse-orlando-nightclub-shooting/os-orlando-pulse-nightclub-shooting-timeline-htmlstory.html

15. Krishnadev Calamur, Marina Koren, and Matt Ford, "A Day after the San Bernardino Shooting," *The Atlantic*, December 3, 2015. https://www.theatlantic.com/national/archive/2015/12/a-shooter-in-san-bernardino/418497/

16. Chris Keller, "San Bernardino Shooting Update: Rifles Used in Attack Were Modified to Be Illegal," December 4, 2015. http://www.scpr.org/news/2015/12/04/56040/san-bernardino-shooting-update-rifles-used-in-atta/

17. Greg Ellifritz, "Recognizing the Sound of Gunfire," Active Response Training, 2017. www.activeresponsetraining.net. Greg Ellifritz posts several articles on this site that are relevant to the topic.

18. "Mandalay Bay Attack: At Least 59 Killed in Deadliest US Shooting," *Guardian*,

October 17, 2017. https://www.theguardian.com/us-news/2017/oct/02/las-vegas-active
-shooter-harvest-country-music-festival

19. "Oklahoma City Bombing," History.com, 2009. http://www.history.com/topics/
oklahoma-city-bombing

20. Mary Beth Sheridan, Doug Struck, and Marc Fisher, "Boston Marathon Bomb
Blasts Kill at Least Three, Leave Scores Injured," *Washington Post*, April 15, 2013.
https://www.washingtonpost.com/world/national-security/boston-marathon-bomb-blasts
-kill-at-least-three-leave-scores-injured/2013/04/15/5b2b5d8a-a607-11e2-b029-8fb7e977
ef71_story.html?utm_term=.59dc24554a9f

21. Peter Martinez, "TSA Issues Security Warning about Vehicle-Ramming Threat,"
CBS News, May 4, 2017. http://www.cbsnews.com/news/tsa-issues-security-warning
-vehicle-ramming-threat/

22. Angela Dewan, Jason Hanna, and Euan McKirdy, "Attack in Nice: Truck Driver
Identified as 31-Year-Old Tunisia Native," CNN, July 16, 2016. http://www.cnn.com/
2016/07/15/europe/nice-france-truck/index.html

23. Holly Yan, "Vehicles as Weapons: Melbourne Part of a Deadly Trend," CNN,
December 21, 2017. http://www.cnn.com/2017/03/22/world/vehicles-as-weapons/index
.html

24. Tina Moore, Larry Celona, and Danika Fears, "8 Killed as Truck Plows into Pedestrians in Downtown NYC Terror Attack," *New York Post*, October 31, 2017. https://nypost
.com/2017/10/31/8-killed-truck-pedestrians-downtown-nyc-terror-attack

25. "Japan Is Normally So Safe That Today's Knife Attack Was the Worst Mass Assault
since WWII," Quartz Media, July 26, 2016. https://qz.com/741981/japan-is-normally-so
-safe-that-todays-knife-attack-was-the-worst-mass-assault-since-wwii/

26. Stephen Rex Brown, "Man Who Went on Mass Stabbing in Japan Was Released
from Mental Hospital Months before Attack," *New York Daily News*, July 27, 2016. http://
www.nydailynews.com/news/world/japan killer-released-mental-hospital-stabbing-arti
cle-1.2728788

27. Pamela Engel, "ISIS and Al Qaeda Have Specifically Called for the Type of Attack
That Just Happened in London," Business Insider: Politics, November 1, 2017. http://
www.businessinsider.com/isis-Al Qaeda-london-attack

CHAPTER 3

1. Mike Wood, "Why 'Run, Hide, Fight' Is Flawed," PoliceOne.com, June 15, 2016.
https://www.policeone.com/active-shooter/articles/190621006-Why-Run-Hide-Fight-is
-flawed/

2. City of Houston, "Run. Hide. Fight," July 23, 2012. https://www.youtube.com/
watch?v=5VcSwejI1200

3. https://www.merriam-webster.com/dictionary/escape

4. https://www.merriam-webster.com/dictionary/fight

5. Keith Somerville, "Mystery Remains over CIA Deaths," BBC News, November
15, 2002. http://news.bbc.co.uk/1/hi/world/americas/2416677.stm

6. Michelle Castillo, "Colo. Shooter Purchased Guns Legally from 3 Different

Stores," CBS News, July 20, 2012. http://www.cbsnews.com/news/colo-shooter-pur chased-guns-legally-from-3-different-stores

7. Gal Tziperman Lotan, Charles Minshew, Mike Lafferty, and Andrew Gibson, "Orlando Mass Shooting: Timeline of Events," *Orlando Sentinel*, May 31, 2017. http://www .orlandosentinel.com/news/pulse-orlando-nightclub-shooting/os-orland0-pulse-nightclub -shooting-timeline-htmlstory.html

8. "IED Attack: Improvised Explosive Devices," Department of Homeland Security, News and Terrorism: Communicating in a Crisis. https://www.dhs.gov/xlibrary/assets/ prep_ied_fact_sheet.pdf

9. CNN Library, "1993 World Trade Center Bombing Fast Facts," CNN, last updated February 21, 2017. http://www.cnn.com/2013/11/05/us/1993-world-trade-center-bomb ing-fast-facts/index.html

10. Sara Morrison and Ellen O'Leary, "Timeline of Boston Marathon Bombing Events," Boston.com/News, January 5, 2015. https://www.boston.com/news/local-news/ 2015/01/05/timeline-of-boston-marathon-bombing-events

11. Annette Witheridge, Rachel Quigley, Lydia Warren, and Louise Boyle, "Grisly New Evidence Photographs Show the Shrapnel That Was Blasted towards Boston Mara thon Victims by Deadly Pressure Cooker Bomb," *Daily Mail* (UK), April18, 2013. http:// www.dailymail.co.uk/news/article-2310768/Boston-bombings-2013-photos-shrapnel -blasted-deadly-pressure-cooker-bomb.html

12. CNN Library, "Terrorist Attacks by Vehicle Fast Facts," CNN, last updated June 22, 2017. http://www.cnn.com/2017/05/03/world/terrorist-attacks-by-vehicle-fast-facts/ index.html

13. Tom Winter, Corky Siemaszko, Phil Helsel, and Jonathon Dienst, "New York Ter rorist Attack: Truck Driver Kills Eight in Lower Manhattan," NBC News, November 1, 2017. https://www.nbcnews.com/storyline/nyc-terrorist-attack/least-one-person-dead-in cident-lower-manhattan-n816166

14. "Traffic Safety Facts: 2014 Data," U.S. Department of Transportation, National Highway Traffic Safety Administration, May 2016. https://crashstats.nhtsa.dot.gov/Api/ Public/ViewPublication/812270

15. CNN Library, "September 11, 2001: Background and Timeline of the Attacks," CNN, August 24, 2017. http://www.cnn.com/2013/07/27/us/september-11-anniversary -fast-facts/index.html

16. Kenneth Pletcher, "Tokyo Subway Attack of 1995," *Encyclopædia Britannica*, November 2, 2014. https://www.britannica.com/event/Tokyo-subway-attack-of-1995

17. Terry Macalister and Richard Halpin, "Radioactive Materials Lost in More Than 30 Incidents over Past Decade," *Guardian*, May 5, 2013. https://www.theguardian.com/ environment/2013/may/05/radioactive-materials-lost-30-incidents

18. "Truck Carrying Radioactive Material Stolen in Mexico, 9 States on High Alert," Fox News World, April 25, 2017. http://www.foxnews.com/world/2017/04/25/truck-car rying-radioactive-material-stolen-in-mexico-9-states-on-high-alert.html

CHAPTER 4

1. "Former Marine Helps Dozens Escape Orlando Nightclub Attack," CBS This Morning video, June 14, 2016. https://www.youtube.com/watch?v = OjHhXRj9D6M

2. Alex Harris, "911 Heard Pain and Panic from Those Hiding inside Pulse Nightclub during Massacre," *Miami Herald*, updated November 20, 2016. http://www.miamiherald.com/news/state/florida/article116038018.html

3. Ben Brumfield, "Connecticut Teachers Were Heroes in the Face of Death," CNN, December 18, 2012. http://www.cnn.com/2012/12/17/us/connecticut-shooting-teacher-heroism/index.html

4. Corky Siemaszko and Miguel Almaguer, "'Why Won't He Stop Shooting?' San Bernardino Terror Attack Survivors Speak," NBC News, December 7, 2015. http://www.nbcnews.com/storyline/san-bernardino-shooting/san-bernardino-shooting-survivors-speak-n475756

5. Rong-Gong Lin II and Rubaina Azhar, "Man Planned Christmas Attack on San Francisco's Pier 39, Was Inspired by Islamic State, FBI Says," *Los Angeles Times*, December 22, 2017. http://www.latimes.com/local/lanow/la-me-terror-attack-plot-san-francisco-20171222-story.html

6. Al Abidin, "5 Ways to Survive Edged Weapon Threats: Know How to Effectively Respond to an Unexpected Knife Attack," *Police: The Law Enforcement Magazine*, March 18, 2010. http://www.policemag.com/channel/weapons/articles/2010/03/5-ways-to-survive-edged-weapon-threats.aspx

7. CNN Library, "Terrorist Attacks by Vehicle Fast Facts," CNN, updated November 6, 2017. http://www.cnn.com/2017/05/03/world/terrorist-attacks-by-vehicle-fast-facts/index.html

8. "Traffic Safety Facts: 2015 Data," U.S. Department of Transportation, National Highway Traffic Safety Administration, February 2017. Report No. DOT HS 812 375. https://crashstats.nhtsa.dot.gov/Api/Public/ViewPublication/812375

9. Joe Ruiz and Doreen McCallister, "Events Surrounding White Nationalist Rally in Virginia Turn Fatal," NPR, August 12, 2017. http://www.npr.org/sections/thetwo-way/2017/08/12/542982015/home-to-university-of-virginia-prepares-for-violence-at-white-nationalist-rally

CHAPTER 5

1. "The Off-Duty Cop Who Tried to Take Down Pulse Nightclub Killer: Bodycam Pictures Reveal First Desperate Minutes of Massacre," Associated Press, April 14, 2017.

2. Sanchez, R., "Connecticut School Shooting: Six-Year-Old Stayed Alive by Playing Dead," *Telegraph*, December 17, 2012 http://www.telegraph.co.uk/news/worldnews/northamerica/usa/9750471/Connecticut-school-shooting-six-year-old-stayed-alive-by-playing-dead.html

3. "Report of the State's Attorney for the Judicial District of Danbury on the Shootings at Sandy Hook Elementary School and 36 Yogananda Street, Newtown, Connecticut on December 14, 2012," Office of the State's Attorney, Judicial District of Danbury, November 2013. http://health-equity.lib.umd.edu/4223/

4. David Kohn, "What Really Happened at Columbine," CBS, April 17, 2001 https://www.cbsnews.com/news/what-really-happened-at-columbine

5. "Oklahoma City Bombing," History.com, 2009, accessed March 8, 2018. http://www.history.com/topics/oklahoma-city-bombing

6. CNN Library, "Boston Marathon Terror Attack Fast Facts," CNN, updated March 29, 2017. http://www.cnn.com/2013/06/03/us/boston-marathon-terror-attack-fast-facts

7. "Crossroads Mall Stabbing Timeline," *Star Tribune*, October 6, 2016. http://www.startribune.com/crossroads-mall-stabbing-timeline/396224681

CHAPTER 6

1. "Survey on Gun ownership," Crime Prevention Research Center, 2017. https://crimeresearch.org/tag/survey-on-gun-ownership

2. http://www.handgunlaw.us/

3. USA Carry Staff, "Concealed Carry Permit Reciprocity Maps," USA Carry, National Concealed, July 11, 2017. https://www.usacarry.com/concealed_carry_permit_reciprocity_maps.html

4. Thomas C. Frohlich and Samuel Stebbins, "12 States Where Anyone Can Carry a Concealed Weapon," July 18, 2017. http://247wallst.com/special-report/2017/07/18/12-states-where-anyone-can-carry-a-concealed-weapon/2

5. Katherine A. Fowler, Linda L. Dahlberg, Tadesse Haileyesus, Carmen Gutierrez, and Sarah Bacon, "Childhood Firearm Injuries in the United States," *Pediatrics*, June 2017. http://pediatrics.aappublications.org/content/early/2017/06/15/peds.2016-3486

6. R. A. Band, D. N. Salhi, D. N. Holena, E. Powell, C. C. Branas, and B. G. Carr, "Severity-Adjusted Mortality in Trauma Patients Transported by Police," *Annals of Emergency Medicine*, June 2017. https://www.sciencedaily.com/releases/2014/01/140102112039.htm

7. https://thefiringline.com/library/blades/knifelaws.html

8. https://www.akti.org/state-knife-laws

9. "Best Personal Protection Devices for Women," ExpertSecurityTips.com, 2018. http://www.expertsecuritytips.com/best-personal-protection-devices-for-women/

10. Kyle Lemmon, "Self Defense: What to Carry If You Don't Want to Carry a Gun," ASecureLife.com, updated April 11, 2017. https://www.asecurelife.com/self-defense-without-a-gun/

11. "What Is Pepper Spray?" Pepper Spray Store, 2017. https://www.pepper-spray-store.com/pages/whatis

12. "The 'Taser' Is a Serious Weapon, but What the Name Stands for May Puzzle You," Dictionary.com: Everything after Z, 2017. http://www.dictionary.com/e/taser

13. "How to Use a Stun Gun," Total Armor: Stun Gun Defense Products, 2018. https://www.stun-gun-defense-products.com/buy-stun-gun/How-to-Use-a-Stun-Gun.html

14. "6 Safe Ways to Use a Taser," TBO Tech: Self Defense Products, 2017. http://www.tbotech.com/blog/6-safe-ways-to-use-a-taser

CHAPTER 7

1. Sheena McKenzie, "Chilling Video Shows Paris Attacker Trying to Shoot Woman, Gun Doesn't Fire," CNN, November 19, 2015. http://www.cnn.com/2015/11/19/world/paris-attacks-cctv-footage-woman-gunman-daily-mail/index.html

2. http://learnersdictionary.com/definition/luck

3. https://www.merriam-webster.com/dictionary/chance

4. Cassi Alexandra and Jeff Costello, "Pulse Nightclub Attack Survivors a Year Later: 'I Might Still Be in Shock,'" ABC News, June 12, 2017. http://abcnews.go.com/US/pulse-nightclub-attack-survivors-year-shock/story?id=47870249

5. Matt Rogers, "VT Tragedy: A Survivor Tells His Story," Christian Broadcasting Network (permission by Zondervan), 2008. http://www.cbn.com/books/vt-tragedy%3A-a-survivor-tells-his-story

6. Alex Johnson, Pete Williams, Chris Jansing, and Alison Stewart, "Worst U.S. Shooting Ever Kills 33 on VA. Campus," MSNBC.com and NBC News, updated April 17, 2007. http://www.nbcnews.com/id/18134671/ns/us_news-crime_and_courts/t/worst-us-shooting-ever-kills-va-campus/#.WdJT4a1e63A

7. Frederic D. Schwarz, "1922: The Herrin Massacre," *American Heritage*, May/June 1997. http://www.americanheritage.com/content/1922-herrin-massacre

8. Erin Harris, "On This Day: 21 Killed in McDonald's Massacre," Finding Dulcinea: Librarian of the Internet, July 18, 2011. http://www.findingdulcinea.com/news/on-this-day/July-August-08/On-this-Day--21-Die-in-McDonalds-s-Massacre.html

CHAPTER 8

1. Amanda Lenhart, chapter 2 of "Teens, Technology, and Friendships: How Teens Hang Out and Stay in Touch with Their Closest Friends," Pew Research Center, August, 6, 2015. http://www.pewinternet.org/2015/08/06/chapter-2-how-teens-hang-out-and-stay-in-touch-with-their-closest-friends/

2. Marc J. Tassé, "Defining Intellectual Disability: Finally We All Agree . . . Almost," American Psychological Association, September, 2016. http://www.apa.org/pi/disability/resources/publications/newsletter/2016/09/intellectual-disability.aspx

3. "Health Statistics," Department of Health and Human Services, NIII, National Institute of Diabetes and Digestive and Kidney Diseases, August, 2017. https://www.niddk.nih.gov/health-information/health-statistics/overweight-obesity

4. Saeed Ahmed, Doug Criss, and Joe Sterling, "'Hero' Exchanged Fire with Gunman, Then Helped Chase Him Down," CNN, November 7, 2017. http://www.wral.com/resident-confronted-texas-church-shooter-and-chased-him/17093805/

5. Pete Williams, Tom Winter, Andrew Blankstein, and Tracy Connor, "Suspect Identified in Ohio State Attack as Abdul Razak Ali Artan," NBC News, November 26, 2018. https://www.nbcnews.com/news/us-news/suspect-dead-after-ohio-state-university-car-knife-attack-n689076

CHAPTER 9

1. Shimon Prokupecz, Eric Levenson, Brynn Gingras, and Steve Almasy, "Note Found Near Truck Claims Manhattan Attack Done for ISIS, Source Says," CNN, updated November 6, 2017. http://www.cnn.com/2017/10/31/us/new-york-shots-fired/index.html

2. Jane J. Lee, "7 Other Sports-Related Attacks," *National Geographic*, April 16,

2013. https://news.nationalgeographic.com/news/2013/03/130415-sports-marathon-olym pics-bombers-culture/

3. Patrick McGee, Manny Fernandez, and Jonah Engel Bromwich, "Snipers Kill 5 Dallas Officers at Protest against Police Shootings," *New York Times*, July 7, 2016. https:// www.nytimes.com/2016/07/08/us/dallas-police-officers-killed.html

4. "Deadly Car Attack, Violent Clashes in Charlottesville: What We Know Now," *USA Today*, August 13, 2017. https://www.usatoday.com/story/news/nation/2017/08/13/ charlottesville-protests-what-we-know-now/562911001/

5. "LAX Shooting Kills TSA Officer, Wounds Others," CBS News, November 1, 2013. https://www.cbsnews.com/news/lax-shooting-kills-tsa-officer-wounds-others

6. Clay Biles, *Unsecure Skies*, Amazon Digital Services, July 15, 2014. https:// www.amazon.com/Unsecure-Skies-Clay-Biles-ebook/dp/B00LUSK62I

7. "Army Major Kills 13 People in Fort Hood Shooting Spree," History.com, November 5, 2011. http://www.history.com/this-day-in-history/army-major-kills-13-people-in -fort-hood-shooting-spree

8. Dan Lamothe, "Army Details the Strange, Downward Spiral of Fort Hood Shooter Ivan Lopez," *Washington Post*, January 23, 2015. https://www.washingtonpost.com/news/ checkpoint/wp/2015/01/23/army-details-the-downward-spiral-of-the-fort-hood-shooter -ivan-lopez/?utm_term = .f540322ba3d1

9. "US School Violence Fast Facts," CNN, updated September 17, 2017. http://www .cnn.com/2013/09/19/us/u-s-school-violence-fast-facts/index.html

10. Melinda Liu, "Not Just Sandy Hook: China's Terrifying Knife Attacks," Daily Beast, December 12, 2012. https://www.thedailybeast.com/not-just-sandy-hook-chinas -terrifying-knife-attacks

11. Jimmy Kilpatrick, "Should First Aid and CPR Be Taught in Schools?," *Education Views*, November 2016. http://www.educationviews.org/aid-cpr-taught-schools.

CHAPTER 10

1. Ranna Parekh, "What Is Posttraumatic Stress Disorder?" American Psychiatric Association, January 2017. https://www.psychiatry.org/patients-families/ptsd/what-is -ptsd

2. Jessica Hamblen and Laurie B. Slone, "Research Findings on the Traumatic Stress Effects of Terrorism," U.S. Department of Veteran Affairs, National Center for PTSD, updated February 23, 2016. https://www.ptsd.va.gov/professional/trauma/disaster-terror ism/research-findings-traumatic-stress-terrorism.asp

3. Jessica Hamblen, "Terrorist Attacks and Children," U.S. Department of Veteran Affairs, National Center for PTSD, updated February 23, 2016. https://www.ptsd.va.gov/ professional/trauma/disaster-terrorism/terrorist_attacks_and_children.asp

4. "PTSD and DSM-5," U.S. Department of Veteran Affairs, National Center for PTSD, updated February 21, 2017. https://www.ptsd.va.gov/professional/ptsd-overview/ dsm5_criteria_ptsd.asp

5. "Post-Traumatic Stress Disorder (PTSD): Self-Management," Mayo Clinic, February 18, 2017. https://www.mayoclinic.org/diseases-conditions/post-traumatic-stress-disor der/manage/ptc-20308566

6. Jay M. Pomerantz, "Can Posttraumatic Stress Disorder Be Prevented?" *Psychiatric Times*, April 1, 2006. http://www.psychiatrictimes.com/ptsd/can-posttraumatic-stress-disorder-be-prevented

7. Deborah A. O'Donnell, Mary E. Schwab-Stone, and Adaline Z. Muyeed, "Multidimensional Resilience in Urban Children Exposed to Community Violence," National Library of Medicine, National Institutes of Health, 73(4):1265–82, July/August 2002. https://www.ncbi.nlm.nih.gov/pubmed/12146747

8. "Talk to Someone Now," Suicide Prevention Lifeline, 2018. https://suicidepreventionlifeline.org/talk-to-someone-now/

9. Nikhil Kumar, "Boston Marathon Bombing: How Critically Injured Jeff Bauman's Memory of 'Man in the Cap' Gave FBI Vital Clue," *Independent*, April 20, 2013. http://www.independent.co.uk/news/world/americas/boston-marathon-bombing-how-critically-injured-jeff-baumans-memory-of-man-in-the-cap-gave-fbi-vital-8580950.html

10. Jeff Bauman with Bret Witter, *Stronger*, New York: Grand Central Publishing, 2014. https://www.hachettebookgroup.biz/titles/jeff-bauman/stronger/9781478920397/

11. Michael Pearson, Greg Botelho, and Pamela Brown, "Navy Yard's Gunman Psychological Issues, Motive Focuses after Shooting," CNN, updated September 17, 2013. http://www.cnn.com/2013/09/17/us/navy-yard-shooting-main/index.html

12. DeNeen L. Brown, "'I'm a Warrior and a Survivor,'" *Washington Post*, September 6, 2014. http://www.washingtonpost.com/sf/local/2014/09/06/im-a-warrior-and-a-survivor/?utm_term = .70207c6c93a7

13. María Paz García-Vera, Jesús Sanz, and Sara Gutiérrez, "A Systematic Review of the Literature on Posttraumatic Stress Disorder in Victims of Terrorist Attacks," *Psychological Reports, Sage Journals*, July 7, 2016. https://www.ncbi.nlm.nih.gov/pubmed/27388691

CHAPTER 11

1. "FBI Knew Al Qaeda Pilots Training in U.S.," *Washington Post*, March 7, 2006. http://www.washingtonpost.com/wp-dyn/content/article/2006/03/07/AR2006030700216.html

2. Phillip Shenon, "Traces of Terrorism: The Warnings; F.B.I. Knew for Years about Terror Pilot Training," *New York Times*, May 18, 2003. http://www.nytimes.com/2002/05/18/us/traces-of-terrorism-the-warnings-fbi-knew-for-years-about-terror-pilot-training.html

3. Dan Collins, "FBI Was Warned about Flight Schools," CBS News, May 15, 2002. https://www.cbsnews.com/news/fbi-was-warned-about-flight-schools

4. Ann O'Neill and Sara Weisfeldt, "Psychiatrist: Holmes Thought 3–4 Times a Day about Killing," CNN, June 17, 2015. http://www.cnn.com/2015/06/16/us/james-holmes-theater-shooting-fenton/index.html

5. David Shortell, "Report Finds Missed Chances to Help Newtown Shooter Adam Lanza," CNN, November 23, 2014. http://www.cnn.com/2014/11/21/justice/newtown-shooter-adam-lanza-report/index.html

6. Gary M. Jackson, "Predicting Malicious Behavior: Tools and Techniques for Ensuring Global Security," Hoboken, NJ: John Wiley & Sons, 2012. http://www.wiley.com/WileyCDA/WileyTitle/productCd-1118166132.html

7. Barbara Demick, "New York Attack Suspect's Family Was 'Very Mysterious,' Neighbor Says," *Los Angeles Times*, November 1, 2017. http://www.latimes.com/nation/la-na-new-york-sayfullo-saipov-profile-20171101-htmlstory.html

CHAPTER 12

1. Steven Bucci, James Carafano, and Jessica Zuckerman, "60 Terrorist Plots Since 9/11: Continued Lessons in Domestic Counterterrorism," Heritage Foundation, July 22, 2013. http://www.heritage.org/terrorism/report/60-terrorist-plots-911-continued-lessons-domestic-counterterrorism

2. Hanson O'Haver, "How 'If You See Something, Say Something' Became Our National Motto," *Washington Post*, September 23, 2016. https://www.washingtonpost.com/posteverything/wp/2016/09/23/how-if-you-see-something-say-something-became-our-national-motto/?utm_term = .23d6c86cab93

3. "If You See Something, Say Something," Department of Homeland Security, December 2017. https://www.dhs.gov/see-something-say-something/what-suspicious-activity

4. U.S. Dept of Justice, "Texas Resident Arrested on Charge of Attempted Use of Weapon of Mass Destruction," The FBI Federal Bureau of Investigation, February 24, 2011. https://archives.fbi.gov/archives/dallas/press-releases/2011/dl022411.htm

5. "Umar Farouk Abdulmutallab Sentenced to Life in Prison for Attempted Bombing of Flight 253 on Christmas Day 2009," Department of Justice, February 16, 2012. https://www.justice.gov/opa/pr/umar-farouk-abdulmutallab-sentenced-life-prison-attempted-bombing-flight-253-christmas-day

6. "Terrorist CBRN: Materials and Effects," CIA.gov/library, updated June 19, 2013. https://www.cia.gov/library/reports/general-reports-1/terrorist_cbrn/terrorist_CBRN.htm#04

7. "Nerve Gas Attack on Tokyo Subway," History.com: This Day in History, 2010. http://www.history.com/this-day-in-history/nerve-gas-attack-on-tokyo-subway

8. "Emergency Preparedness and Response," Centers for Disease Control and Prevention, last updated August 17, 2017. https://emergency.cdc.gov/bioterrorism

9. "FBI Concludes Investigation into 2001 Anthrax Mailings," CNN, February 19, 2010. http://www.cnn.com/2010/CRIME/02/19/fbi.anthrax.report/index.html

10. Andy Sharp, "North Korea Begins Tests to Load Anthrax Onto ICBMs, Report Says," Bloomberg: Politics, December 19, 2017. https://www.bloomberg.com/news/articles/2017-12-20/north-korea-begins-tests-to-load-anthrax-onto-icbms-asahi-says

11. "What Is Anthrax," Emergent BioSolutions, December 2017. http://www.biothrax.com/

12. "Ricin Poisoning," MedicineNet, reviewed February 14, 2017. https://www.medicinenet.com/ricin/article.htm

13. "Kinds of Botulism," Centers for Disease Control and Prevention, updated June 9, 2017. https://www.cdc.gov/botulism/definition.html

14. "Radiation Sickness," Mayo Clinic, 2017. https://www.cia.gov/library/reports/general-reports-1/terrorist_cbrn/terrorist_CBRN.htm#04

15. Joby Warrick, "Use of Weaponized Drones by ISIS Spurs Terrorism Fears," *Washington Post*, February 21, 2017. https://www.washingtonpost.com/world/national-security/use-of-weaponized-drones-by-isis-spurs-terrorism-fears/2017/02/21/9d83d51e-f382–11e6–8d72–263470bf040 1_story.html?utm_term = .0bd662f0cf94

16. https://travel.state.gov/content/travel

Index

Page references for figures are italicized

About the Author

Gary M. Jackson, PhD, is a behavioral psychologist who is currently president and CEO of ANBECO, LLC. Dr. Jackson's career has spanned academia as a professor, director of research and development and treatment development in various clinical settings, research psychologist within the U.S. Secret Service Intelligence Division, operational intelligence officer and chief of three advanced technology branches within the Central Intelligence Agency, vice president and director of research and development for a major psychological test development company, Director of the Center for the Advancement of Intelligent Systems (CAIS) for the American Institutes for Research, founding president and CEO of Psynapse Technologies in Washington, DC, and chief scientist at SAIC and Leidos. He has also authored several books, including *Predicting Malicious Behavior: Tools and Techniques to Ensure Global Security* (2012). You can visit his website at massvictim.com, or follow him on twitter at @DrJacksongm.